Reedbed Management for Commercial and Wildlife Interests

RSPB

BRGA

ENGLISH NATURE

Broads Authority

Written by
Carl Hawke and Paul José

External Editorial Steering Group
Jane Madgwick (Broads Authority)
Rob Andrews (Broads Authority)
Charles Cator (British Reed Growers' Association)

Internal Editorial Steering Group
Roger Buisson (RSPB)
John Sharpe (RSPB)
John Wilson (RSPB)
Paul José (RSPB)
Carl Hawke (RSPB)

Citation
For bibliographic purposes this book should be referred to as *Reedbed Management for Commercial and Wildlife Interests* under the authorship of C J Hawke and P V José

The techniques described or referred to in this book do not necessarily reflect the policies of the partner organisations or individuals involved in its production. A great deal of the information presented originated from the experiences of individual reedbed managers and must therefore be considered on a site-specific basis.

No responsibility can be accepted for any loss, damage or unsatisfactory results arising from the implementation of any of the recommendations within this book.

The use of proprietary and commercial trade names in this guidebook does not necessarily imply endorsement of the product by the partner organisations.

Published by The Royal Society for the Protection of Birds,
The Lodge, Sandy, Beds SG19 2DL

Design by
Philip Cottier

Typesetting and page mark-up by
Harry Scott, Pica Design

Figures by
Rob and Rhoda Burns, Drawing Attention

Printed by Mc Corquodale

RSPB Ref: 24/1008/98–9

ISBN No: 0 903138 81 6

Cover photographs:
Reedbed: FLPA
Swallowtail caterpillar: John Markham (RSPB)
Reed leopard moth: James Cadbury
Bearded tit: Roger Wilmshurst (RSPB)
Marsh sow thistle: Heather Angel
Bittern: Jonathan Wilson

Acknowledgments

The Royal Society for the Protection of Birds, the Broads Authority, the British Reed Growers' Association and English Nature acknowledge that this guidebook has only been made possible as a result of the prodigious efforts of many people and organisations who so willingly gave of their time and information.

The partner organisations are particularly indebted to Carl Hawke who, with Paul José, wrote and compiled the book. Paul José was the Project Manager.

Additional thanks are due to steering group members Jane Madgwick, Rob Andrews, Charles Cator, Roger Buisson, John Sharpe and John Wilson.

We also acknowledge funding from British Gas plc towards the publication of this book.

General acknowledgments

Thanks are due to the large number of individuals who also provided considerable input including reviewing the text, provision of photographic material and general support of the project.

Additional comments on components of the text were provided by:
Glen Tyler (RSPB), Ken Smith (RSPB), Matt Self (RSPB), Sarah Niemann (RSPB), Jane Brookhouse (RSPB), Anita Donaghy (RSPB), Tony Baker (RSPB), Dave Beaumont (RSPB), Dave Sexton (RSPB), Kevin Bayes (RSPB), Stephanie Tyler (RSPB), Graham Hirons (RSPB), Ian Douglas (Northumberland Wildlife Trust), Jo Parmenter (BA), Sylvia Haslam (Cambridge University), John Satchell (Norfolk reedcutter), Andy Brown (EN)

Persons contributing management information and time
Kevin Peberdy (Wildfowl & Wetlands Trust), Ken Smith (INCA and ICI), Bob Rust (Imperial Chemical Industries), Lionel Grooby (Lincolnshire Trust for Nature Conservation), Paul Kirby (Lincolnshire Trust for Nature Conservation), Andrew Credland (Lincolnshire Trust for Nature Conservation), Cliff Waller (English Nature), Norman Sills (RSPB), Rob Macklin (RSPB), Mike Blackburn (RSPB), Paul Burnham (English Nature), Ian Craig (Tayreed Company), Tim Appleton (Leicestershire and Rutland Trust for Nature Conservation), Sally Mills (RSPB), Harry Paget-Wilkes (RSPB), Martin Slater (RSPB), Dave Flumm (RSPB), Colin Harvey (British Steel), Bob Lord (English Nature),

Ian Robinson (RSPB), Bruce Anderson (RSPB), Mark Smart (RSPB), Andrew Grieve (RSPB), Dave Rees (RSPB), Mike Pollard (RSPB), Tony Raven (Broads Authority), Eric Edwards (Broads Authority), Bernard Bishop (Norfolk Wildlife Trust), Reg Land (Norfolk Wildlife Trust), Stephen Bradnock (Norfolk Wildlife Trust), Richard Starling (Norfolk Wildlife Trust), Brent Pope, Stephen Moyes, Ron Harold (English Nature), Robin Lang (National Trust), Frances Cattenach (North Wales Wildlife Trust), David Reed (Dyfed Wildlife Trust), Neil Wyatt (Wiltshire Wildlife Trust), Neil Bedford (Essex Wildlife Trust), Michael Boxall (Hampshire Wildlife Trust), Bob Chapman (Hampshire Wildlife Trust), J A Askew & Partners, Surrey Wildlife Trust, Reedbed Technology Ltd, M R Boardman, Robert Brunt (Dorset Wildlife Trust), Francesca Griffith (Shropshire Wildlife Trust), Victoria Scott (Cornwall Wildlife Trust), John Martin (Bristol, Bath and Avon Wildlife Trust), Bill Jenman (Sussex Wildlife Trust), Mike Harding (Suffolk Wildlife Trust), P Joiner, Capt. K Watt, Ben Green (Severn Trent Water), Peter O'Duffy, Phil Grice (English Nature), Martin Drake (English Nature), Roger Key (English Nature), Brian Wheeler (University of Sheffield), Mary Painter (RSPB), Anthony Merritt (Wildfowl & Wetlands Trust), Vicky Emerson, Susan Campbell, Phil Grice (EN)

Finally, thanks and apologies to any individuals and organisations who contributed in any way but whom we have inadvertently failed to acknowledge.

Foreword

Reedbeds are of outstanding importance. They provide a home to some of our rarest, most threatened and most spectacular wildlife. Arguably, the most important species is the bittern, a highly secretive and enigmatic species whose fortunes are inextricably linked to those of reedbeds. The bittern breeding population has plummeted in recent decades, with just 20 'booming' males in 1995 compared with around 80 in the 1950s. The plight of the bittern has highlighted both the decline in quality and the loss of our reedbeds. High priority is now therefore, being given by both Government and voluntary conservation organisations, to halt this decline and place the bittern population on a more healthy footing. Initiatives such as English Nature's Action for Bittern project, aim both to improve the management of existing reedbeds and to create new ones in suitable localities for the benefit of bitterns and other wildlife of reedbeds.

Reedbeds also provide one of the forgotten crops of the British countryside, and there is increasing recognition that commercial cutting of reed is by no means incompatible with wildlife interests. Reedbeds can be managed for both to the benefit of all. This is a clear application of sustainable development whereby management of an environmental resource to meet the needs of the present can be undertaken without compromising the ability of future generations to do the same.

I am pleased to be associated with this new guidebook. I sincerely hope that it will encourage the appropriate management of reedbeds to meet the requirements of people and wildlife.

The Rt Hon John Gummer MP
Secretary of State for the Environment

Contents

▲ 1. Permanently wet reedbed. An almost pure stand of reed (yellow iris in the foreground) often referred to as 'reedswamp'.

2. Summer cutting has largely suppressed reed in this area which has only shallow surface water in summer. This has encouraged greater plant diversity, eg greater water dock, rushes. This is an example of the many kinds of reedbed habitat often referred to as 'reedfen'. ▼

4. Marsh harrier (male) – this species requires a large hunting area but only a portion of it need be reed, usually in which to build a nest.

Kevin Carlson (Nature Photographers Ltd)

P R Perfect (RSPB)

▲ 3. Reedbeds generally have all the requirements for nesting reed buntings which can occur at high densities.

5. Fenn's wainscot moth. The caterpillars feed in the open on the stems and leaves of reed and may drown if dislodged in swamp conditions. The eggs are the overwintering stage and are laid on reed stems. ▼

Paul Waring

6. The wainscot grass veneer moth is widely distributed in the UK but restricted to swamps dominated by reed and/or reed sweet-grass. The caterpillar pupates inside the stems.

R S Key

▲ 7. Short-winged conehead. This species of bush cricket is not specific to reed but may be found in large numbers in some reedbeds. The female uses the long ovipositor to pierce the reed stems and lay its eggs on the inside.

8. The ground beetle *Agonum thoreyi* is a common inhabitant of damp litter in reedbeds. ▼

R S Key

9. *Macroplea mutica*, one of many species of beetle characteristic of reedbeds.

Ivan West (Broads Authority)

▲ 10. Adult swallowtail butterfly on milk parsley. The female lays its eggs on milk parsley on which the caterpillars feed. This species is restricted to the fens of East Anglia and the British race occurs nowhere else in the world.

11. Reed-dominated fens in the Broads often support a range of ferns including the uncommon marsh fern (left) and the rare crested buckler fern (right). ▼

C Hawke (RSPB)

12. Harvest mouse – a common mammal of reedbeds which uses the stem habitat above the water.

E A Janes

INTRODUCTION

Introduction

Background

This book is a practical guide to the techniques of reedbed management, rehabilitation and creation that integrate commercial and wildlife interests. The publication of the guide is timely for several reasons:

- Loss of reedbed habitat and neglect of remaining reedbeds has focused concern on the reduced wildlife interest of this threatened habitat (EN 1994a). Estimates of habitat losses vary but may be as high as 40% since 1945 (Bibby *et al* 1989). High priority is currently being given by conservation organisations to halt and reverse this decline. Concern has been highlighted by the plight of the bittern, a species which in the UK is highly dependent on reedbeds, which numbered only 20 booming males in 1995.

- A steady growth in the thatching industry has resulted in the demand for quality cut reed exceeding supply in the UK, such that the majority of reed for thatching is currently imported. This situation presents a major opportunity to create new reedbeds and rehabilitate degraded ones for the benefit of wildlife and commercial interests.

- Opportunities have arisen for reedbed creation and rehabilitation as a result of changes in agricultural policy, including the establishment of Environmentally Sensitive Areas, Tir Cymen (Wales) and the Habitat Scheme.

- The responsive attitude of the British Reed Growers' Association and conservation organisations in recognising that the commercial and wildlife interests of reedbeds are highly interdependent.

- Rapidly expanding interest in the use of constructed reedbeds as environmentally sensitive water treatment systems. This includes the ability of large reedbeds to act as buffer zones and remove nutrients from agricultural drainage and sewage treatment works discharges.

- Current interest in floodplain habitats and wetland restoration in the UK and Europe as a whole (RSPB 1994).

This book is a tool for everyone involved in the management of reedbeds; a practical guide which has drawn upon the experiences of reedbed managers throughout the UK. The aim is to encourage the management of reedbeds to meet the requirements of both wildlife and people by:

- presenting the options available
- presenting the best practice management techniques
- enabling managers to make informed decisions

The book achieves this through a straightforward layout, extensive cross-referencing and use of figures, tables and photographs where appropriate. This should enable the reader quickly to find the information sought.

Structure of this book

The text is separated into four parts. Part 1 highlights the importance of planning for management and creation. This section considers what should be done once the potential to modify existing management, rehabilitate a site or to create a new reedbed has been recognised. It explains how to evaluate a site and examines the range of physical, chemical, wildlife and legal factors that may influence the decisions that can be made.

Part 2 describes reedbed management and rehabilitation techniques and gives examples of the best practices for relevant site conditions. It is subdivided into water management and vegetation (ie reed) management. The water management section examines how the regime of a site is influenced by natural processes and can be managed for the benefit of commercial and wildlife interests. Problems associated with water quality and practical solutions are presented. The wildlife value of ditches and open water in reedbeds is described with guidance on best practice management. Reed management looks at cutting techniques, examining advantages and disadvantages in terms of frequency and timing. Other techniques including herbicide use, burning and scrub management are detailed. Part 2 is completed with a section on bed regeneration for rehabilitating degraded reedbeds.

Part 3 examines the creation of new reedbeds on arable, disused land or land with low or no current wildlife value. It is subdivided into sections on engineering operations and vegetation establishment techniques. The section on engineering techniques highlights the benefits of land forming and how dams, bunds and new ditches should be constructed. The principal techniques of reed establishment are described including natural expansion, seeding and planting seedlings, rhizomes and stem cuttings. An overview of the use of constructed wetlands, principally reedbeds, for the treatment of water and industrial effluents completes Part 3.

The general text is underpinned by Part 4, comprising 17 case studies, each describing one or more management or creation techniques which have been undertaken at sites around the UK. The order of these parallels the structure of Parts 1–3. The management and rehabilitation case studies are concluded by a study of integrated management at Walberswick National Nature Reserve. This is one of many sites referred to elsewhere in the text, which are used to illustrate how a range of management techniques can be successfully integrated. These include water management, single wale cutting, and scrub and carr management.

Finally, the Appendices consist largely of addresses of organisations from whom it may be possible to obtain further help and guidance. A map is also included, showing sites in the UK where a range of management and creation techniques have been or are being undertaken, illustrating the high level of interest in reedbeds in the UK today.

Reeds and reedbeds

Distribution and origins

Reedbeds are comprised largely of the common reed *Phragmites australis*, a tall, perennial and flood-tolerant grass. Its distribution is widespread throughout Europe, Africa, Asia, Australia and North America between 10 and 70° latitude. Although normally associated with lowlands, it has been recorded at 3,000 m in Tibet (Crook *et al* 1983).

In the UK, the most extensive reedbeds are found in two main locations:

- river floodplains
- low-lying coastal plains

River floodplains are lowland valley floors containing a river that regularly floods. Reedbeds may develop on ronds, cut-off channels, seasonally wet low-lying areas or even in sections of slow-flowing river such as meanders. They may remain wet all year if the soil is peat (and therefore water retentive), because water is artificially held on the site or because the site is also spring fed.

Reedbeds on coastal plains have developed where incursion of sea water has been prevented, usually by the construction of bunds or sea defences, and a freshwater/brackish environment developed on the landward side.

Reedbeds also occur in other situations, many man-made. These may be divided into a further three categories (Bibby and Lunn 1982):

- artificial sites, eg clay pits/gravel pits
- natural lake margins
- estuaries.

Historical distribution

Reedbeds were once extensive in the now arable fens of eastern England until the major drainage schemes of the 17th century began (Everett 1989). Intensification of drainage between 1945 and 1970 led to further deterioration of the remaining reedbeds. Lack of management exacerbated the situation. A net loss of 5–10% of reedbed in England between 1979 and 1993 has been estimated by the RSPB (RSPB 1994) with activities such as grazing, waste tipping and built development implicated. For the UK as a whole, losses between 1945 and 1990 were estimated by Bibby *et al* (1989) at 10–40%.

Current distribution

A 1994 survey by the RSPB revealed some 926 reedbed sites in the UK, totalling approximately 6,530 ha, mostly fragmented into small blocks of less that one hectare (Painter 1994). This figure hides a more serious issue for UK reedbeds, that of neglect owing to a lack of management resulting in an overall deterioration of the quality of the habitat and the reed itself. As a result, reedbed is one of the rarest habitats in the UK, even more so than lowland heath and primary raised bog.

According to Bibby and Lunn (1982), only 15 sites exceeded 40 ha in a survey of England and Wales in 1979 and 1980, accounting for only 1,140 ha of the total. The extensive tidal reedbed of the Inner Tay estuary in Scotland, at 410 ha, constitutes the largest area of contiguous reed in the UK. Throughout the Norfolk and Suffolk Broads is an estimated 2,500 ha of open fen, a significant proportion of which is reed-dominated (Madgwick *et al* 1994).

Reedbeds in the UK are geographically important in a global context being some of the farthest west in Europe. UK reedbeds tend to be much smaller than those of the Netherlands and the Czech Republic for example. However, they contain a great range of habitat structure and species diversity per hectare which makes them of high conservation value within Europe.

Biology of reed and growing conditions

The natural cycle of reed is for a seed to produce a shoot which itself bears seed, the means by which the species colonises new areas. Seed production in UK reed is very variable and tends to be less on degraded sites where the reed is poor quality. Some seed-heads (panicles) may contain no seeds at all or a proportion may be infertile, the degree depending on growing conditions. Once a plant has established from seed, it spreads by vegetative propagation from a rhizomatous root. The rhizome grows both horizontally and vertically through the soil and sometimes across the soil surface. The rate of growth of a horizontal rhizome can vary greatly, depending on growing conditions, and may be several metres in one season. In April, new shoots emerge from the rhizome, growing vertically to produce stem, leaves and flower. The flowers are fully formed by August–October and seed is set by November. In water-logged soil the green aerial parts provide food and oxygen for the rhizome in summer, whereas in winter the hollow, dead stem functions as a 'snorkel', permitting the rhizome to survive in flooded conditions. In the UK, individual reed stems can grow up to 3.5 m tall. In winter, the aerial parts die and harden to form a rigid cane. The dead stems may persist for two to three seasons whereafter they break off close to the ground to form a litter layer which takes several years to decompose (Haslam 1972).

Within any site, however, the way in which reed grows will vary because of different conditions across the site. The principal factors affecting reed growth may include:

- climate and geographical location
- soil type
- water quantity and quality
- reed genotype.

The success of reed can be attributed to its ability to grow in a wide range of damp conditions, even demonstrating considerable salt tolerance (Ranwell *et al* 1964).

Reedbed habitats

Areas of reed and associated plant species can contain a diverse range of habitats. Reedbeds that normally have 20 cm or more surface water in summer are often referred to as 'reedswamp' (Wheeler pers comm). The wettest areas may contain reed and little else, thus being of low botanical interest but potentially of high invertebrate value (Fojt and Foster 1992). Colour Plate 1 shows an example of a wet reedbed.

Reedbeds with water levels that are normally at or below the surface in summer are often referred to as 'reedfens' (Colour Plate 2). However, the term reedfen is used most frequently to describe the great range of vegetation communities on calcareous peat where reed is nearly always present (Madgwick pers comm).

In practice, there is no clear distinction between reedswamp and reedfen, although the National Vegetation Classification distinguishes four main types of 'reedswamp' and at least 16 types of reed-dominated tall-herb fen (Rodwell 1995). However, reed may be a component of other types of swamp and wetland habitats and is frequently associated with saw-sedge swamps for example. Of the 30 fen communities that occur in England and Wales, 21 were recognised as occurring in the Broads (Wheeler 1980). More recently, Parmenter (in prep) has described 26 communities in the Broads with which reed is associated. Because of the complexity and diversity of these 'reedfen' communities and their importance in conservation terms, it is essential that they are managed to protect the special interest of each type. However, the techniques for management will be common across most types with variations in degree and timing.

This book focuses on the management of 'reedswamps' and reed-dominated, tall-herb fens, collectively referred to as reedbeds (unless otherwise specified). Saw-sedge beds are also addressed because of their wildlife and commercial importance and because of the strong association they have with reed and the thatching industry.

Value for wildlife

Many animals and plants rely on reed for some or all of their life cycle. In Britain, some 40 species of insect feed solely on reed (Fojt and Foster 1992). Table 1 gives some examples of important reedbed associations between wildlife and reed.

Reedbed is a nationally scarce habitat and any plants and animals that rely on them must therefore be equally scarce. 'Reedswamps' support characteristic communities of nationally uncommon birds and invertebrates (Bibby and Lunn 1982). Because they support many nationally rare and threatened species, 'reedfens' are often considered more important for plants and invertebrates than for birds (Burgess and Evans 1989). Figure 2 in Part 2 illustrates that despite clear structural differences, there is considerable overlap between habitats in the species

Table 1: Relationships between wildlife and reed

Species	Reed association
Invertebrates:	
Reed leopard moth	Larva feeds and hibernates in stems for two seasons before emerging as adult.
Twin-spot wainscot moth	Overwinters as egg on reed stems.
Dromius longiceps (beetle)	Lives in dry reed litter.
Plants:	
Milk parsley	Occurs on 'reedfens' of East Anglia.
Marsh pea	Occurs on 'reedfens'.
Marsh sow-thistle	Occurs in drier 'reedswamps'.
Birds:	
Bittern	Nests and feeds in reedbeds.
Bearded tit	Nests in uncut reed with litter layer.
Marsh harrier	Nests and feeds in reedbeds with open water.
Mammals:	
Harvest mouse	Nests and feeds among reed stems.

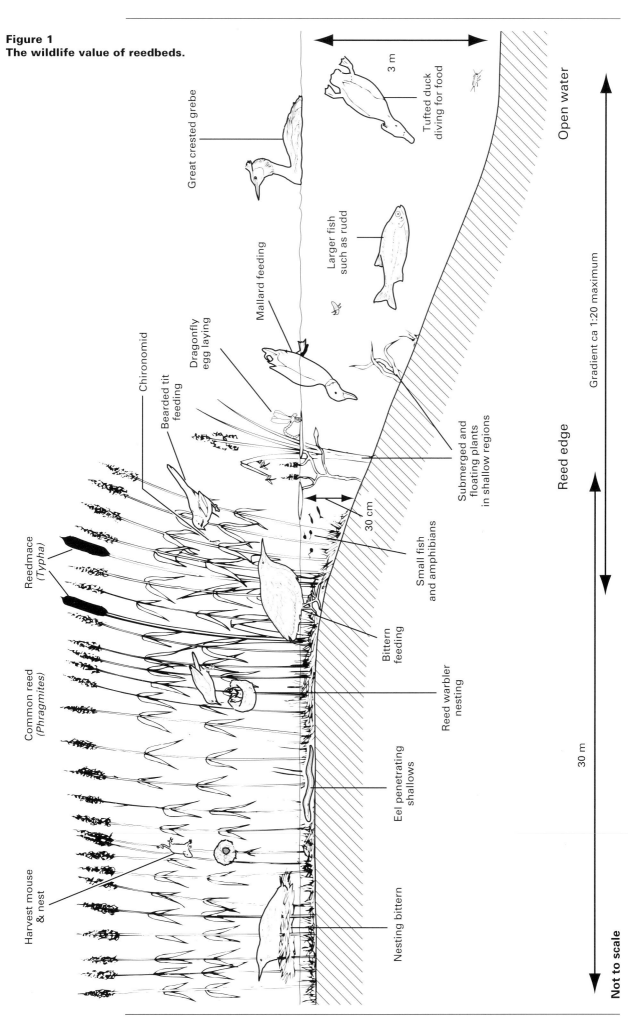

Figure 1
The wildlife value of reedbeds.

Great crested grebe

Tufted duck
diving for food

3 m

Larger fish
such as rudd

Open water

Chironomid

Bearded tit
feeding

Dragonfly
egg laying

Mallard feeding

Gradient ca 1:20 maximum

Reedmace
(Typha)

Submerged and
floating plants
in shallow regions

Reed edge

Common reed
(Phragmites)

30 cm

Small fish
and amphibians

Bittern
feeding

Reed warbler
nesting

Harvest mouse
& nest

Eel penetrating
shallows

30 m

Nesting bittern

Not to scale

they support, which can have important implications for management. The following section is an overview of some of the key species found in reedbeds.

Birds

In the UK there are four species that are highly dependent on reedbeds for their survival: reed warbler, bearded tit, marsh harrier and bittern. A species of international concern is the aquatic warbler, which occurs in significant numbers during autumn on the reedbeds of the south coast of England. Other species of national conservation interest include hen harrier, Cetti's warbler and Savi's warbler but many other species use reedbeds and their associated habitats, notably reed bunting (Colour Plate 3), sedge warbler and many species of water birds, eg teal, water rail. Figure 1 illustrates the wildlife value of reedbeds, in particular for birds, and the importance of the reed/water margins for many species.

The plight of the bittern (Plate 1) in the UK is reflected very much in the fortunes of reedbeds (Tyler 1994a). Prior to the large-scale drainage schemes of the 17th century, bitterns must have been more widespread and abundant than now. Bitterns increased in the late 1800s and early 1900s in the Broads (Ellis 1965) but then declined steeply in the 1970s possibly as a result of pollution, disturbance and habitat deterioration (Day and Wilson 1978). By the mid-1980s the situation was similar throughout the UK, bittern numbers falling owing to a deterioration in habitat. This trend is reflected throughout the majority of Europe, although countries with the largest populations have poor information on trends (Tyler 1994b).

Despite becoming extinct as a British breeding species in the 19th century, the marsh harrier (Colour Plate 4) recolonised Britain in 1915 peaking at about 50 pairs by the late 1950s (Bibby and Lunn 1982). This was followed by another decline such that by 1971 there was only one pair left breeding in Britain. The evidence suggested that pollution by organochlorine pesticides was largely responsible since a remarkable recovery took place following the withdrawal of these chemicals. By 1990

Hellio & Van Ingen (NHPA)

Geoff Nobes

Plate 1 The bittern is highly dependent on reedbeds where it feeds on fish, amphibians and large invertebrates. It requires clear shallow water in which to hunt for food, usually on the secluded reed/water margins of ditches and pools. The population of bitterns has declined from a 20th-century peak of nearly 80 booming males in the early 1950s to 20 in 1995.

Plate 2 Greater spearwort is associated with shallower areas where reed is less dominant.

there were at least 87 marsh harrier nests recorded in Britain (Underhill-Day 1993). Occasionally, marsh harriers nest in crops but reedbeds remain their stronghold, with increasing numbers overwintering each year and breeding now confirmed as far north as the Tay Estuary in Scotland.

Severe winters can seriously deplete the bearded tit population; (eg in 1947 when only 2–4 pairs remained in the UK). Such weather-related fluctuations obscure attempts to correlate declines with habitat loss. At Walberswick in Suffolk, the bearded tit population has recovered from the severe winters of the late 1970s, reaching about 30 pairs, but has never returned to the ca 100 pairs it attained prior to this (Waller pers comm). Factors such as food supply must also play a part. The creation of the vast reedbeds of the Polders in the Netherlands developed a large population of bearded tits, and this probably helped the recolonisation of Britain after the 1947 winter (Axell 1966) such that by 1974, O'Sullivan (1976) recorded at least 590 pairs. More recent surveys suggest a minimum population level of 319 pairs now although according to Bibby (1993) 400 pairs is a more likely estimate.

Despite the incompleteness of the picture of population dynamics for the bearded tit, it is clear that its future survival in the UK lies in the protection and management of existing reedbeds and the creation of new ones.

The reed warbler (Plate 2 in Part 2) is a bird of lowland Britain where it can be very common in suitable habitat. It becomes more sparse farther north. Its success lies in its ability to utilise fragments of reedbed, such as the margins of ponds and reed-filled ditches. Indeed, it has been expanding its range in the UK for the last 20 years with an estimated current population of 40,000–80,000 pairs (Kelsey 1993).

Reedbeds also provide safe roosting places for large numbers of birds of certain species. Starlings can build up to enormous numbers in late summer and use a reedbed as a roost throughout the winter, often causing considerable temporary damage by their sheer weight of numbers. At Greater Westhay in Somerset, a roost of 500,000 starlings completely flattened the reeds there in 1994/95 (Hancock pers comm). Swallows and house martins will roost in reedbeds on their way south in autumn, with up to 150,000 recorded on the Inner Tay in some years (Moyes pers comm). Other birds to make use of reedbeds in this way include yellow wagtails, pied wagtails, corn buntings and wrens (Bibby and Lunn 1982).

Invertebrates

At least 700 species of invertebrates have been found to be associated with reedbeds in the UK. Some 64 insect species are known to be dependent on reed to some extent, 40 being entirely dependent (Fojt and Foster 1992). All stages in the succession of a reedbed support important invertebrate communities, although pure stands of wet reed will have lower value in terms of diversity than reedbeds with a drier litter layer (Kirby 1992). Our knowledge, however, is limited largely to those species that are pests of commercial reedbeds, the effects of which have been studied by van der Toorn and Mook (1982).

Moths are perhaps the best known insect group with at least nine species specific to reed and many more on either reed or other reedbed plants, eg the marsh carpet moth (Plate 3). A common and widespread example is the large wainscot, the larvae of which feed inside both the stems and rhizomes of reed, causing considerable damage to commercial thatching reedbeds. In the UK the internationally rare Fenn's wainscot (Colour Plate 5) is found only in the Norfolk Broads and Walberswick in Suffolk, the larvae feeding at first in the stems of reed and later on the leaves. The silky wainscot is locally common in southern and eastern reedbeds of England and is unusual in that the larva is carnivorous, preying on the pupae of other reed-stem moths. The impressive reed leopard moth has a long life cycle, the larva overwintering for two seasons in reed stems. It is confined mostly to East Anglia and Dorset. The fen wainscot is a common species of reedbeds, occurring in large numbers on some sites. Large emergences of the larvae at Blacktoft Sands provide a vital food source for second brood bearded tits. The distribution of common reedbed moths may be a limiting factor for reed warbler distribution in the UK, possibly explaining the species' general absence from Scotland (Grieve pers comm). The wainscot grass veneer (Colour Plate 6) is one of several species of micromoth common in most UK reedbeds.

Other reedbed insects include the fly *Lipara lucens*, whose larvae develop in galls on reed stems and is common on the Teifi in Dyfed and Chippenhan Fen, Cambridgeshire. The short-winged conehead (Colour Plate 7) inhabits many kinds of damp, tall vegetation, including reedbeds. The ground beetles *Agonum thoreyi* (Colour Plate 8) and *Dromius longiceps* hunt amongst reed litter whilst the reed beetle *Macroplea mutica* (Colour Plate 9) tends to occupy the leafy parts of reeds. The British race of the swallowtail butterfly (Colour Plate 10) is a well known but rare insect confined to the Broads where its larva feeds on milk parsley, a rare plant of 'reedfens'. It usually pupates on the stems of nearby reed. Many aquatic invertebrates, including some rare species, live amongst reed in shallow water (Kirby 1992). The water louse, however, is a common crustacean which feeds on reed litter and other detritus, thus assisting with its break-down.

A group of small flies commonly known as non-biting midges, the chironomids, are particularly important for many reedbed birds, notably warblers and bearded tits. These insects emerge as adults in huge numbers and are feasted upon by birds, which use them to feed their chicks. Chironomids are vital for first brood bearded tits and the aquatic larvae of these insects provide food for many other aquatic animals and water birds. Late summer build-ups of the plum aphid on reed provide an important food supply for passage warblers, notably sedge warblers, which need to fatten up prior to undertaking their long flight to Africa.

Plants

In general terms, the number of plant species in a reedbed decreases as the degree of reed dominance increases (Wheeler 1992). However, even in areas where reed dominates there are always other plants to be found. Reedmace is another very tall, wetland plant and can grow well amongst even flooded reed. Yellow iris, bur-reed and rushes are associated with shallower areas where reed is less dominant. The less common cowbane, greater water parsnip and greater spearwort (Plate 3) also thrive best where reed is less dominant. Drier, unmanaged areas of reedswamp may also support hemp agrimony, greater willowherb, and bittersweet and scrub species like willow and alder where succession has progressed further. These and most associated plant species are, however, not dependent on reedbeds for their survival and can be found in many other wetland habitats.

Reed-dominated, tall-herb fens support a greater diversity of plants than 'reedswamps' and include species which are very localised and restricted by their ecological requirements. Marsh pea, fen orchid, milk parsley, crested buckler fern (Colour Plate 11), marsh fern (Colour Plate 11) and *Sphagnum* mosses are examples, but even these are found in wetlands other than reedbeds.

The botanical importance of reedbeds lies in the different communities of plants that form the range of habitats collectively referred to here as reedbeds.

Paul Waring

David Hosking (FLPA)

Fish

The species found in ditches and open water associated with reedbeds are those common to lowland, eutrophic rivers in the UK. These include pike (Plate 4), tench, roach, rudd, bream and eel. Shoals of fry and smaller species like stickleback and minnow occur amongst reed stems and in the shallow margins of open water. The eggs, larvae and fry are a food source for many creatures, from dragonfly larvae to kingfishers. The dominant species vary from site to site. Eels are particularly common at Leighton Moss whereas smaller fish like three-spined stickleback are more common at Minsmere. Both species form an important food source for many animals, in particular bitterns.

Some species may be absent from reedbeds which have become isolated from a river supply and this may have important implications for recruitment of eels for example. Fish that undergo their entire life cycle in the same body of water may be ecologically more important (eg as food for bitterns) in such circumstances.

Amphibians and reptiles

Frogs can be an important food source for larger waterbirds like the grey heron and bittern, but most animals find common toads distasteful. The larvae of amphibians

Plate 3 The marsh carpet moth is a rare species in Britain, associated with fens where the caterpillar's food plant, common meadow-rue, occurs. A range of management techniques to benefit the plant is required, mostly involving suppressing the dominance of reed.

Plate 4 Reedbeds can support many species of fish, including pike which lays its eggs in the shallow margins of ditches. The fry are a potential food source for many animals, including bitterns.

are a food source for many animals, including the predatory larvae of the great diving beetle, and moorhens, which often eat frog spawn. In general, open waters such as ditches or pools are required by most amphibians, although toads will use shallowly flooded reed and sedge beds. Well vegetated ditches may support newts, especially the more common smooth newt, although the less common palmate and great crested newts can also occur. In general, if fish are present, amphibians will be scarce or absent.

The grass snake is a common inhabitant of many reedbeds where it hunts primarily for frogs. It may lay its eggs in piles of cut reed and other vegetation. The rotting vegetation generates heat, which incubates the eggs (Langton 1989).

Mammals

Most mammals found in reedbeds are associated with a range of aquatic habitats. Water voles and water shrews occur on most sites with ditches. Because the harvest mouse (Colour Plate 12) is not strictly a ground-dwelling mammal, it is able to thrive well in wet reedbeds, which may support quite high densities.

The harvest mouse was found often to be the most dominant mammal in reed and sedge in a study carried out in the Broads. Its success in this wetland habitat was attributed to its ability to exploit the aerial habitat offered by reed and sedge and the abundant supply of insects in summer and seed (including reed) in winter (Jowitt and Perrow 1993).

Large reedbeds with adjacent woodland may attract one or more species of deer. Otters may occur on large reedbeds with considerable open water either as ditches or as large pools. As otters eat primarily fish and frogs, sites that support good populations of these will be more suitable. The otter is quite rare in most of lowland England and has been reintroduced to many areas. Some reedbeds already support otter populations but clearly there is scope for this species to colonise additional reedbed sites including newly created ones (RSPB/NRA/RSNC 1994).

Value for people

Especially valuable reedbeds in the UK are associated largely with the management of such areas as a source of reed, sedge, and formerly marsh hay and litter for bedding. Where management has lapsed, the typical reedbed habitats have deteriorated together with their characteristic populations of plants and animals.

This decline has been halted in the most productive reedbeds by a buoyant thatching industry that prefers to thatch with UK-sourced material, where available. Reed is the most durable of thatching materials and sedge the most hardy for the ridging of thatched roofs.

Reedbeds have also recently been recognised as natural 'filters' for the purpose of effluent water treatment, the rhizomes providing the medium to break down both organic and inorganic substances (Hudson 1992).

The continued management of reedbeds is, therefore, of value for socio-economic reasons as well as for nature conservation and human interest in the wildlife they support. It is a prime example of the co-existence of commercialism and conservation with the advantage of improving habitat in a sustainable way.

Reed and sedge for thatching

Common reed has been used as a roofing material in East Anglia for many centuries, once being a free and abundant material (Plate 5). The fact that over 90% of Norfolk's medieval churches were once thatched (Cooper 1972) reflects just how abundant and important reed was to society. This century has witnessed a decline in the use of reed for thatching but the declining use of straw in traditional areas such as the West Country plus a general upturn in the market has renewed interest in reed as a traditional roofing material.

Extensive reed harvesting used to be manually undertaken on many small beds throughout the country to supply a network of thatchers. Today, this has given way to mechanical harvesting on fewer, larger sites. Nevertheless, the industry in the UK continues to provide employment for some 1,000 people, including seasonal work for farm labourers and fishermen for example.

A roof thatched well with good quality reed and capped with saw-sedge can be expected to last at least 50 years and often more than 70 (BRGA pers comm). Many buildings which were thatched in the 1920s and '30s still have their thatched roofs today. The thatching of new, luxury homes at Southport in 1995 with reed from the Tay Estuary is indicative of the confidence which remains in reed as a roofing material.

Until recently, premature decay of some thatched roofs was believed to be associated with poor reed quality which in turn was linked with high levels of nutrients in the water in which reed was growing. Initial investigations into the problem were not able to establish such a link (Boar *et al* 1991). Haslam (1994) claims the strength and durability of thatching reed is not affected by high levels of nutrients in the reedbed environment.

In 1989, total UK thatching reed production was estimated at 336,555 bundles (some 64% from conservation managed sites). In the same year, approximately 1.5 million bundles were imported from elsewhere in Europe (Bateman *et al* 1990). This suggests there is a huge home market for thatching reed, a market that at present the UK is unable fully to meet. The management, rehabilitation and creation of reedbeds should be able to redress this imbalance.

Plate 5 Reed being used to thatch a roof in Norfolk.

Roger Tidman

Part 1
PLANNING FOR MANAGEMENT AND CREATION

Contents

1.1 Setting Goals and How to Achieve Them

Reedbeds may be managed and created for commercial or conservation reasons, or more often a combination of both purposes. Increasingly, it is recognised that reedbed management techniques are common to both commercial and wildlife interests on a sustainable basis. The balance between the two will vary according to ownership, financial and practical constraints.

This section considers what should be done once the potential to modify existing management, rehabilitate a site or create a new reedbed has been recognised. This entails ensuring that management, rehabilitation and creation decisions taken are appropriate to the location and its existing or potential wildlife value.

Two goals are the focus of this guide: nature conservation and commercial uses. These objectives can be achieved through:

- modification of current management

- rehabilitation of degraded reedbeds

- creation of new reedbeds.

The following section focuses on how to evaluate a site and ensure the appropriate decisions are made in order to achieve the goals which have been set.

1.2 Site Evaluation and Project Planning

Whatever the ultimate goal for a site, making the most of any opportunity requires careful consideration and planning. The steps in Figure 1 should be followed to make best use of management and creation opportunities. Some sites will have greater potential than others. This may result from a range of factors, which are summarised in Table 1 and outlined below.

Table 1: Points to consider when assessing the potential value of an existing reedbed or land for reedbed creation

Investigate and evaluate existing interest
- gather information on site status/ ownership
  eg - SSSI
      NNR
      arable

- size of site

- proximity to other reedbeds

- geographical location

- existing wildlife value
  eg - presence of notable species

- quality of reed/litter depth as indicator of commercial potential/wildlife value

Investigate and evaluate physical and chemical characteristics.
- hydrology (Appendix 1)
  - soils

- water quality

Determine legal constraints.
- discuss proposals with statutory water management agencies and statutory conservation agencies to evaluate constraints and cost implications

Investigate/evaluate financial/management constraints and opportunities.
- resource/labour available to manage site

- availability of grants (Appendix 2)

(Adapted from Campbell 1994)

Figure 1
Sequence of steps to facilitate optimal reedbed management, rehabilitation and creation.

Recognition of opportunity
to enhance/create reedbed

– Identify broad objective (goal)

Identify people/organisations to advise on nature conservation/commercial aspects

eg Statutory Agencies eg EN, BA, British Reed Growers' Association, RSPB, County Wildlife Trusts

Investigate and evaluate the site

Identifying constraints (Tables 1, 2 and 3)

Evaluate and present choices for:

- modification of current management (part 2)
- rehabilitation of degraded reedbed (part 2)
- creation of new reedbed (part 3)

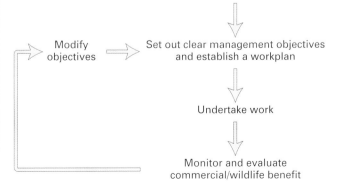

Modify objectives → Set out clear management objectives and establish a workplan

Undertake work

Monitor and evaluate commercial/wildlife benefit

1.2.1   Conservation status and ownership

The starting point for any site assessment should be to collate existing information on its conservation status (is it a designated site eg SSSI/ASSI?). It is always necessary to contact the statutory conservation agency (Appendix 3) if the site is an SSSI/ASSI. This should also yield valuable information about the wildlife value and past/present management practices. The County Wildlife Trusts (Appendix 3) should also be contacted as the site may have regional or county importance for nature conservation. The local knowledge of owners and reed cutters can provide additional valuable information on past site management.

1.2.2   Site size and proximity to other sites

Reedbed size will influence the number and range of species that may be present. In a reedbed some species require a minimum area of reed in order to sustain a viable population.

The habitat size requirement for several breeding reedbed bird species has broadly been determined (Tyler 1992 and Table 23 in Part 2). However, such figures are approximations and are influenced by factors such as habitat quality. Bitterns, for example, appear to prefer reedbeds with extensive shallow margins for feeding (section 2.2.4). Consequently, they may breed in areas smaller than 20 ha (Part 2, Figure 23) where conditions are optimal. It is important to emphasise that even small areas of reed are of value to wildlife. Several square metres of marginal reedbed can support a reed warbler nest and a range of invertebrates (eg Table 12 in Part 3).

1.2.3   Geographical location

All conservation objectives are not applicable to all parts of the UK. The existing distribution of species will influence what wildlife can be attracted to a site. Management work to improve a site for bitterns is more likely to be successful if undertaken in their traditional heartlands currently in the North-west and East Anglia where the remaining pairs regularly breed (Figure 2) despite having declined recently in these areas too (Figure 3). It is therefore important to consider the location of a particular site and be realistic about the species that are likely to occur there.

Figure 2 The distribution of bitterns in the UK (1995).

Bittern breeding areas

Wintering birds most likely here (includes the above)

Frequent winter records

Infrequent winter records

1.2.4 Physical and chemical characteristics

Hydrology is one of the most important factors to consider when examining opportunities for rehabilitation or creation of a reedbed. However, hydrology is often neglected when deciding what to do at a site. The nature of hydrological investigations will depend upon the scale of a project and resources available. The opportunity to rehabilitate a small area of existing reedbed (eg < 1 ha) may simply require a brief field visit to discover an existing sluice is derelict and not working. In contrast a major creation scheme (eg Case Study 13, Ham Wall) may require detailed investigation.

Table 2 shows the range of factors which may be investigated, depending upon the scale of the project and the resources available. At the outset of any project a description of the site, including location of low-lying areas, patterns of water flow and soil type will give invaluable information on the potential of a site. A detailed levelling survey to determine site topography may be unnecessary if you are able to observe the area in flood and make a photographic record.

Determining the availability of water at a site is particularly important when creating a new reedbed. Liaison with staff responsible for water resources and flood defence in the appropriate water management agency may be sufficient to give an indication of overall water availability. However, assessment of a site's water balance (inputs, eg rainfall and river flows, and losses, eg evapotranspiration and seepage) should be considered essential for major schemes. Advice from the Institute of Hydrology, universities and colleges with expertise in this area should be considered.

The ability to hold and manipulate water levels on a site is also important. Liaison with relevant statutory agencies (Appendix 3) should provide valuable information on the nature of existing drainage on a site. Methods for holding and manipulating water levels on a site are examined in section 2.2.1 of the guide and case studies 5, 8 and 14.

**Figure 3
Numbers of booming male bitterns recorded in Britain, 1910–92: total in Broadland and in other sites (from Tyler 1994a).**

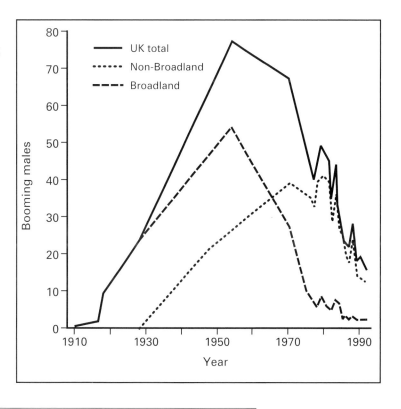

Table 2: Hydrological assessment of reedbed sites

	What to assess	How to assess	Importance/Value
1. Location and description.	Catchment area	OS maps Aerial photographs	Indicates sources/flow of water and low-lying areas suitable for reedbed.
	Soil types	Soil survey maps + auger on site	Soil type will determine the hydrological regime which can be sustained on the site.
			Clay soils because of their low permeability hold water on surface. Surface flooding is essential to maintain wetness. (The presence of clay may promote stronger reed growth.)
			Peat soils are highly permeable. Water levels can therefore be maintained by keeping ditch levels high.
	Topography	Levelling survey or observe area in flood conditions (take photographs). Preflood site before undertaking work.	Indicates low-lying areas and provides information for siting of water level management structures.
	Flow patterns on site	Observe directly and mark on map.	Provides indication of where to site sluices, etc.
2. Overall water availability.	Climatic conditions	Calculations and field measurements. See Appendix 1.	To give an initial indication that there is sufficient water to support the creation of a new reedbed.
			To determine the viable size of reedbed.
			To indicate if winter water storage is required to supplement summer shortages.
	River/ditch levels and seasonal fluctuations	Gauge boards on these may be calibrated to provide actual flow figures. Consult with NRA, etc.	
		Check site for: ● existing embankments/ bunds	These together with topography will affect distribution of water around the site.
		● depth of stream well below field surface; or depth of water table well below field surface.	Where water level well below field surface indicates requirement for: ● sluice construction/ maintenance ● bed lowering ● pumping to maintain water levels.

►

Table 2 cont'd

	What to assess	How to assess	Importance/Value
	Requirements of other water users in catchment	Water management agencies hold information on abstractions and should be able to indicate availability of surface water.	Water requirements of a reedbed may have to be balanced with those of other user groups. This is particularly important in low rainfall and highly populated areas.
	Groundwater	Determine seasonal nature of seepage/ spring flows.	Often a source of high quality/ low nutrient level water, although this is not always the case particularly in eastern England.
		Water table heights can be measured using simple low cost dipwells.	Will indicate through season problem periods of low water levels on a site.
			Caution Assessment of groundwater other than simple water table measurements is notoriously difficult and if required should be undertaken in consultation with experts, eg universities, water management agencies or IoH.
3. Ability to hold and manipulate water levels on a site.	Water levels on site/topography (described above)	Gauge boards/ dipwells (described above).	Water level fluctuations should be appropriate to objective, eg surface levels in existing/proposed reedbed should fluctuate between 5–25 cm for bitterns in summer.
	Determine nature of existing drainage	Liaise with Government agriculture departments and water management agencies.	
		Examine condition of existing water control structures,	
		● check for leakage in bunds	
		● check sluices etc operating effectively.	
		● determine nature of sub-surface drainage.	May provide potential to sub-irrigate a site.
4. Other factors	Impact of flooding/ raising water levels	Liaise at earliest opportunity with water management agencies.	May require bunding of site to protect adjacent land.
Influence of proposals on adjacent land.			

1.2.5   Wildlife value and reedbed quality

The value of a reedbed in both commercial and wildlife terms is affected by its condition. Therefore, on existing reedbed sites an indication of habitat condition and what wildlife is already present will be the most important influence upon management. Table 3 describes a range of easily assessable physical indicators of reedbed habitat condition. Ideally, these indicators should be recorded in map form to provide a record of the existing condition of the site (Figure 4). Such information together with the results of a hydrological assessment form the basis on which management decisions can be made.

A reedbed that already supports a diverse assemblage of wildlife or rare and threatened species is best managed for their benefit. The requirement is to establish whether the habitat is deteriorating such that the wildlife value will be lost if allowed to continue or whether it is ideal as it is and management should continue in its present form. Where the primary objective is to develop the reedbed for commercial reed cutting, the cutting regime and other management may be designed to take the wildlife value into consideration. Other factors to consider for thatching reed include the quality of the reed itself where

Table 3: Physical indicators of reed/reedbed condition

Indicator of conditions	What to assess	How to assess	Indication
Reed quality	Height	Measure directly.	Less than 1.5 m may suggest prolonged single wale cutting, saline intrusion or low nutrient levels. 1.5–2.5 m – 'normal' reed usually as a result of wet conditions or indication of double wale cutting. > 2.5 m may indicate a tidal reedbed or very high nutrient levels.
	Density	Count number of growing stems per square metre.	< 100/m^2 may indicate degraded reedbed 100–200/m^2 may indicate double wale cutting. > 200/m^2 may indicate prolonged single wale cutting.
	Stem thickness (diameter)	Measure butt end.	2–7 mm – thin: less susceptible to attack by stem dwelling invertebrates. 7–12 mm – thick: more susceptible to attack.
	Straightness	Visual	Bent, dog-legged reeds suggest reed with litter layer. No value for thatching and wildlife variable depending on degree of deterioration.

▶

Table 3 cont'd

Indicator of conditions	What to assess	How to assess	Indication
	Hardness	Squeeze butt end (first 10–15 cm) of stem between forefinger and thumb.	Hard reed will be difficult to crush and is suitable for thatching. Soft reed crushes easily. Indicative of growing conditions and management.
Reedbed litter layer	Depth and wetness (see below)	Check for presence and depth by digging.	A deep litter layer (10–30 cm) may indicate the bed is drying out or may indicate lack of past management. If dry at surface in summer may benefit from bed regeneration or raising water levels.
Reedbed water levels	Seasonal variation in water level	Measure winter water level, Oct–March.	Typically as much as 1 m deep (except when drained down for cutting).
		Measure summer water level, April–Sept.	Typically 5–25 cm above surface for wet reedbed eg 'reedswamp'.
			Typically at or just below/above (< 5 cm) surface for 'reedfen'.
			If below these levels then indication bed may be drying out. Wet reedbeds are generally better for wildlife and reed growth.
Scrub	Extent of scrub	Assess visually and mark extent on map.	Scrub indicates a reedbed is drying out. If > 10% of area is scrub, clearance may be required.
Non-wetland plants	Extent	Presence/absence. Mark extent on map.	Presence of non-wetland plants indicates reedbed is drying out.
Open water (including ditches)	Extent	Mark area on map.	May indicate area for potential reedbed expansion if < 1 m deep.
			Presence important for a range of wildlife and for habitat diversity.

factors such as stem height and thickness are generally less important than hardness and straightness.

Assessing which species of animals and plants are present will require specialist help for identifying less common species with which most people are unfamiliar. Assistance may be sought through the statutory conservation agencies, County Wildlife Trusts or individual experts. Some animal groups, eg birds, mammals, amphibians and reptiles, are comparatively well known but more complex groups like plants and invertebrates will certainly require expert help. In reality, it is rarely necessary to conduct an exhaustive survey. Target particular groups – plants offer a good starting point since they provide an indication of the reedbed's condition and what other wildlife is likely to be present. Details of the kinds of plants found in many of the UK's reedbeds are given in Rodwell (1995).

1.2.6 Legal and planning considerations

A range of legal and planning considerations should be taken into account when certain management improvements or reedbed creation are to be undertaken. Table 4 provides a check-list of factors which may need to be considered.

Table 4: Legal and planning considerations

Question	If answer yes
1. Water management Is water supply required from a river/stream or groundwater source? (eg for storage of winter water).	**Action:** Consult water management agency to discuss requirements for abstraction licence.
Will proposals involve: ● retaining water above original ground level? ● raising water above surrounding land? ● altering existing flow regime?	Bunds and dams constructed to impound water may require licensing. If a dam impounds more than 25,000 m³ of water above the level of surrounding land (eg a 1-ha, 2.5-m deep lake) a licence is required. Additionally, construction will require the supervision of a chartered civil engineer.
	Where proposals may affect drainage of neighbouring land, land drainage consent may be required.
	Action: Consult water management agencies to discuss licensing requirements.
	Their staff should also be able to provide informal advice on sluice, dam design, etc.
Can surplus water be discharged into water course without a discharge consent?	Yes, usually this is acceptable unless the discharge causes a marked deterioration in water quality.
	Action: Liaise with water management agencies.
2. Wildlife Interest Is the site a SSSI/ASSI*, non- designated site?	**Action:** Consult statutory conservation agency staff. For sites of local interest consult County Wildlife Trusts.
Are any protected plants/animals likely to be destroyed/disturbed?	**Action:** Consult statutory conservation agency.
3. Public rights of way Is proposal likely to divert or block existing public right of way? eg footpath, bridleway or by-way?	**Action:** Consult local authority.
4. Planning matters Is material (eg spoil) likely to be transported on/off site via a public highway?	**Action:** Consult local authority.
Is excavated material to be sold or used to construct bunds?	Consult mineral planning authority or local planning authority.
Will the proposal affect landscape/drainage of area?	Discuss with local planning authority. This is essential where the area is a designated AONB or in an ESA, in which case MAFF should also be consulted. In a National Park, the National Parks Authority should be consulted.

Footnote: * Special Protection Areas (SPAs) and Special Areas of Conservation (SACs) have additional safeguards requiring the involvement of planning authorities. Further advice should be sought from statutory conservation agencies.

1.2.7 Resource constraints

From the outset, it is important to consider the resource implications of any management or creation proposals. The costs of feasibility studies, engineering works and management should be examined. It is important, therefore, to establish the resources needed to meet the objectives, or to modify the goals in accordance with available resources.

Resource considerations may include:
- design and feasibility studies, eg
  - hydrological survey
  - wildlife survey

- one-off capital costs
  - land forming, eg bund and ditch construction
  - installation of water control structures

- ongoing management costs
  - labour/staff costs to undertake reed cutting/scrub control, etc
  - servicing/maintenance of machinery

- survey and monitoring costs.

1.2.8 Project proposals and management plans

Whether proposals for a site relate to improved management or creation, it is often useful if the background and reasons for any work are put in writing. This can be as a short project proposal or where there are longer term management implications as a management plan. Ideally, either should contain the following sections (Merritt, 1994):

- site description

- site evaluation

- rationale behind site proposals and objectives

- prescriptions to achieve objectives and workplans

This framework will help with the long-term planning of resources and labour. The process enables constraints to be identified and clear goals to be set. Much information can be collated in the form of maps and diagrams. Figure 4 shows a real example developed as part of a preliminary site assessment. More detailed guidance on the management planning process is available in Alexander (1994). Appendix 6 sets out the categories in the nationally promoted Countryside Management System which can be adopted where a detailed management plan is required. An additional benefit of producing a management plan is that the necessary work for a five-year period can be agreed with the statutory conservation agency and the provision of financial assistance may be facilitated.

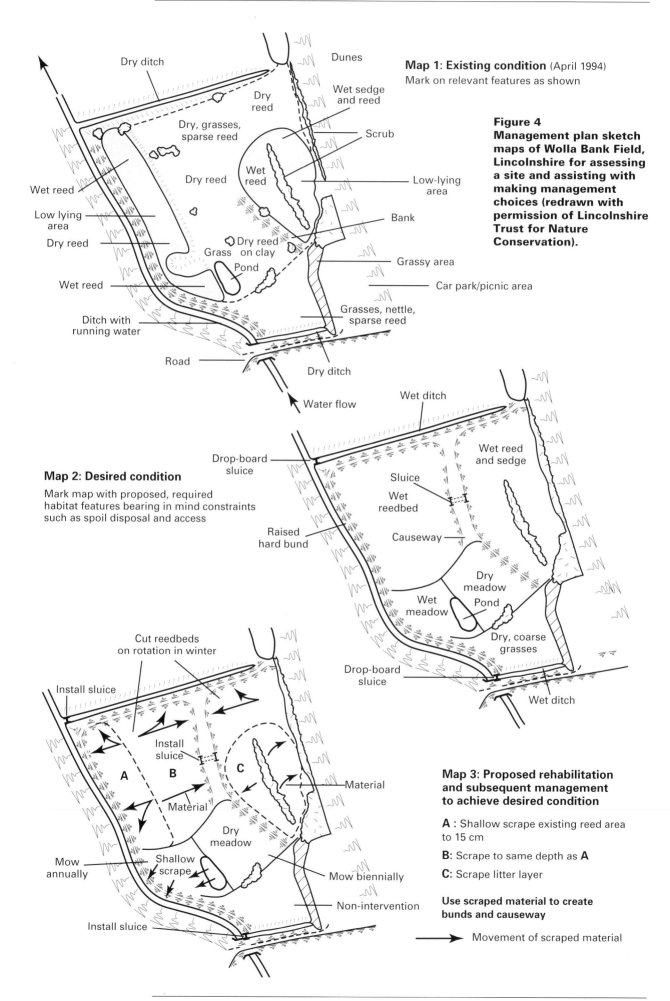

Map 1: **Existing condition** (April 1994)
Mark on relevant features as shown

Dry ditch
Dunes
Dry reed
Wet sedge and reed
Scrub
Dry, grasses, sparse reed
Wet reed
Dry reed
Low-lying area
Wet reed
Low lying area
Dry reed
Bank
Dry reed
Grass on clay
Pond
Grassy area
Wet reed
Car park/picnic area
Ditch with running water
Grasses, nettle, sparse reed
Road
Dry ditch
Water flow

Figure 4
Management plan sketch maps of Wolla Bank Field, Lincolnshire for assessing a site and assisting with making management choices (redrawn with permission of Lincolnshire Trust for Nature Conservation).

Map 2: Desired condition

Mark map with proposed, required habitat features bearing in mind constraints such as spoil disposal and access

Wet ditch
Drop-board sluice
Wet reed and sedge
Sluice
Wet reedbed
Raised hard bund
Causeway
Dry meadow
Wet meadow
Pond
Dry, coarse grasses
Drop-board sluice
Wet ditch

Cut reedbeds on rotation in winter
Install sluice
Install sluice
A
B
C
Material
Material
Mow annually
Dry meadow
Shallow scrape
Mow biennially
Non-intervention
Install sluice

Map 3: Proposed rehabilitation and subsequent management to achieve desired condition

A : Shallow scrape existing reed area to 15 cm

B: Scrape to same depth as **A**

C: Scrape litter layer

Use scraped material to create bunds and causeway

→ Movement of scraped material

1.3   Making Choices

Having evaluated a site, careful consideration should be given to the choices available to improve existing management, rehabilitate an existing site or to create a new reedbed.

Table 5 gives examples of starting points and introduces the management and creation techniques which may be applied

to reedbeds. Parts 2 and 3 of the guide provide detailed information on the benefits, advantages, disadvantages and resource implications of these techniques. While guidance is provided as to the choice of management techniques to achieve specific goals, the decision lies with the reedbed manager.

Table 5: Making choices

Example Starting Point	Management Options	Section	Case Studies
1. Improving existing management Some cutting of reed undertaken. Open water/ditches occasionally managed. Small area with scrub encroaching. Site perceived to be drying out to a limited degree.	Water management:	2.2	
	● Check operation of water control structures to ensure water level prescriptions met.	2.2.1	1, 5, 8
	● Implement appropriate ditch management eg rotational slubbing.	2.2.3	6, 11
	Reed/vegetation management:	2.3	
	● Reduce litter layer by cutting.	2.3.1	4, 5, 6, 7, 8, 11
	Optimise cutting regime in relation to goal. Implement rotational cutting regime and where single wale cutting is undertaken consider adopting double wale. A minimum of 20% of reed area should be left uncut in a single year for the benefit of wildlife.		
	● Undertake scrub management, eg rotational coppicing.	2.3.5	3, 9, 10, 11
	● Reduce litter accumulation by rotational burning or by raking.	2.3.4	4, 9, 11
Example Starting Point	Rehabilitation Options	Section	Case Studies
2. Rehabilitation Degraded reedbed perceived to be drying out with low water levels; significant scrub encroachment; poor quality reed; deep litter layer as a result of lack of management.	Water management:	2.2	
	Raise water levels by:		
	● Repairing existing/installing new water management structures, eg sluices.	2.2.1	10, 11, (13)
	● Implement appropriate water level management regime.		1, 5, 8, 11
	● Lower bed level by excavation (see below).	2.3.6	10
	● Reprofile/re-excavate existing ditches on rotation.	2.2.3	2, 10, (14)
	● Establish open water areas.	2.2.4	3, 7, 10, 11
	Reed/vegetation management:	2.3	
	● Reduce litter by burning	2.3.6	9

▶

Table 5 cont'd

	Rehabilitation Options	Section	Case Studies
Rehabilitation continued	● Reduce litter layer by cutting and clearing. (+ as for management options).	2.3.1	4, 5, 6, 7, 8, 11
	● Undertake scrub management, eg by grubbing.	2.3.5	3, 10
	● Bed regeneration. - excavation by digger - excavation by reciprocator mower - mechanical maceration of litter.	2.3.6	10
Example Starting Point	Creation Options		
3. Creation Arable/disused land with no/ limited existing wildlife value.	Engineering operations:	3.2	
	● Land forming where required.	3.2.1	12, 13
	● Bund/dam and ditch creation.	3.2.2	(10), 13, 17
	● Install water control structures, eg sluices.	3.2.3	12, 13, 14, 16, 17
	Vegetation establishment techniques:	3.3	
	● Prepare bed, eg remove unwanted plants.	3.3.1	14
	● Select establishment technique: - expansion of existing reed - seeding - pot-grown reed - rhizomes - stem cuttings.	3.3.2 } 3.3.3	15 12, 14, 16, 17 15 16

Part 2
MANAGEMENT AND REHABILITATION

Contents

2.1 Introduction

Reedbeds in the UK originated naturally or as an indirect consequence of human activity. In some instances they have appeared when agricultural practices have ceased, usually where grazing and water control have been abandoned on low-lying land. Some have been created for specific purposes but throughout the UK there are innumerable ponds, gravel pits and ditches containing reed that colonised naturally. Whatever their origins, many reedbeds have been traditionally managed as natural resources, usually by cutting for thatch, which maintained them as reed-dominated sites, effectively keeping the process of succession in check.

2.1.1 Why manage reedbeds?

The processes of nature are constantly changing. Habitats gradually change as different plants and animals colonise an area and compete for resources. 'Reedswamp' represents the early stages of succession from open water to woodland. Without management a reedbed will gradually dry out, becoming colonised by other grasses and tall herbs such as greater willowherb, nettle and bittersweet, eventually developing into scrub and woodland. This natural process may be accelerated by drainage, water abstraction or isolation from water courses because the resulting drier conditions favour scrub development. In this situation, characteristic reedbed animals and plants will in time be lost and the reed will no longer be of thatching quality.

Reedbed management and rehabilitation will slow down or even reverse succession (Figure 1) in order to maintain a balance of different habitat types or to reinstate one or more habitats, depending on the objectives. Often the dominance of reed is sought, especially where the objective is to provide habitat for reed-specific wildlife such as bittern and bearded tit or to cut reed for thatch. The maintenance of reed domination is probably the single most important aspect of management for reedbed birds (Burgess and Evans 1989).

Without management a reedbed will naturally dry out and turn to woodland. Management or rehabilitation will slow down or reverse this process.

Figure 1 How management influences succession in reedbeds.

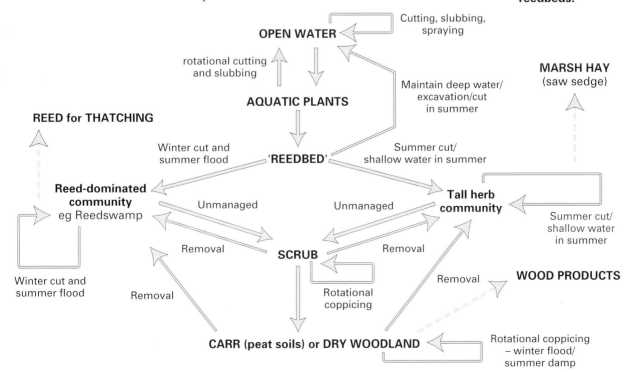

However, the dominance of reed may not always be appropriate or attainable and depends on site characteristics and conservation objectives.

In some reedbeds, areas may have developed a more diverse flora as the bed became less wet/shallower enabling plants other than reed to grow. This may be especially so if the reed was quite recently mown or grazed in summer as was traditional in the Broads (George 1992) and is routine at Leighton Moss in Lancashire (Case Study 8). In the Broadland fens, a great diversity of plant communities in a complex mosaic developed as a result of peat digging and an intricate pattern of winter and summer mowing for fen products. The characteristics of these reedbeds rely on continued management being tailored towards the requirements of important wildlife.

2.1.2 How are reedbeds managed?

The management of reedbeds can be divided into two broad areas: water management (section 2.2) and reed management (section 2.3). Within these, the most fundamental management techniques are control of water levels and reed cutting. Table 1 and Table 2 summarise the effects of managing water level and cutting reed.

Cutting reed in winter allows a crop to be taken without adversely affecting the reeds' growth. Reed is perfectly able to grow in dry soil but has to compete with other vigorous grasses and tall herbs which are absent from flooded soils. The combination of spring flooding and winter cutting maintains reed dominance (Haslam 1972b).

Managing reedbeds to sustain or encourage a more diverse range of plants involves the same principles as for almost pure stands of reed, although the timing of events is quite different. To benefit plants, cutting or grazing may be undertaken in late summer and cut material removed to reduce litter accumulation. Ideally the water level should be at or just below the surface in summer but flooded in winter. Such a regime provides ideal growing conditions for many plants while reducing competition from a few, more vigorous, tall plants such as reed which is relatively intolerant of summer cutting and grazing (Haslam 1972b). This management will gradually reduce the amount of reed in the stand (Gryseels 1989b).

Table 1: Reasons for managing water levels on reedbeds

Control of water levels can be used to:

- encourage reed at the expense of other plant species
- increase the rate of litter break-down (after draw-down)
- facilitate other management practices, especially cutting
- provide an aquatic habitat (in wet reedbed and open water)

Table 2: Reasons for cutting reed on reedbeds

Reed cutting can be used to:

- reduce the rate of litter accumulation
- provide cut reed for commercial purposes
- stimulate the production of new buds
- provide temporary, open, wet habitat
- control reed encroachment into open water

2.1.3 Principal rehabilitation techniques

The rehabilitation techniques employed will depend on the extent of degradation or succession which has taken place. The difference between management and rehabilitation is one of scale; the techniques are essentially the same with the addition of bed regeneration as a major rehabilitation method. The principal rehabilitation techniques are:

● raising water levels

● scrub removal

● bed regeneration.

Bed regeneration can be achieved by a number of means as described in section 2.3.6. In addition, the action of cutting and removal of reed and other vegetation reduces further litter accumulation and is in effect a form of regeneration. Table 3 describes the benefits and disadvantages of the principal rehabilitation techniques.

Table 3: Principal reedbed rehabilitation techniques

Technique	Benefits	Disadvantages	Section
Water Management:			
Raising water levels	Improves habitat for bittern, reed warbler, amphibians, aquatic flora and fauna	Could damage reedfen communities	2.2.1 e
	Encourages reed at expense of other plants	May not benefit bearded tit nest sites	
	Produces better quality reed for thatching	Detrimental to some invertebrates	
Ditch management	Creates open water for aquatic flora and fauna	Detrimental to some aquatic flora and fauna, albeit temporarily	2.2.3
	Creates feeding areas for bittern, bearded tit, water birds and mammals		
	Enhances water management, essential for thatching reed		
Reedbed and vegetation management:			
Reed cutting	Reduces rate of litter build-up	Can be detrimental to some invertebrates and nesting birds	2.3.1
	Increases quality of reed for thatching and nesting birds		
	May benefit certain flora		
	Creates temporary open water		
Reed/litter burning	Reduces litter layer, rankness ⟶ rejuvenates reedbed	Destroys reed-stem and litter-dwelling invertebrates and possibly bearded tit nest sites	2.3.4
Scrub removal	Slows down drying out of reedbed	Could disadvantage Cetti's warbler, sedge warbler, reed warbler, marsh harrier and many invertebrate species	2.3.5
	Enables reed to recolonise		
	Facilitates cutting/harvesting		
Bed regeneration (litter layer removal)	Rejuvenates reedbed ⟶ better quality reed for thatching	Detrimental to litter-dwelling invertebrates	2.3.6
	Creates temporary open water for feeding bittern, bearded tit, water birds (snipe, water rail, moorhen), wildfowl, and aquatic flora and fauna	May destroy bearded tit nesting habitat	

2.1.4 Management for different habitats and species

Management will influence both the type of reedbed and the range of species found within it.

How a reedbed is managed will largely depend on the owner's objectives, financial, physical, chemical and practical constraints as identified in Part 1. The following section overviews how different management techniques influence different reedbed habitats and species. Figure 2 illustrates the range of wildlife associated with a managed reedbed whilst Figure 3 illustrates the main techniques used to manage succession for a range of reedbed habitats.

The most important techniques are cutting and water level management. The simplest way to maintain almost pure reed is to ensure the water level remains above the soil surface all year round. This greatly reduces competition from other plants, enabling the reed to grow freely. The water

Figure 2 Examples of the range of wildlife associated with a managed reedbed.

provides valuable aquatic habitat that supports fish, amphibians and invertebrates, in turn a food source for other animals. A closed, uninterrupted expanse of wet reed would be beneficial to many invertebrates and a small number of other specialist species such as reed warbler, although in plant terms it will be species-poor (Wheeler 1992).

The addition of open water by the construction of ditches, ponds and 'meres' increases the diversity of the habitat and will benefit fish and amphibians which may be exploited by a number of animals including birds such as herons and bitterns. Aquatic invertebrates, plants, birds and mammals will also benefit from the additional aquatic habitat.

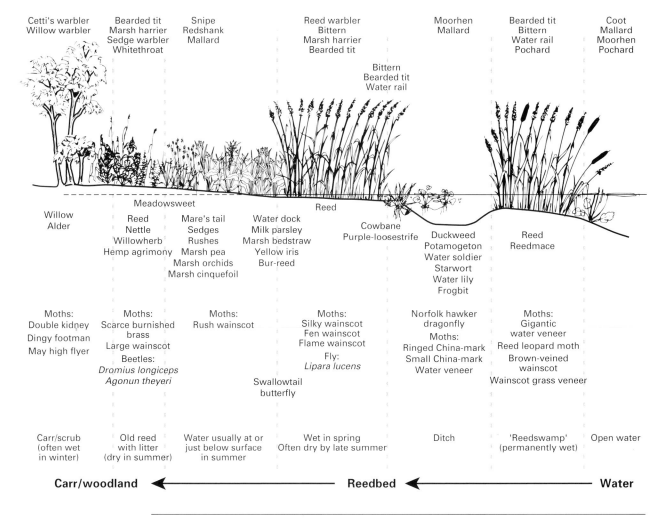

| Cetti's warbler
Willow warbler | Bearded tit
Marsh harrier
Sedge warbler
Whitethroat | Snipe
Redshank
Mallard | Reed warbler
Bittern
Marsh harrier
Bearded tit | Moorhen
Mallard | Bearded tit
Bittern
Water rail
Pochard | Coot
Mallard
Moorhen
Pochard |

Bittern
Bearded tit
Water rail

Meadowsweet
Reed

| Willow
Alder | Reed
Nettle
Willowherb
Hemp agrimony | Mare's tail
Sedges
Rushes
Marsh pea
Marsh orchids
Marsh cinquefoil | Water dock
Milk parsley
Marsh bedstraw
Yellow iris
Bur-reed | Cowbane
Purple-loosestrife | Duckweed
Potamogeton
Water soldier
Starwort
Water lily
Frogbit | Reed
Reedmace |

| Moths:
Double kidney
Dingy footman
May high flyer | Moths:
Scarce burnished
brass
Large wainscot
Beetles:
Dromius longiceps
Agonun theyeri | Moths:
Rush wainscot | Moths:
Silky wainscot
Fen wainscot
Flame wainscot
Fly:
Lipara lucens

Swallowtail
butterfly | Norfolk hawker
dragonfly
Moths:
Ringed China-mark
Small China-mark
Water veneer | Moths:
Gigantic
water veneer
Reed leopard moth
Brown-veined
wainscot
Wainscot grass veneer | |

| Carr/scrub
(often wet
in winter) | Old reed
with litter
(dry in summer) | Water usually at or
just below surface
in summer | Wet in spring
Often dry by late summer | Ditch | 'Reedswamp'
(permanently wet) | Open water |

Carr/woodland ← → **Reedbed** ← → **Water**

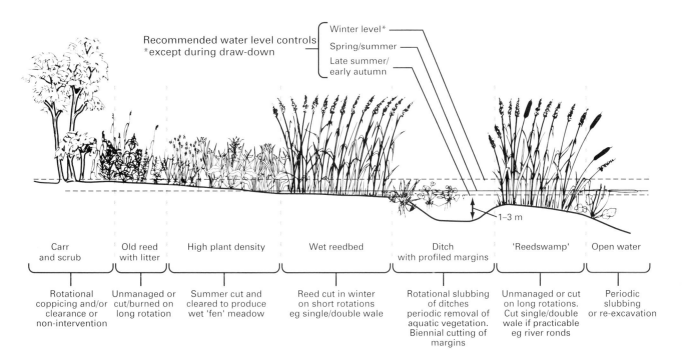

Recommended water level controls
*except during draw-down

Winter level* ————
Spring/summer ————
Late summer/
early autumn

1–3 m

Carr and scrub	Old reed with litter	High plant density	Wet reedbed	Ditch with profiled margins	'Reedswamp'	Open water
Rotational coppicing and/or clearance or non-intervention	Unmanaged or cut/burned on long rotation	Summer cut and cleared to produce wet 'fen' meadow	Reed cut in winter on short rotations eg single/double wale	Rotational slubbing of ditches periodic removal of aquatic vegetation. Biennial cutting of margins	Unmanaged or cut on long rotations. Cut single/double wale if practicable eg river ronds	Periodic slubbing or re-excavation

**Figure 3
The main techniques used to manage succession for a range of reedbed habitats.**

A reedbed managed commercially for thatching materials requires the maintenance of high water levels during the growing season but to facilitate harvesting in winter, the water is drawn down (2.2.1f). Hence, the provision of ditches with control mechanisms such as sluices greatly facilitates commercial management. To sustain reed quality for thatching the reed should be cut annually (single wale) or two-yearly (double wale). After the reed has been harvested the bed should ideally be flooded again to a level just below the top of the cut stubble and raised slowly as the reed shoots grow, ensuring they are not submerged (see also section 2.3.1c).

Whether undertaken annually (or two-yearly as was historically practised) for hay or litter, or on a four-year cycle for saw-sedge, summer cutting reduces biomass and increases plant diversity (Wheeler and Giller 1982a; Gryseels 1989b). Such management suppresses the growth of reed permitting less vigorous plants to thrive.

Clearly, different wildlife groups benefit according to the management undertaken. Selection of management options will therefore entail taking into account the requirements of different groups or species.

Cutting all of a reedbed in one go disadvantages many specialist reedbed species since the absence of standing reed removes the very habitat they depend upon. For example, the reed leopard moth spends two years as a larva inside reed stems and the twin-spotted wainscot pupates inside reed stems (Plate 1) and overwinters on reed as an egg. Both would be lost with the winter cut. Such management does not support breeding birds either, such as reed warbler and bearded tit, which rely on stands of reed for nest sites and cover whilst feeding. In practice this rarely happens across a whole site and uncut reed nearby can act as a wildlife refuge. Rotational cutting such as double wale (or longer rotations with periodic burning), offers the opportunity to help maintain or increase wildlife interest

Plate 1 Split reed stem showing overwintering pupa of twin-spotted wainscot.

Paul Waring

at a site. An integrated approach to wildlife and commercial reedbed management is feasible on all reedbeds but is easier to achieve on larger sites.

Areas of unmanaged reed with a litter layer are often used by bearded tits, which prefer to nest low down amongst dead stems. However, in some sites they use recently cut reed which has only one or two years' worth of litter accumulation and often select such areas for nesting in favour of areas that have not been cut for years or have been unmanaged. At Radipole Lake in Dorset, a shift in cutting areas was accompanied by a notable movement of bearded tits which selected the newly cut areas for nesting. Between 1984–88 the percentage of nests found in the newly cut area increased from 0% to 26% of the population. However, within the wet reedbed at Leighton Moss no bearded tit nests have yet been found in areas which were cut as long as five years ago. Reed litter at this site is slow to accumulate because of the high rate of decomposition. Large reedbeds seem to be preferred by bearded tits presumably because they offer greater nesting and

feeding opportunities, although small reedbeds may occasionally support one or two pairs and small wintering flocks. Cutting strips or blocks of reed on a long rotation will vary the age structure of the reedbed and will prove beneficial to bearded tits and many invertebrates, although this requires a large commitment of labour.

At Strumpshaw Fen in Norfolk, nesting reed warblers (Plate 2) occupied cut areas quite rapidly. By the first spring after a cut the reed was of insufficient height to be of use but after one year's growth nests were recorded at a density of 20/ha. After 2–3 years the density reached 35–40 nests/ha (Burgess and Evans 1989). This demonstrates the rapidity with which this species is able to recolonise cut areas.

The bittern requires large areas of reedswamp to nest in and disturbance-free feeding areas usually just within the reed alongside secluded ditches or pools (Plate 1 in Introduction). Clear, shallow water with an abundant and accessible supply of small fish is also required.

Plate 2 Reed warbler with nest containing chicks.

M W Richards (RSPB)

In order to manage a reedbed which supports a range of wildlife such as reed leopard moth, twin-spotted wainscot moth, bearded tit and bittern, it is necessary to employ a range of management techniques to produce a mosaic of habitat types (Table 4 and Figure 3). It should be recognised that even when optimal habitat conditions are created by management, other factors may prevent colonisation of the target species.

Table 4: Examples of management required for selected species

Species	Habitat requirement	Management technique
Reed leopard moth	Reed stems left for two winters or more	Leave uncut areas or 3-year rotation
Twin-spotted wainscot moth	Reed stems left for one winter or more	Leave uncut areas or 2-year rotation
Bearded tit	Reedbed with litter layer	Leave uncut areas or cut on long rotation
Bittern*	Large reedbed with reed/water edge	Maintain open water. Maintain wet reedswamp by rotational cutting

* Further information on managing reedbeds for bitterns can be found in section 2.2.4a.
In addition, a free leaflet *Reedbed Management for Bitterns* is available from the RSPB (Address in Appendix 3).

2.2 Water Management

The conservation interest and commercial value of a reedbed is influenced by the physical and chemical characteristics of the water environment. Poor water quality and over exploitation of water as a resource by increased abstraction and drainage, has had a serious deleterious effect on UK wetland habitats including reedbeds (Haslam pers comm; Haslam 1994).

In particular, two aspects of water management are important on reedbeds, that of water regime (levels, duration and timing) and of water quality. Section 2.2.1 and 2.2.2 examine these in turn. The first looks at the problems of water availability on sites and how to control and manipulate water levels, and the second at the effects of water quality and measures to improve them.

2.2.1 Regime

Water regime describes the combination of water level (eg surface water depth), the length of time that level is maintained and at what time of the year. The water regime of a reedbed may be influenced by natural processes and by management. These include:

- water supply
  - evapotranspiration
  - rainfall
  - surface flows
  - groundwater

- water distribution
  - sluices (including weirs and pipes)
  - dams and bunds
  - pumps

Figure 4 shows the relationship between supply and distribution and the point where control may be possible.

The water regime will be influenced by the amount of water available and the means of distributing it around the site.

Figure 4 Supply, distribution and control of water on reedbeds.

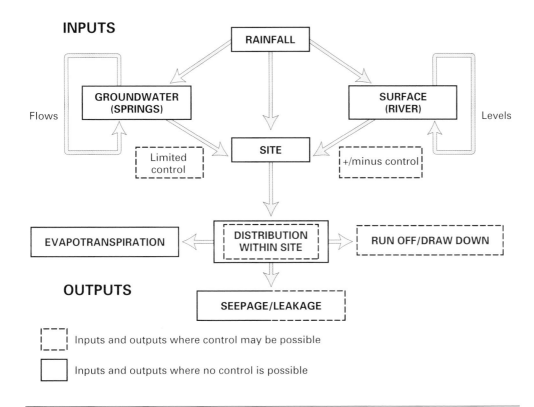

INPUTS

RAINFALL

GROUNDWATER (SPRINGS)   SURFACE (RIVER)

Flows   Levels

Limited control   SITE   +/minus control

EVAPOTRANSPIRATION   DISTRIBUTION WITHIN SITE   RUN OFF/DRAW DOWN

OUTPUTS

SEEPAGE/LEAKAGE

Inputs and outputs where control may be possible

Inputs and outputs where no control is possible

The source of
water supply
available will
determine the
amount of
control and
management
which is
possible.

a) **Water supply**

The water supply for a site is influenced by: climatic conditions, eg rainfall and evapotranspiration (see Part 1); groundwater, eg springs and surface water, eg rivers. The source may affect the quality (section 2.2.2) as rivers and ditches may drain agricultural land (diffuse pollution source) or run through or near an urban area receiving treated sewage effluent and industrial effluents (point-sources of pollution). In addition, water quality is influenced by geology (rock and soil type) and land use (run-off from unimproved grassland is less polluted than that from arable land.)

Managing supply

To what extent the supply can be managed will vary between sites and will be influenced by a range of factors:

● seasonal variations

● water source (eg river, rainfall only, springs)

● access to supply

● losses (eg faulty sluices, damaged bunds, seepage and abstraction)

Natural, seasonal variations of water supply (eg rainfall and evapotranspiration) should be taken into account when determining the appropriate regime for a reedbed. Evapotranspiration will typically be highest in June and July when water levels are naturally at their lowest (see MAFF Technical bulletin 34 – address in Appendix 3). In drier regions of the UK, ie the south and south-east, managing for annual prolonged dry periods may be the safest option. Sites that are primarily fed by rainfall are likely to dry out in mid-summer and will be of value to a different range of wildlife from that sustained by reedbeds which remain wet in summer. In such circumstances it may be appropriate to consider storage of winter water to supplement supplies. For example at Minsmere in Suffolk, the height of a dam was increased to enable large quantities of water to be held on one reedbed to supply an adjacent, lower lying reedbed and open water as it dries out over the summer (Robinson pers comm).

Access to the water supply is the key factor in management. A site which lies below the level of its supplying river and is separated by a sluice should be able to receive water all year round but draw-down would be achievable only by pumping. However, one which is at the same level as the river may only be able to receive water when flows are high in winter or spring and retain water on site throughout the dry mid-summer spell. The scenarios are numerous, which is why an understanding of the hydrology of a site and its water requirements, as determined by assessment, is essential for planning water management.

Potential losses of water from a site will have already been assessed and rectified where possible, eg by repairs to leaking sluices and bunds (Part 1, Table 2). Seepage, eg through ditch bottoms and bund bases, may be difficult to prevent, but where feasible should be assessed and taken into account when determining the water requirements of the site.

Most spring-fed sites have the advantage of a continual water supply. In Suffolk, the small, valley fen site at Market Weston is supplied by four springs arising on site. Springs may not flow all year, however, or at least flows may diminish during summer as a result of low rainfall and reduced aquifer recharge. At Market Weston the situation is further compounded by abstraction (Fojt 1994).

Reedbed managers are rarely able to influence control of river levels (except through the relevant statutory authority, eg the NRA, navigation authorities), which tend to be high in winter and low in summer. On a reedbed connected to a river, natural flooding is likely to influence the site in winter, as occurs in most of the Broadland reedbeds. Similarly, at Radipole Lake in Dorset the River Wey floods the reedbeds each winter because its flow is interrupted by tidal sluices on high tide sequences (Slater pers comm). Conversely, reduced summer flows mean the reedbed dries out in most years. Separation of a reedbed from its river supply has advantages and disadvantages. Input control by sluices permits optimal management to be implemented but removes the effect of natural or semi-natural flooding cycles which influences the range of reedbed types present. Plate 3 shows the River Yare in Norfolk which supplies the reedbeds at Strumpshaw Fen. Inputs are largely controlled via sluices in winter since the site was isolated by bunds to prevent regular inundation.

C H Gomersall (RSPB)

Plate 3 Aerial view of Strumpshaw Fen, Norfolk showing the River Yare in the foreground. In winter, the river supplies water to the Fen where it is held back to ensure the reedbed surface is wet in spring.

Management of water distribution may be achieved by control of inputs or control of outputs.

b) Water distribution

Water distribution or movement in a site is influenced by:

- topography

- surface flows (eg in ditches)

- regional and local groundwater flows.

The topography of a reedbed is important, influencing both flow and water depth. Reedbeds in depressions on floodplains, in flooded pits or where the bed has been artificially levelled may not have a surface flow. This may reduce the degree of control over lowering the water levels such that pumping may be necessary or cutting delayed. Reliance on evapotranspiration and seepage to lower water levels may constrain management in wet years.

Knowledge of groundwater levels and gradients (direction of flow is usually down a valley/towards the river) can be very valuable particularly when creating new reedbeds. Such information is vital to enable excavation work, eg bed lowering, to be undertaken to the right level. However, it is difficult to make accurate predictions and the advice of a hydrologist should be sought. The natural hydraulic gradient should be taken into account when designing new reedbeds. Tiered wetlands, eg Figure 5a, where water levels in the upper tier can be deliberately lowered by draining down to the next tier, should take into account such natural gradients.

**Figure 5 a – f
Examples of hydrological systems on UK reedbeds ▶**

a) Continual supply and flow, bunded system (three hydrological units).

a) Continual supply and flow; bunded system (three hydrological units)

Features:
Continual water supply = flow
Water level control by bunds and sluices
Isolation from saline incursion
eg Walberswick NNR, Suffolk

Surge tide · Sea wall · Spring level · Bunded hydrological units with internal ditches (not shown) · Gradient · Run-off · Springs · Non-return valve · Sectioned sluice pipe · Winter draw-down level

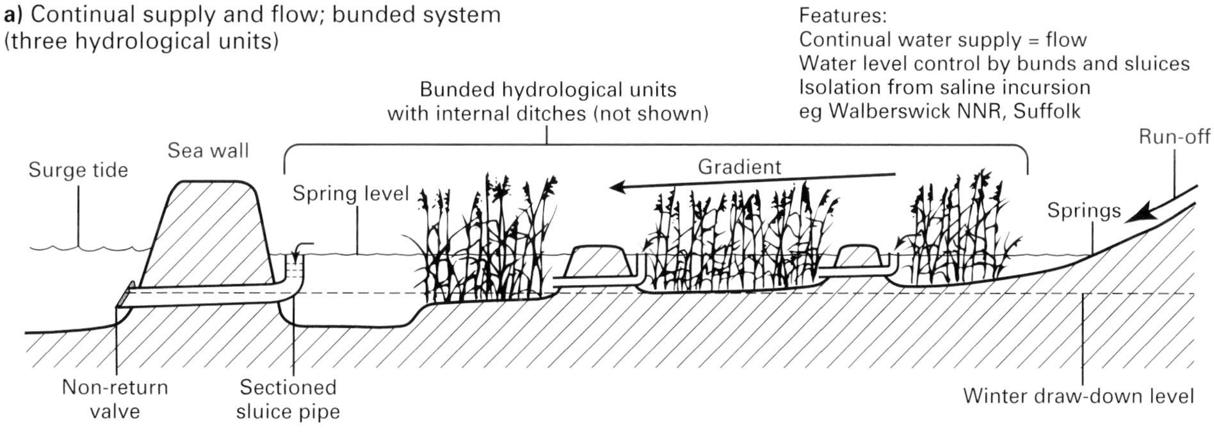

b) Continual supply and flow; drop-board sluice control
(single hydrological unit)

Features:
Continual water supply = flow
Water level control by sluice at outlet
eg Leighton Moss, Lancashire

Distribution by ditches (not shown)

Run-off

Maximum
winter level

Springs

Summer level

Drop-board sluice
in water channel

c)

Features:
Variable water supply–tidally influenced
river plus some spring and run-off
Seepage through peat soil.
No or minimal water level control
eg some Norfolk Broads reedbeds

Rond

Gradient

Run-off

Winter flood level

Mean
summer level

Springs

River

'Soke' dyke

d)

Features:
Water stored in upper reedbed to supply
lower one during summer deficit
Levels controlled by sluices
Constant water supply=Flow
Summer deficit=No flow
eg Minsmere, Suffolk

Swivel pipe sluice
through brick dam

Run-off

Winter level

Drop-board sluice   Scrape   Summer level   Deep water storage reedbed   Springs

b) Continual supply and flow, drop-board sluice control (single hydrological unit).

c) Continual supply and flow, naturally flooded by river.

d) Continual spring supply. Part of reedbed used for winter storage. No continual flow.

e) Occasional supply from tidally influenced river or broad. No continual flow.

f) Occasional supply from river only. No continual flow. Often dry in summer.

e)

Features:
Supply controlled through sluice
Supply not constant = no or intermittent flow
Level controlled by sluice on outlet
eg Hickling NNR, Norfolk
Ranworth Flood, Norfolk

Pen-stock sluice on outlet

Summer level

Flat bed

Winter level (draw-down for cutting)

Bund

Bund

Supply channel from broad or river

Drainage ditch

Internal ditch

Grip

Grip

Internal ditch

Drop-board sluice on inlet

f)

Features:
Supply mainly from river
(tidally influenced)
Water level control by sluice on inlet
Maximum held back for spring
Winter surplus run off when possible
eg Radipole Lake, Dorset

Winter level

Winter flood

Summer level

Flexipipe sluice

River

Many reedbeds have existing structures which enable water levels to be controlled and manipulated. The main aim of controlling water levels on a reedbed is to ensure surface water is available in spring and summer. Surface water also suppresses the growth of most unwanted plants and so maintains the dominance of reed. Control of water level in winter enables draw-down to facilitate management.

Assuming an adequate supply of water to a site and good control of distribution, an ideal water level programme would be:

1. Raise water levels on the site as soon as winter cutting has finished (usually late March–early April) to a maximum surface depth on the reedbed of 30 cm.

2. Maintain surface water in the range 5–30 cm throughout spring and summer.

3. Draw-down water level slowly to just below the reedbed surface from October onwards to facilitate management work, principally cutting.

4. Where possible, maintain some wet reed habitat during winter to provide feeding areas for bitterns.

5. In winter, when management is not undertaken, set sluices so that the maximum surface depth on reedbeds does not exceed 1 m.

Evapotranspiration is a natural process which cannot be controlled. However, many UK reedbed managers make use of this 'natural draw-down' as it usually coincides with the period when management work commences.

Figure 6a–d show a range of water level programmes which may be adopted depending on the management objectives and on-site constraints. It should be emphasised that areas of drier reedbed may support a diverse range of plants which will be lost if water levels are raised too high in summer. It may be desirable to manage such areas to benefit these plants rather than for pure reed.

c) Water level control structures

Water levels on a reedbed are controlled by the rate at which water enters and leaves the site. Three principal techniques may be used to control water levels in reedbeds:

- sluices between reedbed and watercourse to control inflow and outflow

- bunding or damming an area or inflow to raise levels

- pumps – which allow water to be introduced from rivers which are lower than the reedbed and/or over enclosing bunds.

Sluices
Sluices are structures that conduct and control the flow of water. They may be self contained or part of larger dams/bunds or weirs where the aim is to regulate as well as impound water (Brooks 1981). They come in a wide range of forms:

- pipes, eg swivel, flexipipe

- drop-board

- lifting gate, eg penstock.

Selection of sluice type may be influenced by a number of factors (Merritt 1994), including:

- the precision of water level control required

- the range of depths required

- the labour available to operate and maintain the structures

- the likely extent of seasonal and other variations in flow

- susceptibility to vandalism

- susceptibility to blockage from debris and plant growth.

The most commonly used sluices on UK reedbeds, particularly nature reserves, are of the drop-board or pipe type. These durable structures enable relatively fine control over water levels at low cost. Figures 7–10 and Plates 4–8 illustrate some of these and Table 5 compares the attributes of the three main types. Further information on different designs of sluices may be found in Brooks (1981), Burgess and Hirons (1990), Hall *et al* (1992), Hammer (1992) and Street (1989).

At Stodmarsh in Kent, a MAFF/NRA funded project enabled a new sluice to be installed on the western reedbed in 1995. The 2-m wide, wooden drop-board sluice replaced a malfunctioning device through which water was continuously lost. It enables approximately 10–15 cm of surface water depth to be maintained in summer where previously the reedbed dried out.

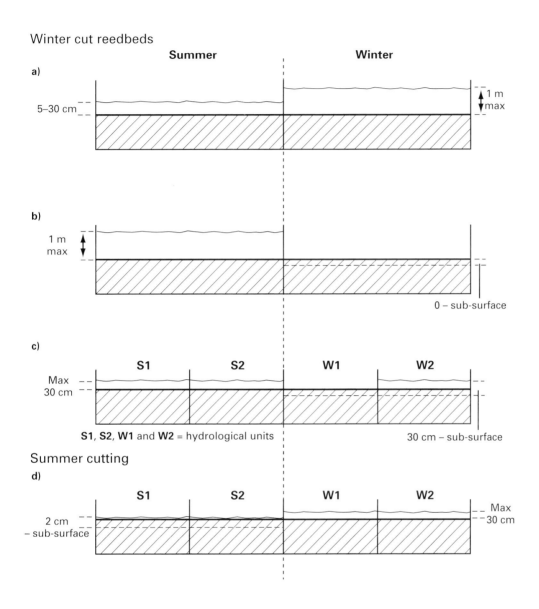

Figure 6 Example water level regimes for different objectives

a) Optimum for reedbed wildlife – idealised regime on sites where reed cutting is not a priority. Summer levels are maintained in the range 5–30 cm where possible with some areas shallower and others deeper to maximise benefits to wildlife. In winter, levels are kept high, usually no more than 1 m on the reedbed itself. However, 30 cm enables bitterns and other wildlife to use the reedbed for winter feeding.

b) Optimum for reed harvest – harvesting reed for thatch is facilitated by complete draw-down of water levels to at or below the ground's surface. This ensures maximum butt length is cut and permits the use of cutting machinery. Summer levels are kept as high as possible to enhance reed growth and reduce competition from other plants. However, a water depth of more than 1 m may inhibit reed growth and in practice few sites are able to achieve more than a few centimetres.

c) Integration for wildlife and reed harvest – summer levels are kept at a maximum of 30 cm depth across most of the reedbed (S1 and S2) with a range of 0–50 cm where possible throughout. In winter, complete draw-down for cutting is required (W1) retaining surface water on separate hydrological units (W2). When cutting is finished on W1, W2 may be drawn-down similarly.

d) Wildlife and commercial (reed, saw-sedge and marsh hay) – in winter, 30 cm depth may be unsuitable for late harvested saw-sedge which may not have regrown sufficiently for the cut ends not to be submerged. In summer, draw-down to just below the surface is best to facilitate cutting and removal and to minimise rutting of the ground by machinery.

a)

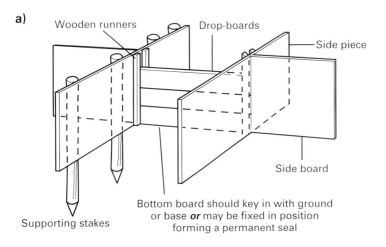

Wooden runners   Drop-boards

Side piece

Side board

Bottom board should key in with ground
or base *or* may be fixed in position
forming a permanent seal

Supporting stakes

Figure 7
A simple wooden, drop-board sluice.
Such sluices come in many sizes and
may have wood, concrete or metal
surrounds although the drop-boards
themselves are usually wood as it swells
when wet, forming a tight seal. It is
important that the sluice is well keyed-
in to the bund or ditch to prevent
seepage and erosion around the sides.

a) 3-D view of structure

b) Top view showing side boards key-in
   to bund.

b)

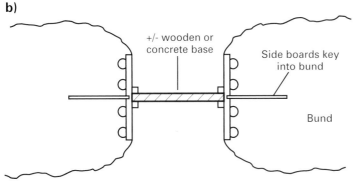

+/- wooden or
concrete base

Side boards key
into bund

Bund

C Hawke (RSPB)

Plate 4 A metal-surround drop-board sluice shown open
during draw-down to enable winter management on a
reedbed in Somerset. ▶

Plate 5 An angled pipe-sluice used to control water levels on
the reedbed at Walberswick, Suffolk. Note the reed litter
which has collected at the entrance of the pipe (left) and the
spare collars (right) which can be added to raise water levels
after winter management. ▼

C Hawke (RSPB)

a)

Wooden drop-boards,
one with 3 reversible, non-return flaps,
which can be placed at any position for maximum control of levels

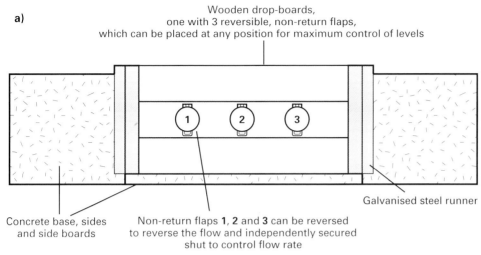

**Figure 8
Kit-form drop-
board sluice with
wooden boards,
concrete
surrounds and
triple non-return
flaps.**

a) Front view

**b) Top view
showing
connection to
feeder pipe and
security grid**

Galvanised steel runner

Concrete base, sides
and side boards

Non-return flaps **1**, **2** and **3** can be reversed
to reverse the flow and independently secured
shut to control flow rate

b)

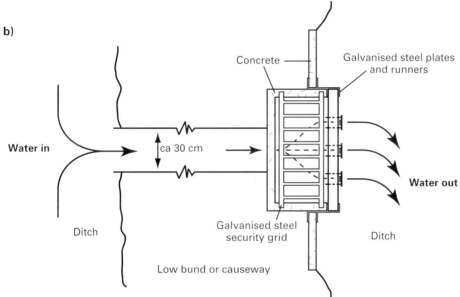

Concrete

Galvanised steel plates
and runners

Water in

ca 30 cm

Water out

Ditch

Galvanised steel
security grid

Ditch

Low bund or causeway

**Plate 6 A swivel-
pipe sluice
maintaining
shallow water on
the reedbed at
Salthouse,
Norfolk.**

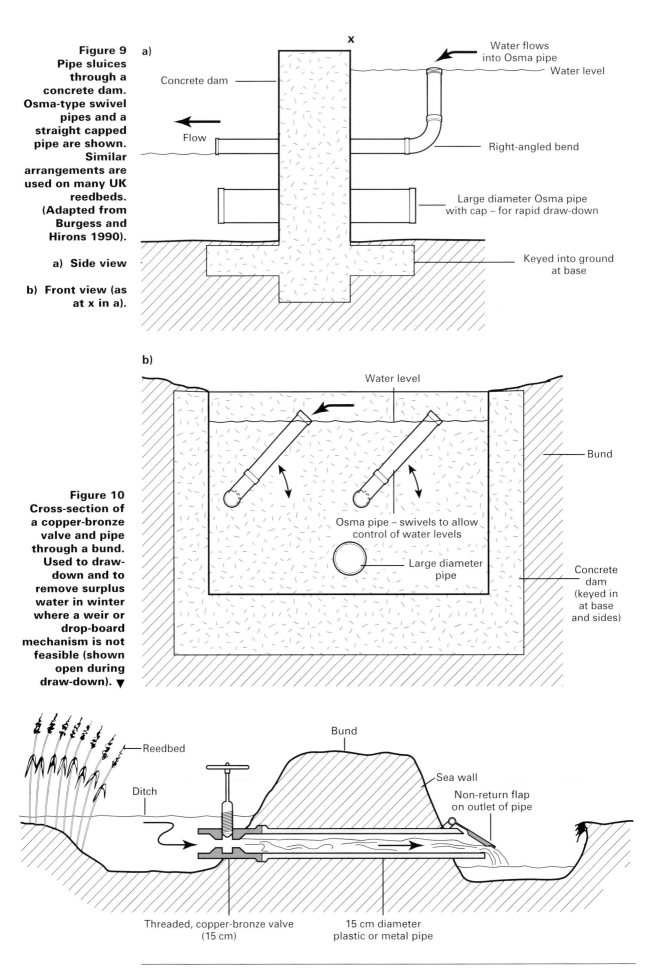

Figure 9 Pipe sluices through a concrete dam. Osma-type swivel pipes and a straight capped pipe are shown. Similar arrangements are used on many UK reedbeds. (Adapted from Burgess and Hirons 1990).

a) Side view

b) Front view (as at x in a).

a)

x

Concrete dam

Flow

Water flows into Osma pipe

Water level

Right-angled bend

Large diameter Osma pipe with cap – for rapid draw-down

Keyed into ground at base

b)

Water level

Bund

Osma pipe – swivels to allow control of water levels

Large diameter pipe

Concrete dam (keyed in at base and sides)

Figure 10 Cross-section of a copper-bronze valve and pipe through a bund. Used to draw-down and to remove surplus water in winter where a weir or drop-board mechanism is not feasible (shown open during draw-down). ▼

Reedbed

Ditch

Bund

Sea wall

Non-return flap on outlet of pipe

Threaded, copper-bronze valve (15 cm)

15 cm diameter plastic or metal pipe

Plate 7 Flexipipes come in many sizes and are a simple, inexpensive method for controlling water levels. This one is used to control the movement of water between the River Wey and the reedbed at Radipole Lake, Dorset.

Plate 8 Lifting gates do not enable fine water level control. This penstock sluice at Hickling in Norfolk holds back water on the reedbed in spring and summer and is opened in autumn to draw-down for cutting.

Table 5: Comparison of relative benefits of three commonly used sluice types on UK reedbeds

Attribute	Sluice type		
	Pipe	Drop-board	Lifting Gate
Flow capacity	■	■■■	■■■■
Water level control	■■■■	■■■	■
Durability	■■	■■■	■■
Adjustment frequency	■■■	■■■	■
Ease of adjustment	■■■	■■	■■■■
Resistance to blockage	■	■■■	■■■
Resistance to vandalism/tampering	■	■■	■■■
Construction cost	■■■■	■■■	■
Design complexity	■■■	■■	■
Ease of installation	■■■■	■■	■
Availability of materials	■■■	■■■	■

Some of these features may vary depending on the design specification, eg concrete or wooden surrounds, the age of the sluice and position/accessibility.
Relative benefits: ■ = poor, ■■ = moderate, ■■■ = good, ■■■■ = very good.
(Adapted from Merritt 1994)

Dams and bunds

These are barriers used to impound water and are usually not designed to be overtopped except where an overflow/spillway is provided. Dams should be constructed using the principles outlined in Table 6. Further information on bund construction is detailed in section 3.2.2.

d) Hydrological units

Many reedbeds are a single unit, ie there is only one input and one output point. However, ideally a reedbed should be divided into more than one unit as this allows finer control over water levels. The advantage of separate hydrological units is that they:

● facilitate management practices

● allow each unit to be managed separately

● make the most effective use of water supply.

An existing reedbed may be divided into units by adding bunds and new ditches. Inevitably, some reed area may be lost but open water and reed edge will be created in the process. Creating a new reedbed offers the opportunity to incorporate units into the design from the outset, eg Ham Wall (Case Study 13). Ideally, each unit should function independently, ie its inputs and outputs should be isolated from other units. In practice, this may not be

Table 6: Principles to consider in the design of bunds and dams

- The crest of a dam should be at least 1 m above the normal water level.

- Earth dams should be constructed to a height 10–15% above the minimum required to compensate for settlement.

- The width of the dam should be at least five times the dam height.

- Banks holding back water should have a gradient no steeper than 1 in 3 (although materials used, small banks and banks not subject to erosion will influence this).

- Dry banks may have steeper gradients of 1 in 2.

- Dams holding back large volumes of water should be crescent shaped with the convex side towards the water body.

- The impermeable core of the dam (usually clay) should key in to the impermeable subsoil.

(Adapted from Merritt 1994)

Raising water levels inhibits unwanted plants which may invade a dry reedbed and allows reed to flourish.

feasible and one unit may depend on another for its water supply which will influence flows, eg during draw-down. Units tend to be interconnected by sluices, flexipipes offering the cheapest and most versatile way of achieving this. Additional independent connections should be installed where possible to the supply channel and outlet channel to enable independent draw-down and water level control within each unit.

The disadvantage of separate hydrological units is that they:

- require control equipment which must be installed and maintained

- may inhibit the free movement of aquatic species such as fish.

On a cautionary note, maintaining water levels using sluices or dams may prevent a continual flow of water through the system. This is commonplace on many UK reedbeds in summer. At Leighton Moss where there is a constant supply of water all year, a flow is maintained over a small drop-board sluice. This gives young eels access to the reedbed, especially during

May, which is the period of their main migration from the sea and up rivers. Lack of recruitment of young eels is thought to be a factor in the decline of the bittern at some UK reedbeds (Tyler pers comm). A range of water regimes for sites with different characteristics, ie single or multiple hydrological units, is illustrated in Figure 5a–f.

e) Rehabilitation by raising water levels

The simplest way to rehabilitate a degraded reedbed is to alter the hydrology of the site by raising water levels. Levels may have dropped as a result of abandoned sluices, diversion of supply or water abstraction. By reinstating the supply and holding water to a level above the reedbed surface, the life of the reedbed will be extended. Plants which have invaded the dry reedbed will die off and further colonisation by scrub will be prevented. However, well established willow and alder may tolerate the flooding. Reed should flourish, although initially sudden changes in water regime may inhibit reed (Haslam 1970). However, it should 'recover' and quickly re-establish itself.

At Leighton Moss in Lancashire, Minsmere in Suffolk and Radipole Lake in Dorset, water levels were raised to reduce the effects of many years of litter build up and silting, increasing the area of wet reed (Burgess and Evans 1989). However, there is a limit to which levels may be raised before undesired flooding occurs, eg of neighbouring land. In addition, periodic exposure of the litter layer to air facilitates decay, reducing the bulk of the detritus. However, recent studies at Leighton Moss have indicated that permanently wet reedbeds accumulate litter more slowly than drier areas because grazing of the litter by invertebrates, particularly waterlouse (*Asellus*), contributes significantly to litter break-down (Graham 1994). Reedbeds which have become dry may require other methods of litter reduction such as those which have been implemented at Minsmere and North Warren (Case Study 10) in Suffolk and at Radipole Lake where the bed surfaces have been lowered by mechanical excavation.

At Preston Marsh in Kent, infilling of the supply ditch from the Little Stour River caused the reedbed to dry out, with a subsequent invasion of scrub, greater willowherb and nettle. Work began in autumn of 1994 to reinstate the supply ditch and clear out the existing ditch network using a contracted digger. The addition of new sluices enabled the water levels to be raised. This action has encouraged reed while inhibiting the nettle and willowherb, and has helped to reduce further invasion by scrub.

f) Draw-down

This is the process by which water is deliberately run off a reedbed so that winter management can take place. This is achieved simply by removing the upper boards from a drop-board sluice or opening any other similar device at the outlet point. It may be necessary to close the water inlet, a facility which will have been built in to a system of hydrological units.

The length of time taken to achieve complete draw-down will vary and depends upon:

● site size

● number of outlets

● size of sluice/pipes

● gradient of the land

● soil type.

Draw-down is achieved at Salthouse in Norfolk by blocking the supply at the first piped-culvert with a plastic bucket. Water remaining on the site drains into the Main Drain leaving the bed dry for single wale cutting. Eventually, the build-up of water behind the blocked culvert overflows onto the reedbed, a situation exacerbated by winter rainfall, although a proportion naturally diverts into another ditch.

The soil at Ranworth Flood (Case Study 5) in the Broads is mostly peat, which holds large quantities of water so that draw-down through a simple drop-board sluice may take several weeks. The sluice is generally opened as early as October in time for cutting in December. On sites with clay soils, draw-down may be achieved relatively quickly as there is only surface water to be drained off. A rapid draw-down may reduce litter accumulation by carrying floating material away. However, too rapid a draw-down may prevent fish and aquatic invertebrates from finding refuge in remaining wet areas of the reedbed. Thus, a gradual draw-down over several weeks is recommended.

Draw-down exposes the litter to the air, enabling a degree of decay to take place, further reducing accumulated litter.

Draw-down may be achieved by running water off a site or preventing it from entering. Gradual draw-down is recommended to reduce any impact on wildlife.

2.2.2 Water quality

Lowland watercourses are frequently polluted by elevated levels of nitrate and phosphate. This is usually a result of fertiliser run-off from agriculture and from treated sewage effluent, which includes many pollutants, including phosphate. Water bodies polluted in this way are said to be in a eutrophic condition. Reed grows well in eutrophic water although high nutrient levels have been implicated in some cases of 'reedswamp' decline in the Broads (Crook *et al* 1983). Also the

susceptibility of reed to decay has been linked with nitrogen levels in reed itself, although not necessarily with nitrogen consumption in the water environment (Boar *et al* 1991).

However, many of the plants and animals of reedbeds and those which live in the ditches and other open water areas can suffer greatly from highly eutrophic water which encourages fast-growing, dominant species such as algae or duckweeds (Plate

Although reed can survive in poor quality water, other wildlife may suffer. Drastic measures may be required to improve water quality. However, water quantity is usually more critical than quality.

Plate 9 Eutrophic water in a supply ditch. A dense growth of duckweed has developed in response to the high quantity of nutrients.

C Hawke (RSPB)

Plate 10 A ditch containing abundant and diverse aquatic plants is indicative of good water quality. The open water is occupied by water lily and water soldier, reed being confined largely to the margins.

Broads Authority

a) Isolation from eutrophic water

Achieving isolation may involve major land forming works, eg the construction of bunds to enclose the reedbed. The primary source of water for Strumpshaw Fen in Norfolk (**Case Study 1**) was the highly eutrophic River Yare but after successful isolation the improvement in water quality has resulted in significant wildlife benefits.

At Stodmarsh in Kent, a clay bund was constructed to enclose 35 ha of the reedbed to permit finer control over water levels and reduce the influence of the eutrophic River Great Stour. Similarly, at North Warren in Suffolk a newly constructed bund now prevents the eutrophic outfall from a nearby sewage treatment works from entering the reedbed.

At How Hill in the Broads, a simple dam was constructed from wooden piles to isolate a ditch from the river. This prevents eutrophic river water entering the reedbed at this point and adversely affecting the diverse aquatic plant and animal life of the ditch.

The disadvantages of isolation of an entire site may include:

- summer shortages in water supply

- prevention of access by fish and other aquatic wildlife

- prevention or reduction of flow across the reedbed and consequent stagnation.

Avoiding summer shortages of water can be a major difficulty and may require supplementing the supply with water from an alternative source such as a bore hole, as at Strumpshaw Fen, or a different river nearby. The last two difficulties may be overcome to some extent by 'flushing' through the reedbed with water from the river in winter, when levels are higher and dilution is greatest, keeping the impact of poor water quality to a minimum. This will remove stagnant water and allow some recruitment of aquatic wildlife from the river water. However, high winter flows may carry polluted silt and care must be taken to ensure flushing is only undertaken

9). Blankets of filamentous algae compete with other species for nutrients but more importantly, prevent other plants from receiving sunlight. Planktonic algal blooms in eutrophic water give it a milky or 'pea-green soup' appearance. This reduction in water clarity means that fish-eating specialists like herons and bitterns cannot see their prey. The decline of aquatic plants in eutrophic conditions results in the loss of habitat for aquatic invertebrates. Many of these are voracious grazers of algae, providing a biological check on algal growth in a stable system. The food-chain is finely balanced and can be permanently disrupted by severe nutrient inputs. A watercourse containing clear water and abundant aquatic plants is generally indicative of good water quality (Plate 10), although much depends on which species are present and the type of watercourse.

Dealing with water quality can be a problem and may require drastic measures, such as isolating areas of conservation value from a eutrophic water supply, phosphate stripping or suction dredging to lower nutrient levels. Even then the recovery of aquatic life is not guaranteed, depending on the severity of the pollution. There are a number of other measures which can be taken to reduce or prevent the impact.

when silt content is at its lowest. Where possible, eel runs should be incorporated into the design of sluices, although these are usually only effective with a continual water supply.

b) Nutrient removal

Phosphate stripping is a process which removes a proportion of this nutrient from sewage effluent at the treatment works before it is discharged into the river. Anglian Water have installed phosphate stripping plants at nine sewage treatment works in the Norfolk Broads in an effort to lower the levels in the Rivers Ant and Bure. It is an expensive technique used for large-scale treatment of phosphate-rich water and has been shown to provide benefits over a 5–10 year period by a reduction in algal levels and some plant recovery.

A small experimental system at Slimbridge in Gloucestershire employs crushed limestone through which nutrient-rich water passes and phosphate is removed by reacting with the limestone (Plate 11 and Case Study 16).

c) Channel orientation

The shape and orientation of channels where they meet with a river can help to reduce the extent of mixing of eutrophic river water with cleaner spring waters, on fens for example. Figure 11a–c show examples of such designs as used in the Broadland fens. In addition, the profile of a ditch will influence the extent to which aquatic plants are able to colonise. Figure 13 and section 3.2.2 (Figures 6 and 7) give examples of ideal ditch profiles for maximising benefits to wildlife.

An abundance of plant life will help maintain clear, good-quality water by trapping suspended solids, breaking down many pollutants and providing the habitat necessary to support algae-grazing invertebrates. Therefore, it is important that ditch clearing work is done on a rotation or only partially, as described in section 2.2.3. A range of techniques that minimise the impact of ditch management on aquatic vegetation is described by Newbold *et al* (1992).

Plate 11 A chalk 'cascade' on the Slimbridge water treatment wetland helps remove phosphate.

C Hawke (RSPB)

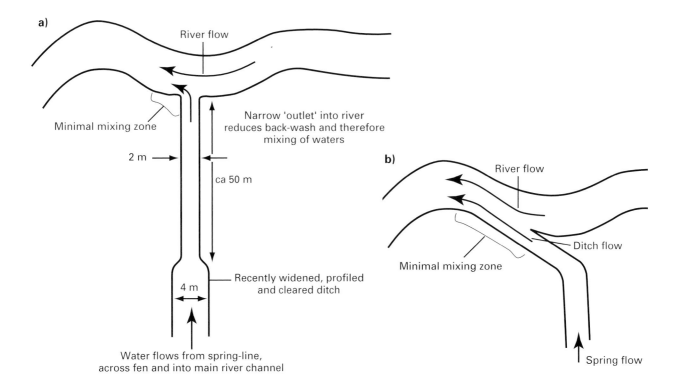

a) River flow

Minimal mixing zone

Narrow 'outlet' into river reduces back-wash and therefore mixing of waters

2 m

ca 50 m

4 m

Recently widened, profiled and cleared ditch

Water flows from spring-line, across fen and into main river channel

b) River flow

Ditch flow

Minimal mixing zone

Spring flow

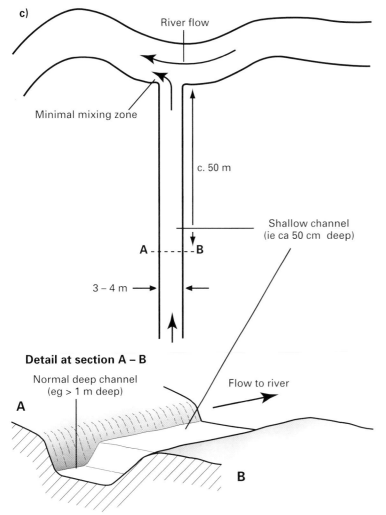

c) River flow

Minimal mixing zone

c. 50 m

Shallow channel (ie ca 50 cm deep)

A - - - - - - B

3 – 4 m

Detail at section A – B

Normal deep channel (eg > 1 m deep)

Flow to river

A

B

**Figure 11
Channel orientation and profiles to minimise mixing of eutrophic river water with low-nutrient ditch water.**

a) **'Bottle-neck' design. Principle of functioning is:**

- **Narrow neck reduces degree of mixing with main channel.**

b) **Angled-outlet design. Principle of functioning is:**

- **Outlet angled in downstream direction reduces degree of mixing.**

c) **'Shallow-neck' design. Principle of functioning is:**

- **Shallow section of channel reduces degree of mixing with main channel.**

d) Flow

A continual flow of water across a reedbed may prevent stagnation and carry away floating detritus thereby reducing litter accumulation and ageing of the reedbed, eg at Walberswick, Suffolk (Waller pers comm). A flow may be impossible to achieve on many reedbeds, especially in summer when levels may be low. Sites with a continual water supply from rivers and/or springs are most likely to be able to maintain a flow.

Small flows may be achievable by damming the outlet with a drop-board sluice and permitting a constant flow over the sluice, similar to a weir. However, even such a small water loss may be unacceptable in summer, especially in the drier, eastern areas of the UK, and should be balanced against the requirement for flow. As described in section 2.2.2a, flushing through with high winter flows of water will alleviate stagnation.

Flow within a reedbed may be enhanced by the design of ditches and grips/foot drains (Figure 12). Grips are small, spade-sized channels that allow water to flow off and on reedbeds, and are connected to the main water system (Burgess *et al* 1995). Typically, a grip is 30 cm wide along most of its length widening to 1 m where it joins a ditch. A well designed grip may be only 5–10 cm deep at its upper end increasing to 60 cm at its lower end. The flow produced by grips on a site with a continual water supply will reduce the rate of litter accumulation within the grips and the need to maintain them. In addition, the flow oxygenates the water. The effect is to produce reed of a very high thatching quality such as that found at Sutton Broad in Norfolk (Satchell pers comm). In the Broads, grips are considered important for maintaining clear, oxygenated water on spring-fed reedbeds and reducing the accumulation of nutrients in the peaty soils. Details of grip design are illustrated in Part 3, Figure 7c.

Figure 12
Flow during flooding and draw-down.

a) Flow controlled across site to prevent stagnation. When the reedbed has surface water a net flow through the reed is maintained by constant inputs and outputs. This is balanced by the sluice at the output point. The grips and soke dyke enhance the flow by drawing the water through the reedbed towards the sluice.

b) Grips facilitate flow across the site during draw-down. During draw-down, once there is no longer any surface water, the grips and ditches draw water into the interconnecting network towards the lowered/opened sluice.

a) Flooding

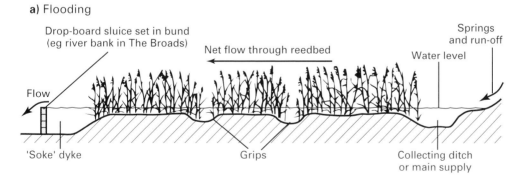

b) Draw-down

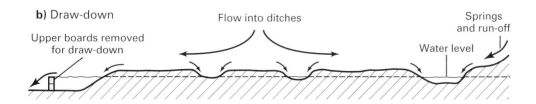

e) Reed-filled ditches

Because of the ability of reed to break down organic substances and utilise certain nutrients, positioned in the supply channel and the first few metres of a reedbed, it will have a cleansing effect on the water throughout the rest of the reedbed. Reed in ditches slows down the flow of water, exposing it for longer to the activities of micro-organisms in the soil. This principle is utilised at Slimbridge in Gloucestershire where long beds of reed and other water plants are used to clean polluted water (Case Study 16). At Far Ings in Humberside, supplementary water from springs supplies the reedbed. The water is highly eutrophic, as evidenced by the massive algal bloom in spring where it first enters a pool containing reedmace. However, after the water has passed through a section of reedbed the algal bloom is absent.

f) The effects of salinity

Reed is able to thrive in brackish water, permitting extensive reedbeds to develop on estuaries such as Inner Tay Estuary in Fife, the Humber Estuary in Humberside and the Blyth Estuary in Suffolk (Plate 12). However, the intrusion of salt water into reedbeds which have developed in fresh water can be highly detrimental, causing die-back of the reed and killing most other wildlife. Reedbeds may take several years to recover from such events (Waller pers comm).

High tides push the fresh water of rivers upstream, causing a gradient of saline mixing. This is a natural and regular occurrence in tidally influenced systems such as the Broads, where after surge tides the peaty soils may retain salt water until late summer, sometimes many miles

upstream of the normal saline limit, eg as far as How Hill on the River Ant (Boar *et al* 1991). In some areas regular flooding with brackish water has led to the development of specialised plant communities (Parmenter in prep).

In the Broadland fens, the influence of saline water from tidal rivers is reduced by the presence of 'soke' dykes (Figure 12). The spoil from the construction and maintenance of 'soke' dykes forms banks which protect the reedbeds and fens from flooding on all but the highest tides. Nevertheless, the peat soil allows considerable seepage through and under the banks. A 'soke' dyke functions as a saline 'sink', effectively containing much of the seepage. It is most effective in conjunction with a good ditch and grip system where the counterflow of water reduces the extent of seepage. 'Borrow' ditches function on the same principle and are usually found on the landward side of sea walls where specialised brackish water communities may develop.

The seepage of sea water under the Blakeney shingle bar in North Norfolk, influences the reedbeds behind it at Cley and Salthouse. Saline reedbed habitats support different specialised wildlife from freshwater reedbeds and are generally less diverse. The brackish reedbeds of the North Solent in Hampshire support virtually pure stands of reed, and the open water largely lacks aquatic vegetation. The absence of sizeable fish and amphibian communities may explain why brackish reedbeds are rarely, if ever, used in the UK by breeding bitterns.

Repairs to leaking sluices and bunds and raising the height of flood walls can prevent direct saline intrusion. However, seepage under these structures through porous soils is difficult to remedy. New bunds may be constructed so that the base is keyed-in to the clay subsoil. At Far Ings in Humberside, saline seepage under the flood wall influences the northern margin of the reedbed and was greatly exacerbated during the drought years of 1989–91. Since the drought has ceased, nearby artesian springs have flowed once more and are used to supplement water supply,

Plate 12 Reed growing alongside saltmarsh plants on the Blythburgh Estuary in Suffolk.

C Hawke (RSPB)

producing a continual flow across the site, partly flushing and partly diluting the salinity (Grooby pers comm).

As far as reedbeds are concerned, it is generally true that water quantity is more important than its quality. Sites with abundant water of a high quality such as Walberswick in Suffolk and Leighton Moss in Lancashire, are able to optimise the management for all reedbed wildlife and commercial requirements. Sites with an abundant but eutrophic or otherwise polluted water supply will still maintain a reedbed or enable establishment of a new reedbed, which will have high wildlife and commercial value. However, sites with prolonged, insufficient water supplies will slowly lose existing reedbed and new reed will establish poorly.

2.2.3 Ditches

Ditches, often created to drain land, are an effective way to distribute water around a reedbed. Additionally, they provide habitat for a range of plants and animals. In the Broadland fens the main purpose of the ditches is access and water distribution on and off the reedbeds. Ditch systems can be used effectively to maintain water levels in a reedbed as well as drain it when draw-down is required for management work.

Water flows along a route of least resistance and therefore may require manipulating to achieve a more even distribution across a reedbed. A reedbed with spring supply and run-off water from surrounding higher land may achieve this naturally but in practice this rarely occurs. Finer control over levels and distribution can be achieved with sluices and dams in the ditches.

Ditches can be important for wildlife without reducing their effectiveness in moving water.

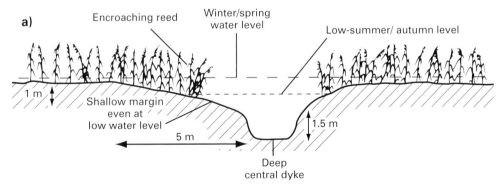

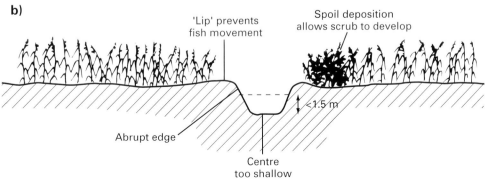

Figure 13 Ditches with the same capacity but different wildlife value.

a) Ditch profile which optimises wildlife benefit

b) Ditch profile with limited wildlife benefit

The profile and depth of a ditch will influence how much water it can carry and how quickly, as well as its effect on water levels in surrounding land. It will also influence the extent of colonisation by plants which in turn will further influence water movements. Figure 13 a and b compares a typical ditch designed both to convey water and optimise benefits for wildlife with one which has minimal wildlife benefits (some other designs are shown in section 3.2.2b). In general, ditches with a graded edge will permit colonisation by emergent plants including reed and provide important secluded feeding areas for many types of wildlife, including bitterns. Provided the centre of the ditch is designed to hold more than one metre depth of water in summer, reed will be prevented from choking the ditch, thus reducing its efficiency at conveying water. Nevertheless, within a few years, ditches will accumulate litter, silt and detritus, which will make them shallower and further prone to colonisation by reed and other plants; they may eventually become almost obliterated if left unmanaged for too long (Plate 14a). In order to retain their effectiveness at conveying water without destroying their wildlife value, ditches can be managed by a variety of means:

- cutting and removal of vegetation

- rotational slubbing

- hand-croming litter

- reprofiling.

a) Cutting and removal of vegetation

This labour-intensive approach is generally practised on small ditches, or from a boat on larger ditches. For example at Stodmarsh in Kent, the larger ditches were cut using a weed-cutting boat but removal of the cut vegetation was done manually using rakes and cromes. This has proved unsatisfactory, and a mechanical weed rake will be used in future.

At Minsmere in Suffolk, a reciprocating brushcutter is used to cut aquatic vegetation under water in depths of as much as 1 m. The cut vegetation is usually then cromed/raked out or left to sink if the aim is to ease the flow of water in the short term.

At Radipole Lake in Dorset, ditch vegetation is pulled by hand on a small scale, targeting larger emergents such as reedmace. This requires water levels to be low, as they are in summer on this site, or for draw-down of a hydrological unit to have taken place. If the soil is soft, pulling vegetation requires little effort but a compacted soil may make the task impossible and increase risk of back injury (see Table 19 for safety points on pulling vegetation).

In addition to clearing reed and other detritus from the ditch itself, periodic cutting and removal of reed from the ditch edges should ideally be undertaken to improve access to the ditch edge for wildlife, including birds such as moorhens, water rails and bitterns. At Leighton Moss in Lancashire, this is done on an alternate, biennial basis, ie one side of a ditch edge is cut in one year while the opposite edge is left and vice versa the following year (Plate 13). Apart from improving access for wildlife, this technique slows down the rate of reed encroachment into the ditch, effectively extending the period of rotational slubbing required. Cutting is usually done from late July–early September using rotating brushcutters on the drier sections and reciprocating brushcutters to cut the lower, wetter strips under water (see also section 2.3.1)

Plate 13 At Leighton Moss the ditch edges are cut once every two years on opposite sides. This reduces encroachment and facilitates access to the ditch edge for wildlife, eg feeding bitterns.

C Hawke (RSPB)

Most cutting equipment cannot reach right to the edge of ditches which means that with time, litter accumulates quite thickly along these narrow stretches. At Hickling Broad and Ranworth Flood in Norfolk, the uncut reed on ditch margins is periodically burned off to remove the litter, thus improving access to the ditch edges for bitterns. Similarly, at Radipole in Dorset and Minsmere in Suffolk, brushcutters are used to clear the reed.

Vegetation cutting is usually done in late summer before it dies off and sinks. Pulling can be done whenever the water level is low enough to allow access and prior to decay of aerial parts of plants. On most sites, these techniques are used as and when necessary and rarely on a fixed cycle. Because the effect of such management is short term, it is performed annually on some sites.

b) Hand-croming litter

A crome is a long-handled fork which has the tynes bent through 90°. Material is raked up with the crome and removed, either being piled elsewhere to decay or added to a bonfire (Figure 14). This is a common practice on small ditches and grips and often an integral part of bed aftercare once an area of reed has been cut. It is particularly a feature of reedbed

management in the Broads and is practised at Martham Broad and Ranworth Flood for example. At Marazion Marsh in Cornwall, small ditches have been reinstated by hand-croming as part of the rehabilitation programme (Flumm pers comm).

This technique is only feasible after draw-down or on dry beds and is usually practised in winter.

R Andrews (Broads Authority)

Plate 14a A choked ditch in the Broadland fens. Scrub has been cut to facilitate access by the digger.

C Hawke (RSPB)

14b Digger re-excavating a choked ditch in the Broadland fens.

Figure 14 Hand-croming litter from a grip or foot-drain.

Crome

Litter-filled grip

Grip cleared of litter

Litter is transferred to a bonfire or left in piles to decay off the reedbed or at the margins

c) **Rotational slubbing**

Slubbing is the removal of many years' worth of accumulated detritus and silt from the bottom of ditches, an operation best carried out by mechanical digger (Plate 14b). Because the use of heavy machinery is expensive and because it causes temporary damage to the ground, this method of management is usually done on long rotations of 5–25 years (Burgess and Evans 1989), depending on the rate of accumulation of material. Hence regular removal of vegetation by cutting and raking helps extend the period of rotation. Similarly, deep ditches (> 1 m) which prevent reed colonising will not require slubbing as frequently as shallower ditches.

Access is a major constraint on many sites. On the peaty soils of the Broadland fens, diggers frequently need to operate on mats to avoid sinking (Plate 14b). On clays and silts access is less of a problem. Many sites have banks alongside ditches caused by the dumping of spoil over many years of ditch clearing; these can be used to track along. A floating digger (called an 'Aquacat') was used at Minsmere and Leighton Moss to slub ditches without damaging the adjoining reedbeds. It can work from within the ditch, using extending sidearms to stabilise itself against the ditch banks. It cannot therefore operate in shallow-profiled ditches and its size prevents it from use in small ditches. It is also expensive to hire.

Many of the ditches of the Broadland fens are navigable by small boats used for fen management. Many ditches have been restored and maintained by slubbing. This work is now almost entirely done by a hydraulic digger but a floating suction-dredger is sometimes used to pump mud and detritus from the bottom of ditches and eject it via a pipe onto the adjoining reedbed as it goes along (Plate 15). This practice is now less common since the spread of detritus was found significantly to alter the characteristics of the open fen habitat for quite a distance from the ditch edge (Madgwick pers comm). Suction dredgers are useful for maintaining ditches where only soft mud has accumulated. The restoration of unmanaged ditches (Plate

Plate 15 This floating suction dredger is occasionally used for mud pumping ditches in the Broads.

14a) requires the use of a hydraulic digger (Plate 14b).

Floating dredgers or diggers on pontoons or barges have been used on reedbeds with large ditches where there is no access on land. However, their use is seriously constrained by expense.

Slubbing to maintain a ditch means that only the soft, accumulated organic matter is removed, material which quite quickly breaks down once dried and exposed to the air. A considerable depth of soil may have developed in long-neglected ditches, posing a problem in terms of its disposal after it is dug out. If possible, the spoil should be removed from the reedbed or used to consolidate permanent access routes or low points in bunds. However, this is often impractical and expensive. Although the spoil can be used to form banks along ditch edges which may become colonised by scrub, nettles, thistles and other plants not normally associated with reedbeds, this is undesirable for wildlife as it may prevent the free movement of fish across a site and reduce its value for bitterns for example. Nevertheless, in the Broads and elsewhere this has been the practice for many years and quite diverse plant communities have developed on the dredgings. In addition, the banks are excellent for access and for stacking cut reed and saw-sedge. By providing gaps in the banks, the problem of restricting flow and access for aquatic wildlife may be overcome. The gaps may be made into culverts, or bridged with planks or liggers (Plate 16).

Distributing the spoil across a reedbed will eliminate such problems but adds to the time and cost and may cause further problems by raising the height of the bed and creating an uneven surface. Because organic material decays readily, this can be flung into the reedbed by the digger on each sweep. However, this could be undesirable as the material may alter the vegetation wherever it lies by changing the soil characteristics and nutrient levels in the immediate area (Madgwick pers comm). In addition, the spreading of spoil in this way may pollute the local soil and water environment (Haslam pers comm).

As the primary function of ditches is to carry water, it would seem logical to ensure that all the ditches on a site were free of vegetation at all times. If such a management approach were adopted, however, this would be seriously detrimental to the aquatic plants and animals the ditches support, and influence the effect the plants have on water quality. In reality, it is neither desirable nor practical to maintain the ditches in this way, which is why ditches are generally managed on rotation so that only a proportion of them are slubbed at any one time, permitting fish and other aquatic wildlife to recolonise. Wildlife benefits will be maximised by regular slubbing to allow the different stages of recolonisation of the ditches to be present on one site at any one time. This ideal situation occurs on some nature reserves but in practice ditch slubbing is done as and when a particular stretch of ditch requires it and may also be seriously limited by financial resources. Because nature does not behave uniformly, this approach often works well, with a succession of ditches managed throughout a site on an irregular basis, thereby spreading the cost of the work.

On a site where the ditches have not been managed for several years, the proportion of ditch length slubbed initially will be greater than on a site with a regular slubbing programme. Despite the variation in litter accumulation between and within sites, the following recommendations may be considered:

C Hawke (RSPB)

- On very overgrown and clogged ditches, remove 25% each year for four years. Alternatively, remove 50%, monitor recovery/development for two years then remove the remainder if appropriate.

- Thereafter, implement a 5–25 year slubbing rotation throughout the site (maximum of 20% in any year).

- Combine the work with routine edge management, vegetation cutting and reprofiling.

Figure 15 shows a schematic representation of a seven-year rotational ditch slubbing programme.

d) Ditch reprofiling

Most ditches traditionally have the profile illustrated in Figure 13b. This shape conveys water well, is easily achieved by mechanical digger and minimises colonisation by reed. The addition of the features illustrated in Figure 13a, greatly enhances the value of a ditch for wildlife without compromising its efficiency. Shallow ditches could also be deepened to reduce the rate of colonisation by plants. Table 7 gives a selection of animals and plants which benefit from such reprofiling. Reprofiling on Cley Marshes in Norfolk and at Stodmarsh in Kent (**Case Study 2**) has been carried out with the specific aim of enhancing feeding sites to encourage breeding bitterns.

Further information on management of ditch and channel vegetation can be found in Newbold *et al* (1992) and the requirements of water plants can be found in the *New Rivers and Wildlife Handbook* (RSPB/NRA/RSNC 1994).

Plate 16 The spoil from ditch creation and subsequent slubbing may be used to construct banks or bunds. Gaps may be left to enable water to flow on and off the reedbed. These may be culverted or bridged. This double 'ligger' in the Norfolk Broads provides access for wheeled cutting equipment as well as for people.

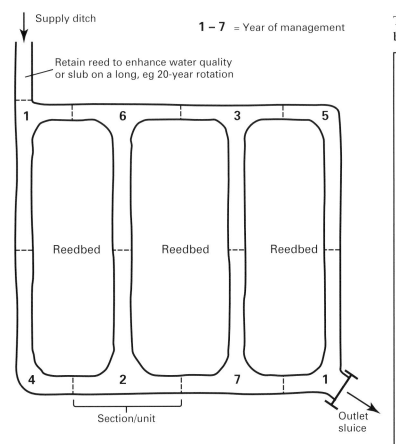

Supply ditch

1 – 7 = Year of management

Retain reed to enhance water quality
or slub on a long, eg 20-year rotation

1   6   3   5

Reedbed   Reedbed   Reedbed

4   2   7   1

Section/unit

Outlet
sluice

▲ **Figure 15**
**Example of a recommended pattern for
a seven-year rotational slubbing
programme. Advantages of a
programme like this include:**

- **Only 10–20% of the total ditch
  length is slubbed in any one year.**

- **One growing season is completed in
  a section slubbed a year earlier
  before the adjacent section is
  cleared.**

- **Ditch wildlife is gradually able to
  recolonise the managed section from
  adjacent vegetated sections of ditch.
  (NB fish populations may take three
  years or more to re-establish in
  slubbed ditches).**

**Table 7: Examples of wildlife that may
benefit from reprofiled ditches**

Plants
    Yellow iris
    Cowbane
    Marsh sowthistle
    Bur reed
    Water plantain
    Lesser water parsnip
    Purple-loosestrife
    Water-mint
    Water-dropworts
    Water dock
    Arrowhead
    Water-lilies
    Pondweeds

Birds
    Bittern
    Grey heron
    Water rail
    Moorhen
    Bearded tit
    Reed warbler
    Mallard
    Teal

Invertebrates
    Dragonflies
    Water beetles
    Water flea
    Cyclops
    Freshwater shrimp
    Mosquitoes
    Midges (chironomids)
    Water snails
    China-mark moths

Amphibians
    Common frog
    Common toad
    Common newt
    Palmate newt

Fish
    Pike
    Rudd
    Eel
    Roach
    Tench
    Sticklebacks

2.2.4 Open water

An area of water without, or with at most
marginal, emergent vegetation may be
described as open water. This section
includes general principles of management
for some types of open water and
encompasses:

- ditches (see section 2.2.3)

- large ponds, lakes, scrapes, meres

- pools, eg 'inversion' (upside-down
  pools), 'turf' ponds, bittern pools.

Plate 17 An aerial view of Leighton Moss, Lancashire showing the extent of open water and reed edge. Much of this has been created and maintained by summer cutting (section 2.3.1 c).

Open water adds to the wildlife value of a reedbed especially if it is of varying depth with shallow, sloping margins. However, it should form no more than 20% of the reedbed area.

Many reedbeds have open water associated with them (Plate 17). Sometimes, open water is created intentionally, to attract wildfowl for shooting or conservation reasons. It may also be a consequence of mineral extraction, formed by gravel or clay pits. Many ponds, reservoirs and lakes have deep water where reed will not colonise, but have reed fringes which may be harvestable for thatch and provide valuable habitat for wildlife.

Shallow (< 1 m), open water will be quickly colonised by reed and eventually lost through the normal process of succession. Management will, therefore, focus on preventing this and may involve the excavation of accumulated detritus/silt and control of marginal vegetation. The techniques for achieving this are described in sections 2.2.3 (Ditches), 2.3.1 (Cutting) and 2.3.3 (Herbicide Use).

Measures to reinstate the silted broads in Strumpshaw Fen and Cockshoot Broad in Norfolk involved the techniques of jetting and mud-pumping which are described in George (1992) and Tickner *et al* (1991).

a) Value of open water for wildlife

The value of open water for wildlife will be greatly enhanced if the water is of varying depth with shallow sloping margins as described for ditches in section 2.2.3 and Figure 16. Within reedbeds, most open water is designed so that the reed margins remain wet all year round where feasible and are graded so that the reed stands in 5–15 cm water depth in summer with increasing depth towards open water. In addition, the amount of reed edge can be increased by providing a varied land form so that the reed edge does not grow in a

straight line (Figure 17). Alternatively, the same can be achieved by a regular programme of cutting so that the reed edge has a scalloped appearance (Figure 16).

Open water is of value to a number of birds, including for example marsh harriers, which hunt over it in search of prey such as coot chicks and ducklings (Tyler 1992). However, the main value of open water is for animals and plants not reliant on reedbeds, especially wildfowl. Table 8 gives a list of birds which might otherwise be absent from a reedbed without open water. For important reedbed species its value lies at the edge where swamp grades into water.

Table 8: Examples of birds that utilise open water in a reedbed

Great crested grebe	Tufted duck
Little grebe	Goldeneye
Cormorant	Moorhen
Grey heron	Coot
Mute swan	Avocet
Bewick's swan	Redshank
Canada goose	Snipe
Greylag goose	Little ringed plover
Mallard	Common gull
Gadwall	Black-headed gull
Pintail	Common tern
Wigeon	Kingfisher
Shoveler	Swallow
Teal	House martin
Pochard	Sand martin

b) The importance of reed/water margins

Recent research by the RSPB on features of reedbeds which influence whether or not a site is occupied by breeding bitterns showed that the length of reed/water edge in a site was very important (Tyler 1994). Bitterns are secretive birds that hunt for fish, amphibians and large invertebrates in the shallow, wet reed margins of open water. In fact, bitterns generally feed in the first few metres of reed in from open water and nest most frequently within 30 m of reed edge/open water (Tyler pers comm).

Figure 16 Example design of reed edge and open water for wildlife benefit.

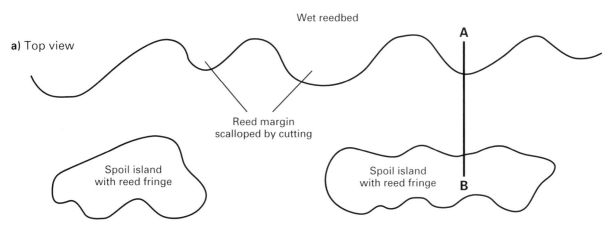

a) Top view

Wet reedbed

A

B

Reed margin
scalloped by cutting

Spoil island
with reed fringe

Spoil island
with reed fringe

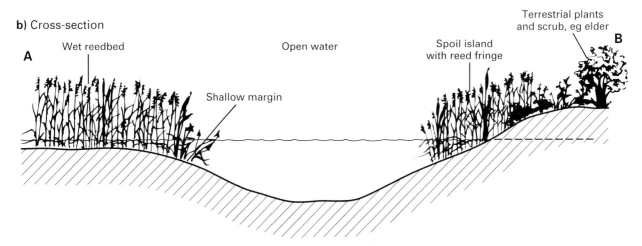

b) Cross-section

A

Wet reedbed

Open water

Terrestrial plants
and scrub, eg elder

B

Spoil island
with reed fringe

Shallow margin

Figure 17 Variable land form, eg ridge and furrow, maximises reed edge effect on open water.

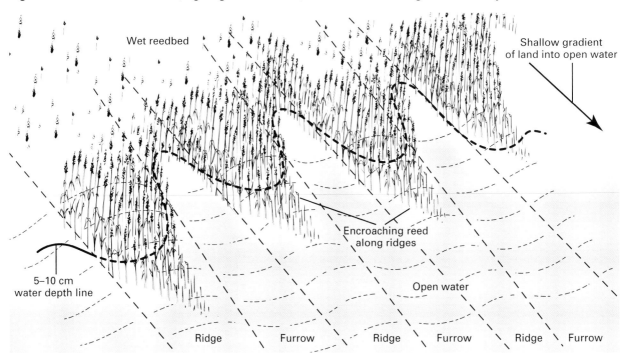

Wet reedbed

Shallow gradient
of land into open water

Encroaching reed
along ridges

5–10 cm
water depth line

Open water

Ridge   Furrow   Ridge   Furrow   Ridge   Furrow

The encroaching edge of reed (and rushes and reedmace when present) into shallow water provides bitterns with ideal feeding habitat because:

● The reed provides cover whilst enabling free movement of the bird through sparser growth than occurs deeper in the reedbed.

● Sunlight is able to penetrate the first few metres of reed and shallow water, which attracts fish, invertebrates and amphibians. In fact, these conditions support a whole food chain.

● Fish such as rudd and eels, are able to penetrate into the reedbed as far as shallow water extends. Eels may penetrate farther if conditions remain sufficiently damp. Many species, pike for example, lay their eggs in the warmer, shallow water at the reed margin.

At Leighton Moss in Lancashire, a study of radio-tagged bitterns between 1988 and 1990 gave some insight into habitat requirements. Open water was calculated to represent an average of 18% of the area used by the birds studied which equated to approximately 260 m of reed edge/ha of the habitat (Tyler in prep and pers comm).

A large pool, a series of small pools throughout the wet reedbed and a system of ditches and grips with shallowly profiled edges will provide the maximum amount of reed edge (Plate 17). This not only benefits bitterns but other bird species such as moorhen, water rail and heron plus, in the shallow water's edge, snipe and dabbling ducks such as pintail, shoveler, teal and mallard. The shallow water permits submerged and floating plants to grow, providing habitat for feeding and breeding invertebrates. Birds such as bearded tit, reed warbler and Cetti's warbler will feed at the edge on insects emerging from the water. Little grebe, coot and pochard will build nests on the edge or a metre or so into the reed. The range of wildlife which can utilise the reed edge-open water zone is illustrated in Introduction, Figure 1.

However, maximum reed edge alone is not sufficient to support breeding bitterns. Other factors such as reed area and quality, water quality and food supply also need to be considered. Table 9 represents a guide to the requirements of bitterns based on both scientific findings and detailed observations over many years. Many of the figures given are extrapolated on the basis of breeding bittern occupancy of a site and the habitats present. Nevertheless, they appear to hold true for the small number of bitterns studied so far.

Table 9: Average proportions of major habitats within reedbeds utilised by breeding bitterns at Leighton Moss

Habitat	Proportion	
Scrub*	8%	}
Reed	72%	}
Open water	18%	} 22 ha
Edge	260 m/ha	}

* represents maximum amount which should be present (Data courtesy Glen Tyler, RSPB).

c) Creation of open water on an existing reedbed site

Open water, close to or within a reedbed greatly enhances its wildlife value by providing additional habitat which can be exploited by a wide range of wildlife. The addition of new areas of open water or the clearing of existing overgrown ditches and pools is the most cost-effective way of increasing the wildlife value of a reedbed (Burgess and Evans 1989). Open water is created by three main techniques:

● excavation by digger

● spraying reed with herbicide (section 2.3.3)

● cutting reed in summer and under water (section 2.3.1 d).

The optimum size of the area of open water will depend on the total area of reed present and as a general guide should be no

Figure 18
Stages of turf pond excavation (drawing by Matthew Dane, reproduced with permission of Broads Authority).

more than 20% of the reedbed area (Table 23). The location within the reedbed is also important. To avoid damaging the existing invertebrate interest, it is advisable to create a pond for example, adjacent to or at the edge of the wetland (Kirby 1992), although even here important communities of plants may be present and should be avoided. On large reedbed sites, the addition of open water at the expense of pure reed, which generally has less wildlife diversity than more mixed areas of plants, will add to the wildlife value without damaging the other reedbed habitats present.

For pools, ponds, meres, scrapes and lakes the basic principles are the same. Soil is excavated from the reedbed using a mechanical digger to produce a hole, which fills with water. Spreading the spoil on existing reed areas or other valuable habitat should be avoided and it may be pushed into the centre and used to construct islands for example, or as at Far Ings on Humberside, dropped into the edge of deeper water to make it shallower (**Case Study 3**). At Strumpshaw Fen in Norfolk, the mud pumped to re-open the Old Broad was deposited on a designated, bunded area of low-value scrub. The construction of bunds may be combined with open water creation as was the case at Walberswick in Suffolk where material was scraped from the reedbed to create a sea wall leaving shallow open water areas on either side (Case Study 11).

Similarly, in the Broadland fens, 'turf' ponds are dug as part of fen restoration work where the peat spoil is used to consolidate existing bunds or to construct new ones to prevent excessive flooding by the tidally influenced river system. The ponds are profiled, allowing reed and a variety of other plants gradually to recolonise the shallow margins (Figure 18). A similar system but on a smaller scale has been used at Redgrave and Lopham Fen on the Norfolk and Suffolk borders where small pools were dug to mimic traditional peat diggings for the benefit of the endangered great raft spider.

At Blacktoft Sands on Humberside, some 20 ha of shallow, coastal lagoons were created by excavating the tidal reedbed, using the spoil to construct islands and a boundary bund, which holds back water after topping up on a high tide. One lagoon of about 8 ha of wet reedbed and 4 ha of open water, is kept as wet as possible by retaining high water levels throughout the year but frequently dries out in hot summers. There is a further 88 ha of tidal reedbed.

Similarly, at Minsmere in Suffolk 20 ha of wader breeding scrape was excavated leaving some 145 ha of reedbed intact. Apart from the aquatic habitat this provided, about 2.5 km of reed edge was added.

At Titchwell in Norfolk, a novel method of creating open water has been developed whereby scraped 'topsoil' (mainly plant debris) was excavated to one side and the subsoil also dug out. The topsoil was replaced in the hole and the subsoil placed on top of it. The weight of this compressed the softer topsoil below, creating a shallow pool. The reed rhizomes in the original topsoil were buried too deep to grow so that reed could recolonise only from the margins. Experimental plots of 10 m x 10 m had achieved nearly complete reed cover again within five years of excavation (Sills pers comm). Similar, but larger 'upside-down' or 'inverted substrate' pools have been created in 1991 and 1993 (see Figure 1 in Case Study 7).

At Far Ings in Humberside, a series of small pools were excavated to produce an encroaching reed margin for the benefit of feeding bitterns and other wildlife (Case Study 3).

2.3 Reed Management

2.3.1 Cutting

Cutting simply involves the severance of the aerial parts (stems and seed heads) of reedbed plants. What varies is:

- time of year

- frequency

- extent.

There are two main cutting periods, summer and winter. Summer cutting is undertaken principally to suppress the more dominant taller plant species thus promoting species diversity and maintaining open water. Traditionally, marsh hay and litter for stock bedding was cropped in summer from mixed, tall-herb fen in the Broads but any similar management is now done solely for conservation purposes and the cut vegetation is usually raked and burned or stacked to decay (Andrews pers comm). Saw-sedge is cut in summer while it is green, which permits sufficient regrowth before damage is done by frosts and floods in winter (Plate 18). Winter cutting removes only the dead parts of reedbed plants. In fact, it tends to promote the growth of better quality reed and the removal of the cut material, either for commercial uses or by burning off, reduces the rate of litter build-up and hence drying

out and subsequent succession. This favours the dominance of reed and a corresponding reduction in species diversity (Wheeler and Giller 1982a+b). Winter cutting is generally favoured over burning as a technique because it enables a crop to be taken and does not damage the litter invertebrate population.

Frequency refers to how often in one season cutting is done, or more commonly, whether cutting is done annually or on rotations of two years or more. Cutting more than once in summer will effectively suppress growth of most plant species and reduces the biomass of the reedbed as a whole. Annual summer cuts, however, are quite common. Harvesting saw-sedge requires cutting on a three or four-year rotation to allow sufficient regrowth and density of new stems. Reed is cut annually (single wale) or biennially (double wale) for thatching and sometimes on longer rotations where wildlife conservation is the principal aim.

The extent of cutting will vary greatly, depending on factors such as resources, the market price of cut reed, the type of rotation employed and the target species or group.

Reed that has not been managed for many years may need to be burned off (section 2.3.4) to reduce the litter and produce a straight-stemmed stand which may then be cut. Reedbeds that are usually dry in the spring and have been invaded by grasses and other unwanted plants may be grazed with sheep. Unlike cattle, sheep are reluctant to eat reed shoots provided there is plenty of other palatable vegetation available. It is important therefore, that stocking densities are low and that the sheep are removed when grazing has become tight. It is important that there are dry refuges for the sheep if flooding is likely. The reed grows well in the absence of competition from other plants and the

Winter cutting favours reed production for thatching and benefits wildlife. Summer cutting increases plant diversity in a reedbed.

C Hawke (RSPB)

Plate 18 A saw-sedge bed in the Broads. The shorter sedge on the right was cut two years ago whilst the taller sedge on the left was cut three years ago and will be cut in its fourth year of growth.

quantity of litter to be cleaned from the reed during harvest is reduced. This technique is practised on reedbeds adjacent to river banks in some parts of the Broads (Satchell pers comm).

Table 23 gives recommended figures for percentages of reed to cut for integrating wildlife and commercial interests.

a) The rotational cutting of reed in winter

The purpose of cutting reed on any rotation is that it:

- enables a structured management regime to be implemented and matched to resources and markets

- produces quality thatching reed

- reduces the rate of succession and eventual loss of usable reed

- benefits wildlife by sustaining the habitat

Single wale

This is when reed is cut every winter and while not strictly rotational, for the purposes of this book is best considered as a one-year rotational method of management.

Single wale cutting is used primarily to produce reed for the thatching industry. Reed from single wale cutting is usually:

- 1–2 m tall

- 2–7 mm diameter (butt end)

- dense (200+ stems/m^2)

- with dense seed-heads.

These are qualities much sought after by thatchers. On reedbeds which have been cut single wale for many years a gradual decline in yield may occur (Ward 1992). At Ranworth Flood in Norfolk (**Case Study 5**) the average yield is 750–1,000 bundles/ha (300–400 bundles/acre) from single wale beds compared with 1,000–1,250 bundles/ha (400–500 bundles/acre) from double wale beds (Haslam 1972a). However, single wale cutting on tidal

reedbeds does not necessarily reduce yields (although stem height is usually shorter than on uncut areas) as experienced on the Tay estuary (**Case Study 4**) where single wale cutting can produce 1,250 bundles/ha (Craig pers comm).

During the first two to three years of single wale cutting, the reed may regrow to 2–3 m tall but after several more years the reed height may be only 1.5–2 m (Satchell pers comm). On drier sites, reed cut single wale for many years may be only 1 m tall. Provided the stems are straight with hard butt ends, reed of different lengths can be used for thatching different parts of a roof. However, different length stems within a single bundle are unpopular with thatchers. The increased number of thinner stems produced by single wale cutting enables the reed to be packed tightly on the roof, a characteristic favoured by many thatchers.

Single wale cutting means that each year the dead reed biomass is removed and does not accumulate as litter. This produces an annual crop that requires minimal cleaning (Pope pers comm), reduces the rate of drying out and succession in the reedbed and facilitates a surface flow of water. A noticeable absence of scrub is a feature of single wale reedbeds, any seedlings being removed in the cut each year (see section 2.3.5).

This frequency of cutting tends to increase the dominance of reed, thereby reducing plant diversity. In particular, species such as milk parsley may be suppressed by such management, which would be detrimental to the swallowtail butterfly whose caterpillar feeds on this plant in the Norfolk Broads. However, experiments on a degraded reedbed at Blankaart in Belgium showed that after four years of annual winter cutting the species diversity was much higher than in unmanaged areas. The reduction in litter and shading encouraged the growth of early, less vigorous plants such as water mint and marsh bedstraw. The intensity of the management inhibited taller plants, such as reed and nettle, which emerged later (Gryseels 1989a).

Certain invertebrate species, notably the wainscot moths or 'reed bugs', can be damaging to reed if they occur in large numbers (van der Toorn and Mook 1982). Single wale cutting removes the overwintering microhabitat for most species, and is an efficient control method. However, there are several species of reed-dwelling moth that are nationally rare and would be unable to survive such frequent cutting. The thinner stems produced by prolonged single wale cutting may reduce infestation by many stem-boring invertebrates.

A degree of rotation can be introduced into a single wale cutting regime if the site has the capacity. Such a system operates at Walberswick in Suffolk (Case Study 11) where each year no more than 30 ha of the total 230 ha of reedbed is cut single wale for thatch. Individual plots vary in size and are cut annually for five years, in which year a 'new' plot (one that has not been cut for at least five years) is established by burning (section 2.3.4). A new single wale regime is established on the regrowth of the burned plot the following season, the old plot is then left uncut for a minimum of five years. The benefits of such a rotation are:

● a single wale crop can be taken for thatching

● small-scale burning regenerates reed uncut for several years but leaves large areas unburned, thus preserving invertebrates and bird and mammal nest sites

● the rotation moves between active and resting plots and never involves cutting more than 12% of the total reed area in any one year. This means that succession to woodland is effectively halted in the single wale cut plots.

According to Burgess and Evans (1989), single wale cutting:

● increases reed vigour, density, flowering and seed production

● promotes structural diversity and provides abundant reed edge for invertebrates and bitterns

● provides winter feeding sites for bearded tits

● provides spring breeding grounds for waders.

Cutting single wale in large, continuous swathes within one site will reduce the amount of standing reed available for the benefit of birds and invertebrates. By reducing the size of blocks and spreading them throughout the reedbed with uncut or double wale cut blocks between, all the advantages described above are retained. In addition, greater benefits are achieved, such as nest sites for reed warblers and bitterns, cover for feeding birds, and protection for eggs and larvae of rare moths and other invertebrates. In practice, it is unusual for a whole reedbed to be cut in one go due to the impracticalities of cutting around ditch edges, on soft ground and in depressions that retain water. Also, reed quality is never consistent throughout a site and varies from year to year, which means that reed of unsuitable thatching quality may be left uncut. Most commercial reedbeds have uncut areas associated with them which have never, or have only periodically, been included in the single wale programme (Plate 19).

Plate 19 A single wale reedbed (fore ground) on the Inner Tay, Fife. Note the taller reed (background) which is left uncut each year for wildlife.

C Hawke (RSPB)

Double wale

This is when the reed is cut in winter once every two years. Bundles of reed cut for thatch contain the dead stems from the previous year's growth, as well as the most recent stems which will be the most suitable for thatching. Double wale cut reed is commonly used for thatching. It is widely available and is the preferred method of cutting management by many reed growers (Plates 20 and 21). Reed cut double wale is usually:

- more than 2 m tall

- 7–12 mm diameter (butt end)

- 100–200 stems/m^2

- with dense seed-heads.

Plate 20 Double wale reed being harvested at Far Ings, Humberside.

K Gray

Plate 21 Cutting reed double wale using a reciprocator mower.

Broads Authority

Plate 22 New shoots growing amongst last year's stems at Teifi, Dyfed. On double wale reedbeds the old stems provide a 'cold frame' effect which benefits the new shoots.

C Haoke (RSPB)

Double wale bundles require some cleaning to remove short stems and any grasses and other unwanted vegetation. In the Broadland fens, invasion by grasses is common in double wale beds but they are easily cleaned out at harvest (**Case Study 6**). This is probably a feature related to periods of dryness in summer, allowing the grass to establish. It also occurs on the North Solent reedbeds which, like the

Broads, have a tidally influenced hydrology, fluctuating both daily and seasonally.

The advantages of double wale cutting are that it offers a period of 'rest' for reedbeds uncut in the rotation and usually produces higher yields. As well as producing high quality thatching reed, double wale ensures there is always some uncut reed for reed-dwelling wildlife so long as an entire reedbed is not cut in one year of a double wale rotation. At Salthouse in Norfolk, 25% of the reedbed area is left uncut in any one year (ie cut double wale) under a management agreement with English Nature. This ensures that 3–4 ha remains standing ready for next spring's reed-nesting birds, harvest mice and reed-dwelling invertebrates.

Double wale also enables biennial and perennial tall herbs such as milk parsley to reach the flowering stage and to set seed. Because of the advantages of double wale to a wide range of wildlife it is the preferred method of commercial harvesting promoted by the Broads Authority (Andrews pers comm) and employed by the Norfolk Wildlife Trust at Martham Broad (Starling pers comm).

Despite some litter accumulation associated with double wale cutting, the cleaned out litter and other bed litter is usually raked and burned as part of bed aftercare and causes little problem.

The more vigorous stems produced in double wale reedbeds can be partly explained by the 'cold frame' effect afforded by the previous year's stems to the newly growing shoots (Plate 22). This gives the second year's growth a head start by protecting it from late frosts and producing taller, thicker and stronger stems (Andrews 1992).

Longer rotations
A long rotation is when reed is cut in every third year or more. Rarely, three-year rotational reed can be cut and sold for thatch, but it is unpopular with thatchers because it contains two years' worth of old, weaker stems (McDougall 1972) and requires more cleaning at the bundling

stage. On nature reserves, longer rotations are frequently employed where the cut reed and litter is raked up and burned (Plate 23) or piled in stacks as alternative habitat for invertebrates, nesting wrens and bearded tits, and possibly small mammals. Grass snakes are often associated with reedbeds and may use such piles of decaying vegetation to incubate their eggs (Langton 1989).

The frequency of rotations and size of plots are usually dictated by resources, especially labour. The frequency is sometimes arbitrary therefore, and not necessarily linked to a known benefit. Similarly, the length of the rotation may depend on the size of the site and how conveniently it divides into manageable plots. Because of such difficulties, cutting at Titchwell Marsh in Norfolk was once carried out on a quite random basis and in small plots. The acquisition of a reciprocator mower in the late 1980s enabled larger areas to be managed on a regular basis and now a range of experimental rotations are in place and being monitored (**Case Study 7**).

More frequent rotations consume more resources in the short term but are likely to be more sustainable since they reduce litter accumulation and scrub invasion which are both costly to deal with if allowed to proceed unabated. Longer rotations may be preferred if certain species require undisturbed habitat; for example the marsh harrier often nests in the same area of reed in consecutive years. Many reed-dwelling invertebrates overwinter in or on parts of reedbed plants and rotations of two to three years or more enable them to persist on a site. However, only small areas of uncut reed or reed stands cut on a long rotation are required to support these species. These areas can be combined with shorter rotations on the majority of the site.

Where wildlife conservation is the primary aim and sufficient resources are available, longer rotations may be beneficial. At Leighton Moss in Lancashire, a 5–10 year experimental, rotational cutting programme was started in 1990 (Wilson 1990). The original aim was to cut between 4–8 ha of the 79 ha reedbed each year. Plots

Plate 23 Burning off cut reed on a bonfire.

Broads Authority

were kept small (ca 30 m–40 m diameter) and were spread throughout the reedbed, mainly in the drier areas where the litter build-up was greatest. Cutting was done in winter with a Honda reciprocator mower and brush cutters and the debris burned on site. The reedbed at Leighton Moss is wet with a slow litter build-up such that the area now cut in this programme has been reduced to 3 ha as it was feared that insufficient areas of reed suitable for bearded tits to nest in were being left. Bitterns use the newly cut and newly growing areas for feeding and marsh harriers regularly hunt the open, cut plots. It is considered that small areas scattered through the reedbed have been more beneficial than one or two larger areas. Increases in breeding coots, water rails and reed warblers have been recorded around the cut areas since the rotation commenced.

A similar 10–15-year programme is ongoing at Stodmarsh in Kent, with fixed rotational blocks throughout the reserve. In addition, a new 2–3-year rotation was started in 1994 associated with a ditch reprofiling project (Case Study 2). An area of 4 ha, of which 1–2 ha is cut each year, is being managed specifically for bitterns which once bred there. Once again, the aim is to prevent a build-up of litter and to maintain a wet, reed-dominated area suitable for bitterns to both nest and feed in.

According to Burgess and Evans (1989), long rotations:

- maintain reed vigour for reed warblers and nesting marsh harriers

- permit litter accumulation for invertebrates and nesting bearded tits

- help reduce succession

- maintain structural diversity and reed edge for invertebrates and bitterns.

Table 10 summarises the benefits of winter cutting rotations on a reedbed.

Table 10: The effects of winter cutting rotations on reed and the benefits for wildlife and thatching

Cycle length (yrs)	Reduces scrub invasion	Maintains vigour	Reduces litter accumulation	Increases stem density	Increases flowering & seed production	Thatching	Wildlife
1	■■■■	■■■	■■■■	■■■■	■■■	■■■■	■/■■
2	■■■■	■■■■	■■■	■■■	■■■■	■■■/■■■■	■■■
3–5	■■■	■■	■■	■■■	■■■■	■	■■■■
7–15	■	■	■	■■	■■		■■■■

These ratings are generalised and are based on a number of sites. Variations may occur between sites and within a site depending on soil type, water regime and weather.
■ = minimum effect   ■■■■ = maximum effect

Reed cutting for thatch may commence in November when the reed has hardened. It generally ceases in March to avoid damage to new shoots. Prolonged submersion of reed stubble can delay growth and is usually avoided.

b) Cutting reed for thatch

Whether cutting on a single or double wale rotation the procedure for cutting and bundling reed is essentially the same. The equipment used will influence the degree of manual labour required. Machines which cut, bundle and tie the reed, eg Olympia harvester (Plate 24a and section 2.3.1 d) reduce the harvesting time and enable bundles to be collected and carried off the reedbeds with comparative ease. Reciprocator mowers with attachments, hand scything and brushcutters enable the cut reed to be wind-rowed, which facilitates bundling. The procedure for cutting, bundling, dressing/cleaning and tying is illustrated in Plates 24a–24e.

Most reed cutters will start harvesting as soon as possible in the season. In most years, cutting rarely starts before November, ensuring the reed is hard and suitable for thatching. In the Norfolk Broads, reed cutting starts in late November and may continue well into March or April (Andrews pers comm). How late cutting can be done without causing damage to new reed shoots varies from site to site and geographical location. Shoots emerge later on drier reedbeds, eg parts of the River Bure in Norfolk where cutting sometimes continues well into April (Satchell pers comm). However, as a general rule cutting rarely continues beyond mid-March to avoid damage to

newly emerging shoots and disturbance to breeding wildlife. On the Tay Estuary, cutting and burning continue until 14 April because of the later breeding season.

On sites where water level control is difficult, January and February are often the most active months when rainfall is lowest or frozen ground facilitates access with machinery.

The point after which the lower leaves, or 'flags', of reeds drop is traditionally used as an indicator that the crop is ready for harvesting (McDougall 1972). Colour is another indicator for reed is rarely cut 'green' for thatching. When the stems are a yellow/brown colour, often shiny, along the entire length apart from the butt end section which may retain a little greenness, the reed crop is ready. If the cut reed is to be dry-stored for a year before use for thatching, cutting earlier with a degree of greenness is feasible, as the hardening process will continue during storage. However, this is usually a preference of individual thatchers (Pope pers comm).

Reed of suitable quality can be cut from very small areas such as on river banks where hand scythes may be used to reach difficult terrain. The size of a block is invariably based on practicalities therefore. However, small areas, eg 20 m x 20 m, cut amongst unmanaged reed or reed cut on long rotations, may produce reed of decreasing thatching quality. This is thought to be because of damage caused by invertebrates which colonise from the uncut edges. Cutting larger plots would reduce this 'edge effect' by concentrating the invertebrates to the first few metres leaving unaffected reed to grow in the middle. Cutting larger blocks double wale would reduce the impact and have improved benefits for wildlife (Satchell pers comm).

The British Reed Growers' Association have produced a leaflet *Buying and Selling Reed* which describes reed qualities for thatching. It is available free from the address in Appendix 3.

Stubble length after cutting

Because the butt ends of the reeds are hardest and form the outer, durable layer of a thatched roof, cutting as close to the ground as possible will ensure the maximum length of butt end is cut. This is best achieved by:

- cutting with maximum draw-down, ie no surface water on the bed

- ensuring the blade is set as low as possible on reciprocator mowers

- cutting using a hand-scythe.

A flat bed will facilitate cutting and maximise the length of butt end cut.

Submersion of the stubble can cause a decreased yield and delay growth in spring (Haslam 1972). On Ranworth Flood, the water level is highly controllable, permitting complete draw-down for close cutting, whereafter the level is gradually increased as new shoots grow in spring. By contrast, the high risk of uncontrolled winter flooding at Radipole Lake in Dorset and on many Broads sites which are influenced by tidally fluctuating river levels, means that the stubble is submerged periodically. Temporary submersion of stubble may not affect yield; on the tidal reedbeds of the Tay, the lower lying reed is frequently inundated and yet the taller, tougher reed grows.

Plate 24a An Olympia reedcutter in action.

R Andrews (Broads Authority)

24b Shaking out unwanted debris from single wale reed at Walberswick in Suffolk.

C Hawke (RSPB)

24c Cleaning litter from double wale reed at How Hill in Norfolk.

C Hawke (RSPB)

24d Retying bundles after dressing the reed at Walberswick, Suffolk.

C Hawke (RSPB)

24e A finished bundle of double wale reed from How Hill, Norfolk.

C Hawke (RSPB)

Cutting sheaf for thatching

Sheaf is a mixture of tall grasses, reed and other plants, which is unsuitable for thatching houses. However, traditionally it was harvested in the Broads to thatch barns and other farm buildings (Cator pers comm). At Ranworth Flood, areas of single wale reedbed where tall grasses are invading, are cut early for sheaf. It is cut and bundled in the same way as quality thatching reed but requires no dressing or cleaning. Because its market value is much lower than for quality thatching reed it is only cut to order. Because sheaf can be cut earlier in the season (late summer to early autumn) the period of employment for contractors is extended. The poorer quality material that constitutes sheaf gives a life expectancy of a sheaf-thatched roof of 20–30 years compared with up to 80 years for a roof thatched with pure, high quality reed.

Summer cutting favours plant diversity. It can also be a tool to maintain open water in a reedbed.

c) Summer cutting of reed

The purpose of cutting reed in summer is to reduce its vigour and competitiveness for the benefit of other plants and wildlife. Summer cutting:

- removes the green, growing parts of reed thus depriving the rhizome of energy

- if cut under water, further reduces the vigour of reed and other reedbed vegetation

- usually increases the diversity of plants in a reedbed

- maintains (and extends) open water.

The mechanism by which summer cutting of reed increases plant diversity is the same as for traditional hay meadow management and grazing pastures. The dominant, fast-growing grasses (in this case reed) are cut and removed, permitting the shorter, slower growing species to thrive. The effect of summer cutting will depend on site conditions, in particular the habitat, when cutting commenced. Despite a change in the composition of the vegetation, Gryseels (1989b) found it remained species poor. Nevertheless, the removal of reed from a reed-dominated area:

- reduces shading

- reduces competition for nutrients

- provides physical space for other plants to grow.

On commercial reedbeds summer cutting is rarely, if ever, practised (although spring cuts are sometimes used to regenerate areas of rough reed). On some reedbed nature reserves however, the practice is commonplace and two methods are widely used:

- above-water cutting

- under-water cutting.

Above-water cutting

This technique is practised most often in areas of dry reedbed or very shallow water. Cutting is usually by brushcutter (Plate 25) or reciprocator mower and the cuttings may be raked up into piles to decay or burned off when dry enough. It is important to time the cutting for maximum effect which for reed is during the main growth period April to July although as late as September can still be effective in some years. However, disturbance to breeding wildlife is a major consideration so later in this period is preferable. If reed is cut early, it will regrow, requiring a second or third cut in one season. Four years of cutting in July and again in August failed to prevent reed from regrowing at Blankaart in Belgium. However, eutrophic conditions may have been the cause of this (Gryseels 1989b).

C Hawke (RSPB)

Plate 25 Summer cutting reed at Leighton Moss, Lancashire using a rotating brushcutter.

When first establishing a summer cutting programme, more than one cut in the season will reduce the quantity to be cut the following year and after several years of annual summer cutting the quantity may be so small that raking and removal are no longer necessary (Wilson pers comm). This method of establishing a summer cutting programme is used at Leighton Moss in Lancashire, but priority is given to important nesting reedbed birds by leaving a disturbance-free margin around sensitive areas.

Above-water cutting is less effective at reducing reed dominance than under-water cutting. Both techniques are used at Leighton Moss although underwater cutting is used more widely due to the generally deep water conditions of the site (**Case Study 8**).

Under-water cutting

The rationale for under-water cutting is that it permits vegetation control without the use of herbicides or the need to run off water at a time when it is important for wildlife and usually in short supply. Thus, open water can be maintained or pools formed within the reedbed without any changes to the water regime.

The principle behind under-water cutting is that the reed stems are cut while actively growing and are further inhibited by being submerged in water. This has the effect of:

- removing green, aerial parts which are essential for photosynthesis

- 'drowning' the rhizome by depriving it of oxygen (Andrews and Ward 1991)

- reducing shoot growth the following spring.

This method may be used to create new, permanent areas of open water within a reedbed, which would produce additional reed/open water edge (section 2.2.4 b). This can benefit a range of wildlife, especially birds, fish and aquatic invertebrates and plants.

Important considerations when undertaking under-water cutting include:

- after the first cut, subsequent cuts should be during the growing phase (April–September)

- stubble must remain submerged throughout remainder of season

- cutting should be directed to minimise disturbance to wildlife.

Many other plants, including reedmace and rushes, can be controlled using this method.

The only practical method of cutting under water is using a reciprocator mower or reciprocating brushcutter. Cutting by hand-scythe is difficult because of the resistance offered by the water itself. However, as the number of shoots drops considerably after each cut a hand-scythe can be used very effectively on later cuts (Wilson pers comm). Rotating brushcutters spray the operator with water making working conditions unpleasant and unsafe.

Reciprocators permit one operator to cut relatively large areas quickly, depending on conditions. At Minsmere in Suffolk, an Allen reciprocating brushcutter is used for cutting aquatic vegetation and marginal reed in ditches (Robinson pers comm). The advantage of reciprocating brushcutters is that they operate effectively and safely in deep water (up to 1 m) whereas mowers are limited by water depth and topography. At Leighton Moss in Lancashire, a Honda mower is used with a 1-m bar to cut large open areas with up to 30 cm water depth (Figure 1 in Case Study 8 and Plate 27).

Plate 26 A Seiga cutter as used by the Tayreed Company on the Inner Tay Reedbed.

C Hawke (RSPB)

Because these mowers are wheeled vehicles they can damage soft substrates (Waller pers comm) and frequently become bogged down, a problem which can be greatly alleviated when double or triple wheels are fitted (Wilson pers comm). A sharply undulating surface can lead to the bar slicing into the substrate, damaging the blades.

The skids on the reciprocator mower's bar must be adjusted so that the stubble is of an even length and submerged. When cutting large areas with a reciprocating brushcutter, care must be taken to avoid cutting above water on the upswings by cutting more slowly and precisely.

Timing is very important, especially in the first year, when the vegetation will be tall and dense. This is best cut, raked and burned in late summer or winter, followed by the first summer cut in April/May when the shoots are young. During year one, a second and third cut may be necessary depending on regrowth and will greatly inhibit development the following spring. Cuts in subsequent years need only be once, in August/September, when animals have completed breeding and plants of value have set seed.

Some flexibility in the management plan may be required with time as the effect of late summer cutting in shallower areas is to encourage botanical diversity. This may make continued management of the area as open water hard to justify as the benefits of increased plant diversity may be higher. Where appropriate, this may be prevented by ensuring there is surface water all year round.

d) Cutting equipment

A wide range of cutting equipment is used on UK reedbeds, from hand-sickles to large self-propelled reciprocating mowers. The following is a brief description of the most commonly used equipment and Table 11 compares some of the attributes of each type.

Hand-scythes and sickles

The traditional scythe is still used on a limited scale. Its value lies in being able to reach small areas where machinery is unable to operate. Scythe-cut reed has smooth, tapered tips to the butt ends, perfect for thatching. A skilled and fit operator can cut reed as fast as some machinery but scythes have been replaced by reciprocating mowers on most reedbeds. The sickle is a short-handled blade which is inappropriate for cutting reed but is used occasionally where other equipment is unavailable.

Reciprocating mowers

These are machines with cutting bars one, two or three metres long. The bar consists of a static lower blade, and a moving upper blade which is driven from side to side over the static blade, severing the reed stems near ground level. The blades produce square-cut butt ends with frayed tips, which are suitable for thatching. There are

Table 11: A comparison of commonly used cutting equipment

Equipment	Ease of use	Reliability	Terrain	Speed	Result	Cost (£)
Hand scythe	Moderate	Very	All	Moderate	V good	<100
Hand sickle	Difficult	Very	All	Slow	Poor	< 15
Reciprocating mowers:						
Allen	Difficult	Good	Flat/wet	Fast	Good	?
Iseki/Honda	Easy	Good	Flat/wet	Fast	Good	2,000
Bucher	Easy	Very	Flat/wet	Fast	Good	5,000
Olympia	Difficult	Moderate	Flat/wet	Fast	Good	7,000
Seiga	Easy	Good	Flat	V fast	Good	30,000
Brushcutters:						
Rotating	Easy	Good	All	Fast	Poor	<350
Reciprocating	Moderate	Good	All	Moderate	Good	<350

The prices are estimates. Allen scythes and Seiga cutters are no longer manufactured and new versions of Olympia cutters are hard to come by.

several different models of the walk-behind type; the earliest was the Allen scythe. This has largely been superseded by the easier to handle and safer Iseki, Honda (Plate 27), BCS or Bucher (Plate 36a) all of which are usually fitted with a 1-m cutting bar. Often, where reed is cut for thatching, custom-made catching boxes are fitted to facilitate bundling by hand. A wind-rowing attachment is available for use with the Bucher, which also comes in diesel (very hard-working) and petrol versions. The Bucher and BCS are purpose-built mowers, but have a low ground clearance which may cause difficulties in very wet conditions.

The Olympia is a larger walk-behind machine which bundles and ties the reed (Plate 28). It is quite heavy and cumbersome and operates best on large, flat reedbeds. New machines are rare and it is possible that there are only about eight in service in the UK.

The Seiga is a self-propelled machine with a 3-m long reciprocating blade mounted on a cargo rig (Plate 26). There is only one in service in the UK but several operate on reedbeds elsewhere in Europe. There are four- and six-wheeled versions. They are designed for working on large reedbeds such as the Tay Estuary (410 ha) and the massive Lake Kolon reedbed (> 800 ha) in Hungary. Three people are required to operate the machine, which is capable of cutting and tying 2,000 bundles in a day.

Brushcutters (Rotating blade)

These machines come in a wide range of makes and models. Lightweight versions are not recommended for cutting reed. Tri-star (Figure 19a) blades are the most effective although other types will also do the job. An experienced operator can cut and wind-row a large area in a day. Because the butt ends of the reeds are smashed by the blade they are not recommended for cutting reed for thatching.

Brushcutters (reciprocating blade)

These are specialist machines with a fixed reciprocating head (Figure 19b). They are especially suited for under-water cutting (section 2.3.1 c and Case Study 8).

C H Gomersall (RSPB)

C Hawke (RSPB)

Plate 27 A Honda reciprocator mower. Machines of this type are lightweight and easy to operate even in water as shown. Note the custom-made catching rack on the front which retains cut reed upright to facilitate bundling by hand.

Plate 28 An Olympia reedcutter showing the guide arms, cutting bar and bundling tines.

Figure 19
Examples of brushcutter heads for cutting reed

a) Rotating tri-star blade

b) Reciprocating type

a)

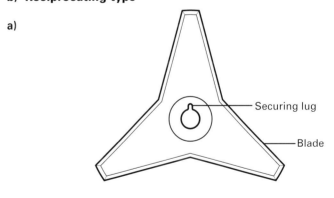

b)

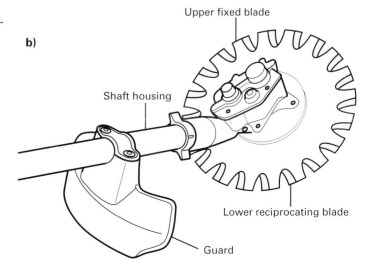

2.3.2 Frosting

Exposure to frost can increase the number of shoots but they may be shorter and thinner. Late frosts may harm the final crop. Single wale cutting may increase the susceptibility of new shoots to frost.

Frost can damage the tissues of most plants including reed. The period when reed is most vulnerable from ground frosts is in April when new shoots are emerging; frosts in May cause less damage (van der Toorn and Mook 1982). However, it is likely that much will depend on the severity of an individual frost or exposure to several consecutive frosts.

Exposure of buds to frost, either on recently planted rhizome cuttings or where rhizomes have been uncovered when the litter layer has been scraped away as part of bed regeneration, may kill both the rhizomes and buds. However, an increase in the number of shoots which develop in the spring may occur (see below) although the time for the shoots to emerge may be delayed by up to one month as replacement buds need to develop (Haslam 1969).

Exposure of the bed surface by cutting and removal of the reed can increase the number of shoots emerging by up to 400%. This occurs when each new shoot killed by frost is replaced by 1–3 new ones. However, the effect is to produce a denser stand of reed with shorter, thinner stems (Haslam 1969). This response could be achieved by ensuring water levels are not raised until the first frost occurs after completion of cutting. In most cutting

seasons, beds will be exposed to frosting as a matter of course. On soft soils such as peat, frozen ground is an advantage, permitting operation of cutting equipment without rutting or bogging down.

Avoidance of frosting may be achieved by:

- cutting double wale or long rotations

- shallow flooding as soon as possible after completion of cutting.

Late killing frosts may produce late replacement shoots with possible harm to the final crop. Very severe frosts may kill up to 100% of the shoots (Haslam 1972b). Shoots 30–50 cm tall will die if affected by frost but taller ones will lose only their immature tips (Haslam 1972a).

Because the litter layer forms a protective shield against frost, single wale cutting (which produces very little litter) may incur a 55% kill from frost while double wale may be as low as 7% (see also section 2.3.1 Double wale).

Haslam (1972b) summarises the effects of spring frosts as causing an increase in shoot density, crop weight and length of emergence period, but a decrease in stem height and diameter.

2.3.3 Herbicide use

Herbicides have been invaluable for controlling reed in the past. However, no herbicide can be recommended for use on reed at present.

The use of herbicides on wetlands has always been contentious from an environmental viewpoint. However, limited resources or limited access for cutting equipment may mean the use of herbicides is sometimes unavoidable. Herbicides are used in reedbed management to control the regrowth of cut scrub (section 2.3.5), reducing competition from other plants when planting a new reedbed (section 3.3.1 a) and in controlling reed itself.

a) Controlling Reed

Spraying growing reeds with herbicide is a very effective method of eliminating reed from an area in order to:

- create open water in an existing reedbed

- maintain open water and ditches by preventing encroachment at the edges.

The use of systemic herbicides such as Dalapon have, in the past, enabled long-term control of reed on several sites in the UK. At Walberswick in Suffolk a large area of open water was created in the middle of a stand of reed some 14 years ago, requiring maintenance spraying at the edges about every five years (Waller pers comm). Similarly, at Leighton Moss in Lancashire, Dalapon was used for many years to maintain ditch edges (4 km/annum), create open water and rides for ringing surveys of bearded tits, although ditch edges are now maintained by cutting. The great advantages of this herbicide were low toxicity, narrow target range and longevity of the effect. Unfortunately, Dalapon is no longer available in the UK and no satisfactory replacement has yet been found. Roundup has been used experimentally at Walberswick but it is non-selective. It kills almost all plants and is toxic to fish. New herbicides are likely to become available with time and new uses in reedbeds may be found for existing ones.

b) Choosing a herbicide

The law restricts the range of herbicides that can be used to control plants in or near water. MAFF (1995) lists those products that are approved for the use in or near water. Newbold *et al* (1992) and MAFF (1985) provide additional information on their use. Within that primary restriction, the selection of a herbicide for use on reeds should consider the following points:

- Choose a herbicide with low user-toxicity.

- Choose a herbicide with low environmental toxicity, or at least one that quickly breaks down into harmless by-products.

- Select a herbicide with a narrow target species range, ie one which kills only reed and other grasses.

- Herbicides are expensive. A systemic herbicide will be more cost effective than a surface acting herbicide. Otherwise, the best option would be to consider summer cutting (section 2.3.1 c).

c) Equipment

The most effective method of applying herbicide to reeds is with a knapsack sprayer. This consists of a tank that holds the diluted herbicide and is carried on the operator's back. A hand-held trigger and

Table 12: Check-points for leaks on most knapsack sprayers

- Diaphragm – check for cracks before each use. Replace every two years.

- Clips on hose – check for leaks and tighten if necessary.

- w = washer points – if signs of leaking, replace immediately.

Figure 20

a) A standard 20-l knapsack sprayer

b) Knapsack sprayer in use on 1-m tall reed shoots

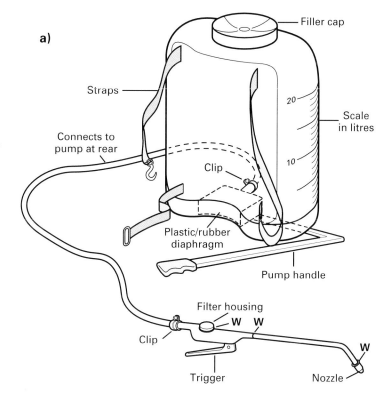

a)

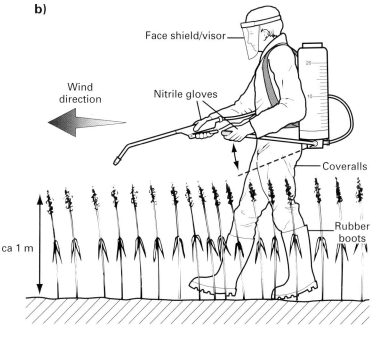

b)

nozzle delivers the herbicide from the tank to the reed (Figure 20 and Table 12). Other smaller spraying devices are available but impractical, requiring repeated refilling unless treating very small areas.

Larger devices such as boom sprayers can be fitted to tractors and ATVs but are expensive and impractical on all but the hardest of grounds and largest of reedbeds. Boat-mounted sprayers are operated by specialist contractors but can deal only with reed fringing navigable water. Weedwipers may similarly be towed behind off-road vehicles but manoeuvring in tight situations can cause unacceptable damage to the ground. Hand-held weedwipers are effective on small areas and for spot treatments where reed is growing sparsely in water.

d) Training

The use of herbicides and spraying equipment requires special training. The Food and Environment Protection Act 1985 regulates the use of herbicides and regulations state that persons born on or before 31 December 1964 are exempt from formal training requirements. Persons born after that date must undergo training and receive a certificate of proficiency in the use of knapsack sprayers (other equipment may require further training) from the NPTC (Appendix 5). The Agricultural Training Board and equivalent organisations offer formal training in all aspects of herbicide use (useful addresses in Appendix 3). MAFF has published guidelines and a code of practice on pesticide use which is available from the Health and Safety Executive or MAFF (Appendix 3 and 5).

e) Method for spraying reed

Knapsack sprayers can hold up to 25 l of liquid (some have smaller capacities), a heavy weight to carry especially with difficult ground conditions encountered on a reedbed. It is advisable to carry no more than 12 l of liquid in any one load to reduce fatigue and back ache. The following approach and points are worth considering:

● **Plan the job**

   - Dilute the correct amount of concentrate for the area to be sprayed.

   - Do not take on too much in one go. Know your own limits.

   - Avoid walking through reed still wet with spray.

   - Be aware of deep water areas. Margins on open water may have to be sprayed from a boat or if possible, draw-down the water level to facilitate access.

● **Spray at waist height (never above shoulder height without a protective hood and visor)** when the reed is about 1m tall. At this height, a stand of reed will usually form a closed canopy ensuring maximum coverage of reed and minimum accidental spraying of non-target species and accidental contamination of the water.

● **Spray the green leaves.** Systemic herbicides are absorbed into the reed and carried throughout the whole plant including the rhizome. The green leaves are active and will absorb the maximum amount of herbicide.

● **Timing** – at Minsmere, July and August are the preferred months, after wildlife has finished breeding (Burgess and Evans 1989). Where disturbance is not a problem, late spring and early summer is a good time but extra care must be taken to avoid spraying water and non-target plants as the reed will be much shorter (eg 30–50 cm tall).

● **Removal of treated reed** – different herbicides take different lengths of time to kill reed. Manufacturers usually give an indication in the notes supplied with the herbicide. Six weeks seems about average but the reed will show signs of withering and browning anyway. If spraying is done in July and August the dead reed is best cut and removed or burned in the autumn. Leaving it to decay *in situ* may cause oxygen depletion of the water (Burgess and Evans 1989).

- **Access after treatment** – each herbicide has a statutory minimum period stated on its label for re-entry of people and livestock into a treated area. This should be considered as an absolute minimum. As a general precaution allow at least six weeks to elapse after spraying before admitting the public into a treated area. Temporarily fence it off if necessary and post explanatory signs. (See also Table 13.)

Table 13: Six important points when spraying a reedbed

> 1 Mix the correct dilution and quantity of herbicide for the job in hand and according to the manufacturer's recommendations.
>
> 2 Prepare the knapsack sprayer (check safety points Figure 20 and Table 12) and herbicide away from the reedbed. A specially designated preparation area may be required for this operation.
>
> 3 Always wear the appropriate personal protective equipment (PPE). Minimum PPE recommended will depend on the herbicide being used but will be at least:
>
>   - coveralls
>   - face mask and/or visor
>   - gloves (eg nitrile, unlined)
>   - rubber boots (eg wellingtons, waders)
>
> The PPE should be designated for pesticide use only.
>
> 4 Avoid spraying in winds of force 2 and above. Ideally, spray on a calm, sunny morning. Never spray in the rain.
>
> 5 Always stand upwind of the direction of spraying.
>
> 6 Do not spray close to footpaths or areas of public access.

2.3.4 Burning

Burning is a traditional reedbed management technique performed in winter when the reed is dead and dry. The rationale for its use is that it is a quick and inexpensive way to remove reed (both cut and standing) and scrub, thus reducing the rate of litter build-up and drying out.

The use of fire for managing reedbeds includes:

- burning cut reed (see also 2.3.1)

- burning cut scrub (see also 2.3.5)

- regenerating degraded reed (see also 2.3.6).

The principal problems with burning are loss of control of the fire, with subsequent destruction of adjacent habitats and good quality reed, and the potential damage to invertebrates. Burning can cause a public nuisance and care should be taken to ensure any nearby housing or roads are not affected. In addition to the general safety points listed in Table 16 an information leaflet is available from MAFF (address in Appendix 3) entitled *Guidance Notes to Farmers when Burning Crop Residues*. Reed is not a crop residue and is exempt from the regulations. Nevertheless, useful advice on procedures and safety is given in the leaflet.

a) Burning cut reed

Figure 21 a and b show two widely used techniques for burning off reed (or scrub) which has been cut from a given area. It is feasible for cut reed to be burned where it falls but the resulting fire would be difficult to control, and stubble and litter would be

Controlled burning can regenerate degraded reed and remove reed, litter and scrub. It has the same effect upon wildlife as cutting and may lead to increased plant diversity and better quality reed.

a)

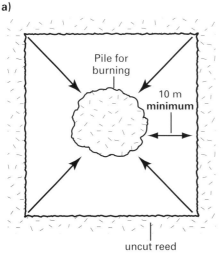

b)

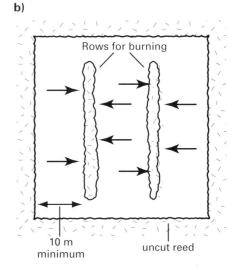

Figure 21
Techniques for burning cut reed

a) Central pile(s). The reed is cut and raked to one central pile (small plots) or several well spaced piles (larger plots). Plot size depends on labour and objective. This confines the burning to one or more focal points, as practised at Minsmere, Suffolk and Hall Fen, Norfolk.

b) Burning in rows. Reed is cut and raked into rows. This spreads the burn and minimises the impact on any one point. May also be used along ditch edges and banks, as at Stodmarsh, Kent and Radipole Lake, Dorset.

burned across the entire area. Raking the reed into one or more piles or rows facilitates control permitting access to all sides of the fire. In addition, burning of stubble and litter is confined to limited areas, minimising the impact on invertebrates.

The method in Figure 21b is simpler than 21a, especially if the reed was wind-rowed when cut, requiring the amalgamation of pairs of rows to produce long bonfires. Method 21a requires the cut reed to be carried to a central point but is safer on very small cut plots, reducing the risk of spread of the fire. On larger cut areas a series of bonfires located around the plot may be used.

Burning cut reed on the bed requires that the bed is not flooded to any great depth. However, a damp or wet bed will prevent the fire from burning deep, or spreading out of control. It is common practice where feasible, to select a raised, dry area within the cut area on which to locate the bonfire. In such a location the reed quality is usually poor anyway and the fire burns more safely on an 'island' surrounded by wet ground. On sites with peat soils it is

essential for the ground to be wet to prevent the peat itself from igniting. Peat fires can be very difficult to extinguish as the burn may continue underground for many days.

b) Burning standing reed

Reed which has been uncut for more than two years, or has never been cut, will be of poor quality in commercial terms but will be of value to a limited range of reedbed wildlife. In order to restore or generate a new growth of straight-stemmed reed with minimal debris, burning the old growth and litter is the only commercially feasible method (Cator pers comm).

On most commercial reedbeds in the UK, reed unsuitable for cutting for thatch is burned off in the spring so that a new harvestable crop is ready for the following winter. This occurs, for example, on the Tay estuary where the area burned each year varies depending on weather and the growth season for reed.

On regularly harvested sites, restoration may be complete within one growing season following burning, as experienced on Ranworth Flood in Norfolk. However, experiences vary considerably with much longer periods required for recovery on sites where reed has been unmanaged for several years, eg two years in the Broads (Andrews 1992), and five years or more on the Tay estuary (Craig pers comm). Conversely, wet reedbeds that have never been cut can produce good quality reed one year after burning, as at Far Ings on South Humberside (Grooby pers comm).

At Horning Marsh Farm (**Case Study 9**) in the Norfolk Broads, burning is the main habitat management technique used by the Broads Authority. After a programme of massive scrub clearance the reed-dominated vegetation began to recover, greatly enhanced by rotational burning of no more than one-third of the total area in any one year. The burning also deals with any scrub regrowth. After five years of this treatment much of the reed is of thatching quality but harvesting would be impractical because of the abundant tree stumps present.

The procedure used in the Broads and on many other sites in the UK involves cutting fire-breaks around the area to be burned to assist controlling the flames (Figure 22). Fire-breaks can vary in width but it is recommended that they are at least 3 m wide (Burgess and Evans 1989). Breaks of 15 m were recommended on the Tay estuary but a compromise of 6 m was established and is now in operation (Moyes 1990). Wider breaks may be necessary on areas where the reed grows very tall (> 3 m) as this will produce fires with larger flames. An additional precaution exercised on the Tay involves flattening the reeds to be burned by driving over the area with a Seiga harvester (not in cutting mode). This reduces the height of the flames and permits finer control. On the Tay, breaks are cut using the Seiga harvester but elsewhere brushcutters and reciprocator mowers are more commonly used. Most reciprocator mowers have a 1-m cutting bar, requiring three passes to cut a break whereas the Seiga requires only a single pass. In the Broads the cuttings are raked and removed for burning later, some being used to start the fire.

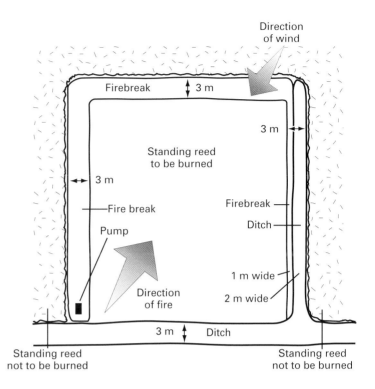

Figure 22 Technique for burning standing reed using fire-breaks and ditches (Table 14).

Wide, reed-free and water-filled ditches act as useful fire-breaks, but if a ditch is less than 3 m wide, an additional break should be cut alongside it.

Prior to starting the fire, the breaks are thoroughly dowsed with water, usually by pumping from a ditch. Wetting continues during the burn. Figure 22 and Table 14 describe the method for a controlled burn in the Broads, in this instance, against the wind. Burning against the wind gives a slower, deeper burn which helps reduce deep litter layers (see 2.3.6 a). It also permits greater control over the fire. Burning with the wind should be undertaken with great care as within only a

Table 14: Procedure for burning standing reed

1 Cut 3-m wide fire-break around plot to be burned. Reed-free ditches may be used as fire breaks if present.

2 Use a pump to draw water from a ditch to dowse the cut fire-breaks.

3 Assess wind direction. Light fire at point diametrically opposite wind direction.

4 Continue wetting fire-breaks with pumped water wherever safe to do so, ie away from smoke and flames.

5 Control margins of fire where necessary using water or fire-beaters.

few minutes of lighting, the flames can reach more than 5 m high (George 1992). The burn is quick and shallow, leaving an unburned stubble and only slightly scorched litter layer. This technique is used more commonly on patches of reed which have been cut or burned recently and the litter layer is thin. A hot, deep burn in this instance could damage new reed buds, delaying shoot emergence by up to two months (Haslam 1972).

Plate 29a Burning standing reed 'with the wind' at Far Ings, Humberside.

K Gray

29b The result of burning standing reed on a wet reedbed at Far Ings, Humberside. The burn has been light and patchy leaving unburned areas as a refuge for invertebrates.

C Hawke (RSPB)

29c By burning a degenerated reedbed a new growth is produced with thicker, straighter stems, as at Minsmere in Suffolk.

C Hawke (RSPB)

Burning with the wind is used at Far Ings on Humberside because the reedbed is very wet and will not burn successfully against the wind (Credland pers comm). Plate 29a shows part of the wet reedbed being burned off with the wind and Plate 29b shows the result of the technique. In spring, new shoots appear and grow straight, unhindered by the absence of litter and old, bent stems (Plate 29c).

c) The effects of burning on wildlife

As with cutting, burning removes the aerial parts of reeds in which many reed-dwelling animals live. Nesting sites for birds and small mammals, cover for feeding bitterns, moorhens, water rails and deer also disappear. Invertebrates that overwinter in or on the stems and leaves of dead reeds will be destroyed and those which occupy the litter layer may be affected if the burn is deep. Some plants may suffer too, although like the reed, most will be losing only dead, dispensable parts. Bryophytes may suffer badly however (Cowie *et al* 1992).

Burning creates temporary open areas of marsh or shallow water, which can be utilised by a variety of birds in much the same way as are open areas created by reed cutting. The open areas provide feeding grounds for bird species including heron, snipe, redshank and dabbling ducks, and even wintering bittern in secluded patches. Before the reed regrows significantly, other bird species such as lapwing and snipe may attempt to nest, although lapwings rarely complete breeding once the reed grows too high (Moyes 1990).

Research by Cowie *et al* (1992) on reedbeds in East Anglia showed that burning led to an increased diversity of plants, benefiting notable species such as marsh pea and milk parsley. In addition, it led to greater flowering of the reed itself and enhanced seed production, which would be of benefit to seed-eating animals, notably bearded tits and reed buntings.

Despite the inevitable destruction of invertebrates in the wake of a fire, experiments at Hickling in Norfolk suggested that burning small plots (in this case 30 x 40 m) in combination with unmanaged and cut plots has no long-term detrimental effect on invertebrate populations since rapid recolonisation occurs from the unburned areas within a year (Ditlhogo *et al* 1992). This follows a common principle for conservation management, ie that most species can be accommodated in a management programme by rotating the work over time and space, allowing wildlife to recolonise managed areas from adjacent unmanaged ones. The negative effects of burning on the arthropod fauna have been described by Hoffman (1980).

Light burns which leave stubble and litter intact are unlikely to affect the majority of invertebrates (Plate 29b), as most dwell in the lower few centimetres of the stem, the rhizome itself or the litter layer. Deep burns on a small scale will have a localised and temporary effect only and will greatly prolong the life of the reedbed by setting back succession. In general, burning removes less litter than cutting and clearance and is a useful management tool, if applied wisely, for both commercial reedbeds and those managed primarily for wildlife. (See also Tables 15 and 16.)

Table 17 compares the effects of burning and cutting reed on reedbed condition and reedbed wildlife.

Table 15: The effects of burning standing reed in spring

- Removes unwanted, poor quality reed and surface litter.

- Increases early shoot emergence and density (Haslam 1969).

- Assists dominance of reed (van der Toorn and Mook 1982).

- Encourages growth of thatching quality reed.*

* The removal of litter and old stems enables new shoots to grow straight.

Table 16: Safety considerations when burning reed

- The procedure should be supervised by someone with experience of burning reed.

- All helpers should understand the risks involved and be positioned upwind of the fire.

- There should be clean water available for treating burns.

- A safe exit route from the burn site should be established in case of loss of control or sudden change in wind direction.

- The location of the nearest telephone should be established in case of an emergency.

- Fire-beaters should be at hand to control the margins of the fire where necessary.

- Always cut fire-breaks.

- Avoid burning in winds above force 2.

Table 17: Summary of the effects of cutting and burning in winter

Effect on:	Unmanaged	Cutting reed	Burning reed
Scrub	Natural succession from open reed to scrub and woodland. Reedbed lost.	Prevents early establishment of seedling trees but cannot restore scrub invaded areas.	Prevents scrub encroachment and may kill existing scrub up to 5 m tall.
Litter	Gradual accumulation making cutting impossible. Reed shoot density declines. Plant diversity suppressed.	Most litter removed allowing growth of other plant species .	Only partially removed depending on wetness of ground at time of burning.
Birds	Eventual loss of habitat for reedbed specialists, eg bittern and bearded tit.	Temporary creation of shallow flooded areas for breeding and feeding waders and reed edge for a range of birds. Temporary loss of habitat for reedbed specialists, eg reed warbler.	Same as for cutting.
Plants	Gradually becomes impoverished with low diversity.	Allows the development of plants typical for physical and chemical factors present.	Same as for cutting but depends on how much litter is removed in the burn.
Reed	Low shoot density. Lower flower/seed productivity. Stems sometimes bent.	Higher shoot density and flower/seed production. Stems more suitable for thatching use.	Same as for cutting with greater benefits from more complete litter burn.
Invertebrates	Gradual loss of reedbed specialists.	Temporary loss of some species which overwinter in reedbeds. Recolonise from adjacent areas.	Some litter invertebrates may survive in wettest areas and with light burns. Recolonise from adjacent areas.
Conservation implications	Gradual loss of reedbed due to scrub encroachment. Loss of reedbed specialists.	Best for overall diversity provided cutting is on a suitable rotation.	Good for restoration of neglected areas and for maintaining open conditions. Can be achieved with a longer rotation than cutting.
Cost	No opportunity in long term to establish commercial harvest. Loss of specialist wildlife.	Only achievable on large areas if there is an economic market for the reed.	Not labour intensive particularly if large areas are burned and where there is no need for fire breaks.

Adapted from R Andrews (Broads Authority, unpublished).

2.3.5 Scrub and carr woodland management

Invasion by scrub is probably the single biggest management problem of UK reedbeds. Neglect, or undermanagement, has permitted the development of scrub on the drier margins which has, with time, encroached upon the open areas as they have dried with years of litter accumulation. Between 1973 and 1987 for example, scrub at Radipole Lake in Dorset increased in extent from 1.0 to 5.5 ha as the site silted up from winter floods by the River Wey. At North Warren in Suffolk, single wale cutting ceased in 1954 and was rapidly followed by scrub invasion which encroached over almost all the 23-ha reedbed (Macklin pers comm).

The species that most quickly and easily colonise reedbeds are willow and alder although others such as birch and bog myrtle can be a problem on some sites. Willow and alder, in particular, flourish on wetlands and support important wildlife themselves, notably invertebrates. In addition, birds such as sedge warblers, willow warblers and the rarer Cetti's warbler utilise scrub for nesting and feeding and marsh harriers make use of taller trees as look-out perches.

Progressive scrub development is generally disastrous for a reedbed and requires management by way of control. Scrub is a problem because it:

- directly competes with reed for nutrients and space

- causes shading

- uses large quantities of water

- produces large quantities of litter

- impedes cutting equipment.

There are several approaches to managing scrub but only the most widely used methods will be discussed in detail. They are:

- raising water levels (see also 2.2.1 e)

- cutting and burning (see also 2.3.4 a)

- grubbing.

The direct methods of cutting, burning and grubbing are the same as for scrub control in most habitats with the added problems associated with working on boggy ground (see Appendix 5). October to March is the usual period in which scrub management is undertaken, after draw-down and to avoid disturbing breeding wildlife.

a) Cutting

By far the most widely used techniques involve cutting scrub in some way or another. Figure 23 shows the sequence of cutting, burning and stump treatment used on most sites. It may facilitate work if reed and other vegetation is cut and cleared first to improve access. Where there is a good labour supply, cutting may be done using bow saws and bill hooks (Table 20) on small to medium-sized scrub (2–10 cm diameter). Larger scrub and carr woodland management requires the use of chain saws (Table 18). Very small scrub and seedlings can either be pulled up by hand (Table 19) or if a large area is involved, cut using a brushcutter. This latter method, however, can encourage a vigorous regrowth and is rarely used unless the cut stumps can be flooded throughout the growing season.

Cut scrub and pulled scrub is nearly always burned off in bonfires. Occasionally, a proportion may be stacked to form 'habitat piles' for wildlife but there is usually too much material for all of it to be dealt with in this way. Larger material can be removed from the site and sold as firewood or for timber products, but the inaccessibility of many reedbeds may make this impractical.

Where cut scrub is to be controlled permanently, the application of herbicide to the stumps is essential. Amcide, Roundup and Garlon 4 are most often used (Andrews

Without management scrub will rapidly invade a reedbed. It can be controlled by cutting and burning, grubbing or by raising water levels.

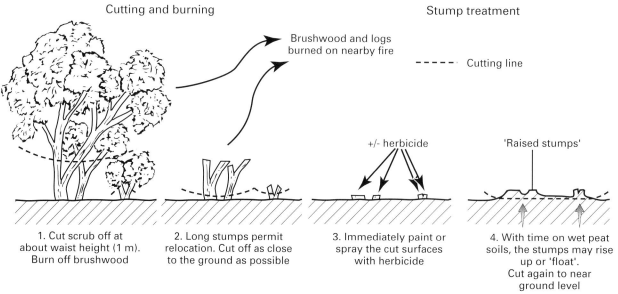

Cutting and burning

Stump treatment

Brushwood and logs
burned on nearby fire

----- Cutting line

+/- herbicide

'Raised stumps'

1. Cut scrub off at
about waist height (1 m).
Burn off brushwood

2. Long stumps permit
relocation. Cut off as close
to the ground as possible

3. Immediately paint or
spray the cut surfaces
with herbicide

4. With time on wet peat
soils, the stumps may rise
up or 'float'.
Cut again to near
ground level

Figure 23
Scrub clearance by cutting, burning and stump treatment as undertaken at Hall Fen, Norfolk.

Table 18: Safety points for use of chain saws on reedbeds

- Use of chain saws requires special training and certification (see Appendix 5 for addresses and further information).

- Always wear appropriate Personal Protective Equipment (PPE). The minimum recommended is:
  - safety helmet, ear defenders and visor
  - chain saw gloves (with Kevlar)
  - chain saw leggings (with Kevlar)
  - chain saw wellingtons (with Kevlar).

- Never operate a chain saw alone. A second person can assist in an emergency.

- Beware of uneven, boggy or slippery ground, tree roots, deep pools, etc.

- Ensure others working in the vicinity are not too close (*at least twice the distance of the height of the tree being felled*).

Table 19: Safety points for pulling scrub in a reedbed

- If the scrub offers excessive resistance, do not continue. Know your limits and avoid damage to your back.

- Check who or what is behind you. Avoid falling backwards onto people and hazardous objects when the roots suddenly give way.

- Always wear work gloves.

Table 20: Safety points for cutting scrub with a bill hook

- Ensure training in correct use has been received before using a bill hook (inexperienced persons should be supervised).

- Do not use a bill hook with a split or loose handle.

- Do not wear standard work-gloves (rigger-type). To ensure a firm grip wear 'gripper'-type gloves or none at all.

- Operate a bill hook at least 5 m away from the nearest person.

- Avoid swinging the bill hook above shoulder height (there should be no need to if the bill hook is sharp and used correctly).

1992) either sprayed or painted onto the cut surfaces to prevent regrowth. Willow can be very persistent and may regrow even after treatment, requiring a second application (Burgess and Evans 1989). As with spraying reed (2.3.3), special training is essential for carrying out such work. To avoid missing cut stumps, on Hall Fen in Norfolk, large-scale cutting is done by leaving long stumps about 1 m high (convenient for cutting at waist height) for easier relocation. When the stumps are finally cut to ground level, a second operator stands ready to apply the herbicide immediately afterwards (Raven pers comm). The herbicide contains a marker dye which indicates that a stump has been treated. It is recommended that the treated stumps are not flooded for at least six weeks after application of herbicide. Each year, some 20–25 ha of scrub is cleared by this method in the Broadland fens by supervised teams of volunteers.

It is important that, where possible, the stumps left after final cutting should not protrude more than 2 cm above the soil surface. This is most easily achieved with a chain saw, which slices through the base of a cluster of stumps. Low stumps facilitate the operation of reed cutting equipment later on and increase the chances of submersion when the water level rises, preventing regrowth the following spring. Maintaining high spring water levels in this way is so effective in preventing regrowth that at Leighton Moss in Lancashire cut stumps are rarely treated with herbicide. In addition, browsing deer keep other scrub regrowth in check throughout the reedbed.

At Haweswater Moss in Lancashire, a site which once held breeding bitterns, the scrub invaded to the point where virtually all the reed was lost. A programme of clearance using contractors in 1993 and 1994 has removed approximately 8 ha of mature scrub/carr woodland. The regrowth from the first year's work was only partially grazed by deer such that a considerable proportion remained. The deer population is probably too small to deal with all the regrowth in one season and the remainder has been cut with a brushcutter. It is hoped that water levels

can be raised sufficiently to suppress the regrowth on the second year's cutting.

On peat soils, which hold water like a 'sponge', the removal of the weight of the scrub by cutting may cause the stumps eventually to rise or 'float', as the soil water table rises (Figure 23). This phenomenon is commonplace in the Broads and requires additional clearance if machinery is to be operated on the bed (Andrews pers comm).

Scrub removal by cutting has been a major activity on most nature reserve reedbeds over the past 20 years or more. At Strumpshaw Fen in Norfolk 10 ha of scrub and carr was removed between 1975–87 (Burgess and Evans 1989) equivalent to nearly 50% of the total scrub area on the reserve at the time. At Walberswick in Suffolk, scrub removal from the freshwater reedbed was at its height during the 1960s–1980s and now requires only occasional effort to keep it in check (Waller pers comm). At Marazion Marsh in Cornwall, scrub cutting in the winter of 1993/94 produced immediate benefits the following spring with reed regrowing vigorously where there was once scrub (Flumm pers comm). More recently, scrub has been cut and removed from the ditch edges on Ranworth Marsh and Ward Marsh in Norfolk, in a 10–20-m wide strip, made possible by a management agreement with EN because of its SSSI status. On the Hundred Acre Reedbed at Hickling in Norfolk, scrub removal by cutting and burning is central to the rehabilitation programme of the dried out reedbed (Plate 30).

C Hawke (RSPB)

Plate 30 Rehabilitating the Hundred Acre Reedbed at Hickling, Norfolk by scrub cutting. Note the long stumps awaiting cutting to ground level immediately prior to treatment with Amcide or Garlon 4.

b) Rotational coppicing

Where some scrub is to be retained to provide a range of habitats within a reedbed, cutting the scrub or carr on a rotation is an option (Figure 24). Coppicing is a traditional, sustainable, broadleaf woodland, management technique involving the cutting of a tree to leave only a stump between 1–30 cm high. This is undertaken in autumn or winter, when the tree is dormant. The following spring, new buds will develop and shoot from the cut stump (Figure 25). The rationale for coppicing is that it:

- prolongs the life of carr

- produces a renewable crop

- avoids the use of herbicides

- benefits wildlife.

The length of a coppicing cycle will depend on a number of factors:

- resources – places high demand on labour

- purpose – timber crop or wildlife or both

- species.

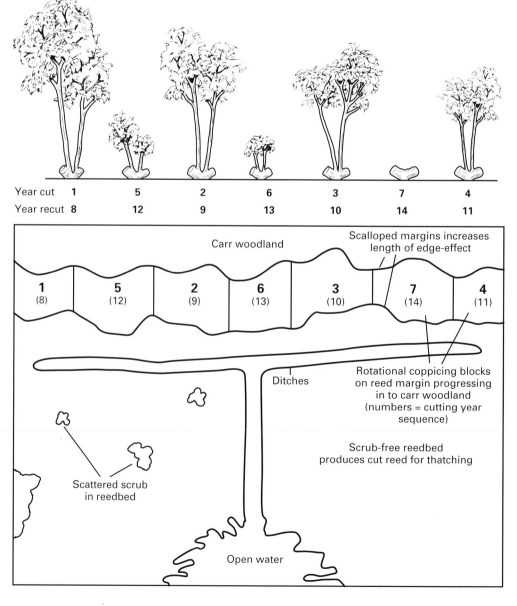

Figure 24 Sequence of a seven-year coppicing rotation.

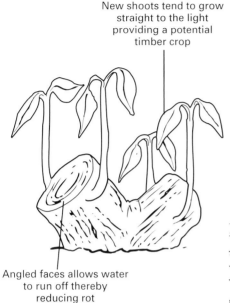

New shoots tend to grow straight to the light providing a potential timber crop

Angled faces allows water to run off thereby reducing rot

Figure 25
A coppiced willow or alder stump with one year's regrowth.

On most sites, the resources available are the major influence upon the cutting cycle. Where resources allow, willow and alder scrub is usually cut on a four-year rotation for the purposes of control within a reedbed. This produces patches of scrub of varying ages and enables it to be contained within defined limits (Plate 31). Alder woodland may be cut on longer rotations of up to seven or eight years if a timber crop is required or longer if not.

The demand for timber products (including willow for basket making for example) has declined greatly such that very little is managed specifically for such purposes nowadays. However, on Ranworth Marshes in Norfolk, a Forest Enterprise Woodland Grant enables the landowner to pay a contractor to coppice 5 ha of mature carr each year, the total area in the scheme being 135 ha. The contractor is able to supplement his income by selling the timber and has an agreement to coppice the regrowth for timber products in years to come. At Stodmarsh in Kent, a small area of alder and willow carr is cut on a traditional eight-year coppicing and pollarding rotation for wildlife benefits.

Figure 24 illustrates the age structure produced by a coppicing rotation by the end of the first cycle and how this can be

integrated into a scrub/woodland management programme for a reedbed. This provides habitat for a range of wildlife, notably invertebrates and birds but also enables plants to colonise. In addition, a saleable timber crop may be produced. A seven-year rotation as illustrated is one of simple alternate blocks, repeated in subsequent recuts.

D Shipp (Broads Authority)

Plate 31 The How Hill Volunteers coppicing and burning off scrub encroaching at the reedbed margin.

c) Grubbing

Where resources permit and the scrub problem is large, grubbing with a mechanical excavator is more effective, quicker and less expensive in the long term. The technique is simple, in that the excavator digs out or pulls out whole trees and bushes, including the roots (Plate 32a).

Nowhere has this method been more fully utilised than in the Broads, usually in conjunction with 'turf pond' creation (Madgwick *et al* 1992) as part of fen restoration work, or at the same time as ditch management. Despite there being 2,500 ha of open fen in the Broads, 3,000 ha of carr woodland remains, most of which was once open fen too. The scrub has invaded many old peat diggings and dried them out. The aim is to recreate the turf pond and allow it to recolonise. The biggest problem is where to put the grubbed up material. In most instances, it is pulled into the path of the excavator, by the machine itself, which rides over it (increasing traction and reducing the risk of sinking) crushing it in its wake. The grubbed scrub is piled along the banks of the turf pond or ditches and spoil from the digging placed over it. This is flattened with the excavator's bucket, which reinforces the bunds. Bunds created in this way are low and wide so that they may be used for access at a future date and can be

Plate 32a Removing scrub using a digger in the Broadland fens.

R Andrews (Broads Authority)

32b The scrub is used to construct a bund/access route for the digger. The digger slubs the ditches as it goes, placing this over the scrub bund and crushing it down.

C Hawke (RSPB)

32c The result is scrub cleared (left), ditch slubbed (right) and bund/bank consolidated and accessible (centre).

C Hawke (RSPB)

maintained by cutting to benefit plants. This procedure is illustrated in Plates 32 a, b and c.

This large-scale clearance is used on relatively young alder carr and willow scrub. In other areas the same technique is used to lower the surface of a reedbed (section 2.3.6).

On a section of Catfield Fen owned by Butterfly Conservation, a large area (some 5 ha) of scrub-invaded fen has been cleared using the grubbing method, resulting in the creation of an area of apparently open water (about half was due to scrub removal

and half shallow peat digging). However, with time the reed fen communities will re-establish in the cleared areas.

At North Warren on the Suffolk coast, scrub has been grubbed out using excavators as part of a programme of reedbed regeneration (Case Study 10). During the winter of 1993/94 alone, the excavator produced 30 large piles of scrub from an area of about 6 ha. The scrub was subsequently burned off in bonfires the following winter.

Winching is another form of grubbing but is much more time-consuming and only small numbers of trees can be removed in a day. The technique involves the use of a Tirfor winch or similar, equipment that requires special training in its safe use and operation (contact ATB for details of courses – address in Appendix 5).

At Far Ings and Barton Reedbed on South Humberside, both part of the Barton Pits SSSI, a tractor and steel cable system is used to winch medium sized scrub (10 cm diameter) from parts of the reedbed which are inaccessible for a digger and where coppicing or herbicide use is not the aim (see Case Study 3, Figure 2). As well as removing the scrub this technique creates small pools in the reedbed, which are of value to wildlife.

Table 21: Scrub on commercial reedbeds

On reedbeds which have been cut single or double wale for many years, there will be no scrub present. Because of the frequency of cutting, scrub never gets beyond the seedling or sapling stage and is removed with the cut. If cutting is to resume or start on a scrub-invaded reedbed, all the scrub must be removed from the harvestable areas. Scrub left at the margins will act as a seed source but will be inconsequential if the cutting regime is maintained. In addition, it will be of benefit to wildlife. There is some 350 ha of largely scrub-free commercial reedbed and sedgebed in the Broads.

At Salthouse, a commercial reedbed in north Norfolk, there is no marginal scrub but occasional elder bushes appear. These have been brought in by roosting starlings, the seeds being deposited in their droppings. Elder does not grow in wet conditions, only those seeds falling on dry ground will germinate.

2.3.6 Bed Regeneration

The principle of bed regeneration involves the reduction of accumulated reed litter and soil by physical removal, which effectively returns the habitat to an earlier stage of succession. A thin layer of litter (5 cm) may benefit wildlife and reduce competition from other wetland plants. Deep litter layers (30–100 cm) inhibit reed growth, dry out the reedbed and allow other plants to colonise. Eventually reedbed habitat will disappear. There are a number of approaches to the problem; they vary by degree and method and may include a combination of techniques on any one site.

An alternative method to those described here is to raise water levels, where supply permits, a technique which has already been described in section 2.2.1.

Small-scale litter reduction is achievable using fire, the basis of which has been described in section 2.3.4 but the techniques are further detailed below.

The rationale for bed regeneration is that it:

- sets succession farther back than most other management methods

- enables large areas of degraded reedbed to be treated in one go

- reduces the long-term, annual resource commitment for the site

- enables new design features, eg bunds and sluices, to be incorporated.

Because the removal of litter by excavation or deep burning is a drastic management approach, the succession in the reedbed is pushed back much farther than by say, cutting alone. Excavation produces open, shallow water essentially taking succession back to its beginning.

Depending on the technique used, large areas of reedbed can be easily treated. This may offset the considerable cost of excavation work as subsequent management may no longer require annual inputs.

The benefits of bed regeneration include:

- reduction in height of bed surface (litter layer)

- increased water depth (and wetness of reedbed)

- creation of temporary, shallow open water

- removal of seed bank of invasive plants

- improved quality of reed for wildlife and thatching.

The main disadvantages of excavation of a reedbed are high cost and problems of spoil disposal. In addition, heavy machinery may not be able to access all sites. Consequently, burning dry litter may be a cheaper alternative and feasible in inaccessible areas where it is neither possible nor cost-effective to operate large equipment.

a) Burning litter *in situ*

The requirements for this technique are:

- very dry litter

- small, manageable plots (< 0.5 ha)

- light wind

- access to water for dampening fire-breaks.

The technique for burning is described in section 2.3.4 and involves ensuring a deep burn is achieved by burning slowly against a light wind.

At Stodmarsh in Kent a degree of litter burn was achieved when cut reed was burned off in rows on a dry reedbed and succeeded in igniting the litter beneath, spreading laterally. Burning against the wind to reduce litter has been used in the Broads with some success but does require the litter to be exceptionally dry, which increases the risk of loss of control of the fire. If insufficiently dry the burn will be incomplete and only partially reduce the

Bed regeneration involves lowering the reedbed surface by burning, raking or excavation of the litter layer. It can produce a wet reedbed with more vigorous reed.

litter, which may be satisfactory in some instances.

One potential drawback of the technique is the resultant massive release of nutrients in the form of ash which may encourage undesirable plant species to colonise from seed already in the reedbed or from an adjacent source. Species such as rosebay willowherb and nettle are quick to colonise although the risk is removed if the bed is subsequently flooded. On a small scale, such difficulties are usually manageable.

b) **Hand-raking**

Figure 26 Bed regeneration by excavation of litter layer/topsoil by a digger.

Because of the labour-intensive nature of this technique, it is rarely used, although on small plots (less than 0.25 ha) it may be practicable. Dry litter can be hard to rake and the presence of roots, runners and stubble may damage lightweight wooden rakes, and injure operators.

At Minsmere in Suffolk, wet litter is raked with metal cromes as part of the rotational cutting programme (Lambert pers comm). The reed is cut and burned and the litter raked out as far as is practical to do so. The raked litter is piled along the margins of the cut area where it drains dry and eventually oxidises. Alternatively, dry litter can be burned in piles or rows shortly after raking. (See also Figure 14.)

c) **Excavation by digger**

The principle behind this technique is the removal of years of accumulated litter to a level just above the rhizome depth. This lowers the surface of the ground in relation to the water level, creating wet reedbed ideal for new reed growth while restricting or eliminating other species, particularly scrub (Figure 26).

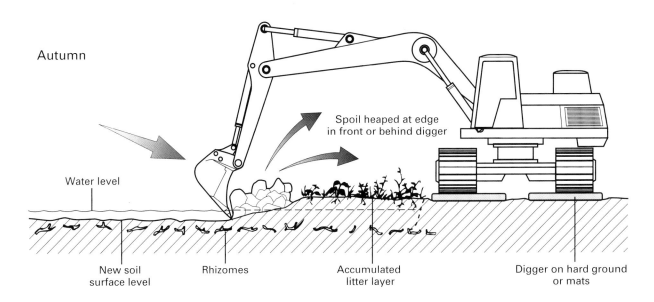

Autumn

Spoil heaped at edge
in front or behind digger

Water level

New soil
surface level | Rhizomes | Accumulated
litter layer | Digger on hard ground
or mats

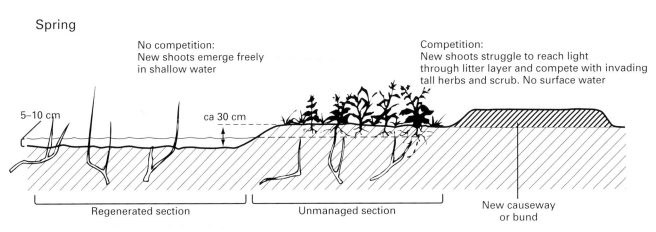

Spring

No competition:
New shoots emerge freely
in shallow water

Competition:
New shoots struggle to reach light
through litter layer and compete with invading
tall herbs and scrub. No surface water

5–10 cm

ca 30 cm

Regenerated section | Unmanaged section | New causeway
or bund

On most UK reedbeds the rhizomes are about 30–40 cm below the litter surface, although this varies with previous management, age of the reedbed and factors such as silting which need to be assessed (see Part 1). The technique is most cost-effective on seriously degraded reedbeds with 20 or more years of accumulated reed litter. While on site, the digger can be used to remove scrub, dig/re-excavate ditches, create pools and construct bunds, thus maximising digger time. Draw-down of the water level to at or well below (30 cm+) the surface facilitates the work of the digger as does the use of a 'weed bucket', which enables water to drain out of each scoop.

Experimental digs to establish rhizome depth on the area to be excavated are advisable to avoid accidental removal of the rhizomes. A safety margin of some 5–10 cm ensures the rhizomes are undamaged and not exposed to the air where they will be open to frost damage.

Despite low ground pressure, diggers are heavy and on some sites may be restricted to hard ground or mats. Peat soils and hover are more prone to problems of diggers sinking whereas silts and clays offer a firmer base for the digger to work on. Nevertheless, damage to the rhizomes beneath and compression of the soil are not desirable and so tracking movements of the digger across the bed should be kept to a minimum. Long-reach diggers are able to scrape material from farther away on either side of a tracking line, which reduces the number of tracking routes required to complete the job. On some sites the spoil may be used to construct a firmer base in front of the digger as it tracks forward. On others, spoil may be placed behind the digger as it works its way out of the reedbed, and profiled to form bunds or access tracks as was undertaken at Cley in Norfolk. Digger operators who have undertaken similar work before will be aware of the problems and requirements but operators new to such a technique may require close supervision as mistakes cannot be easily remedied and will add to the cost. Table 22 summarises some precautions to consider when using a digger on hazardous ground.

Plate 33 Bed regeneration at Minsmere, Suffolk using a digger to excavate the litter layer.
C Hawke (RSPB)

At Minsmere, work began in autumn 1994 to regenerate 60 ha of degraded reedbed, a programme which will span four years (Plate 33). In 1994, 11 ha was excavated to an average depth of 30 cm. This depth represented nearly 40 years' worth of accumulated reed litter. The spoil was used to construct low, enclosing bunds to create interconnected, hydrological units. The immediate result was for the area to 'flood' as the water level beneath the litter was exposed. New, swivel-pipe sluices were installed at the same time to improve control over water levels. The area had previously been prepared by cutting the old reed and burning it off in piles and dry litter was also burned *in situ* (although this was only partial, owing to varying dryness) to reduce the amount of material to be bunded. The digger tracked minimally across the area and was able to gain access on a permanent, hard track. The same machine then proceeded to North Warren, close to Minsmere, to carry out the second phase of bed regeneration work, which also entailed the addition of new sluices and ditches (**Case Study 10**).

Table 22: Some precautions when using a digger on soft ground

- Check the site over on foot first to establish potentially hazardous spots or have an assistant walk ahead of the machine in the first instance.

- Plan the job to minimise movements across soft ground.

- Where possible, work on the firmest ground on the site, eg the margins.

- Many tasks may be performed from the tops of bunds, causeways, hard tracks, etc (although this may limit the extent of any operation).

- On waterlogged and very soft soils, working on mats should prevent the machine from becoming stuck.

Plate 34 At Blackwater on the North Solent NNR, the bed has been excavated and the spoil used to create a bank at the edge (right).

C Hawke (RSPB)

Plate 35 Reed regrowth after bed regeneration by excavation of litter at Radipole Lake reedbed in Dorset.

C Hawke (RSPB)

Plate 36a At Hall Fen, Norfolk a diesel Bucher reciprocator mower was used to excavate the litter layer where the ground was unsuitable for heavy machinery. These powerful mowers can slice 10 cm or more into the litter.

C Hawke (RSPB)

36b The excavated litter is placed in piles to drain and be burned later.

C Hawke (RSPB)

36c The result is an area of open water (compare with unexcavated area on the left) in which a reinvigorated reedbed will grow in the spring.

C Hawke (RSPB)

Similarly, on some of the North Solent's reedbeds, English Nature carried out bed regeneration work starting in the autumn of 1991. The absence of management for more than 20 years developed a litter layer 65 cm deep, which produced poor, thin stands of reed, making cutting with normal harvesting machinery impossible (Venner 1994). A 17.5-tonne Hymac with wide, long tracks and a wide bucket was used to scrape back the litter layer from 20 m within the bed to the margins where the spoil was dumped and tracked down into a low bank which had reduced to a few centimetres high within one year (Plate 34). Within a month, the reed began to regrow. Subsequent winter flooding produced a new, clean crop of reed with more than 370 stems/m^2. The success of this trial encouraged additional regeneration work on other areas of the North Solent NNR's reedbeds.

Bed regeneration at Radipole Lake in Dorset took place over a two-year programme with variable results. The reed has regrown well in one plot but has proved slower in another (Plate 35), possibly because the excavation was slightly deeper (Slater pers comm).

d) Excavation by reciprocator mower

A technique developed by the Broads Authority utilises powerful diesel reciprocator mowers. Bucher mowers are available in both petrol and diesel models but the petrol version is not powerful enough for the task. Plates 36 a, b and c illustrate the technique, which enables litter removal from wet, reed-dominated tall-herb fen where it is not possible to lower the water levels and diggers are unable to access. It is used throughout the 'reedfens' of the Broads to regenerate badly degraded areas with low to moderate scrub invasion (up to 25% scrub cover). Because it is less drastic than excavation by digger, it can be used on more sensitive areas which support important habitat features and plant species.

e) Mechanical maceration of litter

This technique involves the use of a single-bladed rotary swipe on a four-wheel drive tractor with flotation tyres. The swipe cuts the deep reed litter into a mulch but leaves it on the reedbed (Lang pers comm). Hence, there are no problems with spoil disposal. On reedbeds where there is a flow of water or where water levels can be raised, the litter may disperse to some extent. The effect of mulching the litter may also enhance the rate of decay by bacteria, fungi and invertebrates. Its application is limited to reedbeds where there is suitable access, a relatively flat surface and water level controls.

It is a relatively expensive technique and less effective than excavation by digger. In terms of cost-benefit it is probably not practicable for regenerating small reedbeds. This technique has been tried by the National Trust and English Nature at Horsey in Norfolk.

2.3.7 Summary – the integration of management

An integrated approach to management will enable the interests of both wildlife and commercial cutting to be incorporated. Table 23 suggests what proportions of a site should be managed in a particular way to achieve integration. This approach has been successfully practised at Walberswick in Suffolk for nearly 25 years (**Case Study 11**).

Table 23: Suggested habitat management to optimise wildlife and commercial benefits

Management	Habitat size requirement	Area Managed (proportion)	Wildlife likely to benefit											
			Bittern	Bearded tit	Marsh harrier	Reed warbler	Wetland plants	Aquatic inverts	Reed inverts	Other inverts	Dryland plants	Harvest mouse	Water vole	Otter
			20 ha	20 ha	100 ha	<1ha	<1 ha	<1ha	<1ha	<1ha	<1ha	<1ha	<1ha	(>20 ha)
Open Water/ Ditches (5 cm–2.5 m deep with shallow margins)		10—20%	–	–	★	–	★	★	–	–	–	–	★	★
Reed/Water edge	260m/ha minimum		★	★	–	★	★	★	–	–	–	–	★	★
Wet Reedbed (10-30 cm deep)		60%	★	★	★	★	★■	★	★■	–	–	★	★	–
Dry Reedbed		15—20%	–	★	★	★	–	–	★	–	★	★	–	–
Single wale cutting		<50%	★	★	★	★	–	–	–	–	–	–	–	–
Double wale cutting		>40%	★	★	★	★	★	–	★	–	–	★	–	–
Longer rotations		>10%	★	★	★	★	★	–	★	–	–	★	–	–
Burning (as an alternative to or in conjunction with cutting)		<33%	★	★	★	★	★	–	–	–	–	–	–	–
Scattered scrub/trees		<10%	–	–	★	★	–	–	–	★	★	–	–	–
Carr/Reed Edge (where present)		5%	–	–	–	★	–	–	–	★	–	–	–	–

■ = may benefit some species only   ★ = significant benefit   – = no significant benefit identified

Part 3
REEDBED CREATION

Contents

3.1 Introduction

In the past reedbeds have been created for a range of reasons, in particular to increase reed production for commercial purposes, eg thatching and also as cover for duck shoots and to protect mudflats from erosion. The extensive reedbeds of the Inner Tay were thought to have been planted by prisoners of the Napoleonic War to protect the estuary's mudflats from tidal erosion. A large area of mudflats on the upper Humber estuary is rumoured to have been aerially sprayed with reed seed prior to World War II and created what is known today as the Blacktoft Sands SSSI, an RSPB reserve of some 108 ha of reed. The purpose was to claim the land for agriculture. The reedbeds of the North Norfolk coast at Cley and Salthouse were originally planted as cover for duck shooting. At East Chevington in Northumberland, reed was transported from Hickling in Norfolk to create a reedbed from which reed was harvested to thatch haystacks.

More recently, interest in reedbed creation as low cost, environmentally sensitive systems for water and industrial effluent treatment purposes has increased. In the USA and Europe the ability of reed to break down pollutants has long been recognised as potentially useful and constructed water treatment systems have been in place for many years. Efforts to create reedbeds specifically for wildlife conservation date back at least 20 years in the UK. Concern over the decline in quantity and quality of reedbeds and the wildlife which depends on them, has increased interest in reedbed creation as a way of spreading the risks and maximising the chances of protecting key species. Similarly, creation is seen as a way of increasing the reed resource in the UK to supply the demand of the thatching industry. Figure 1 shows the sequence of events for the creation of a reedbed.

Considerable expertise already exists on reed establishment and on constructed reedbeds for water treatment systems. However, techniques for the creation of large, 'natural' reedbeds for other purposes are still largely experimental.

Reedbed creation is not new. However, the need to increase the area of reed for wildlife and commercial interests, and its use in the treatment of effluents has seen a recent increase in interest in reedbed creation.

Figure 1 The sequence of events when creating a reedbed.

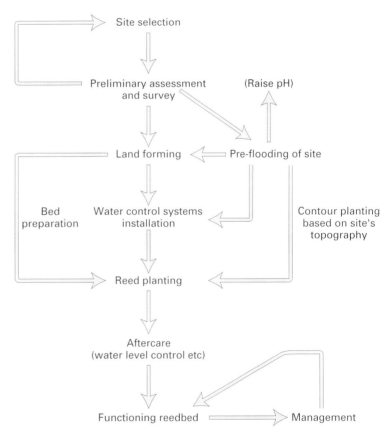

Reedbed creation enables reed to establish more quickly than by natural expansion alone (Table 1). Compared with most other habitats, eg woodland, reedbeds can be created quickly, often taking less than five years to reach full cover. Creation is essential in wildlife terms to secure the future of the bittern (Table 2) in the UK and to increase production of UK-produced reed for thatching (Table 3).

Of the UK production total, some 64% of thatching reed is produced from reedbeds of designated conservation importance (Bateman *et al* 1990). There is a high potential to increase this further, in particular on newly created reedbeds.

Three thousand hectares of created, double wale reedbed (Table 3) has the potential to support:

● 75 booming male bitterns (ca 20 ha/pair)

● 30 marsh harrier nests (ca 100 ha/pair) (this is a conservative estimate – see below)

● at least 700 pairs of bearded tits (ca 30 pairs/100 ha)

● an enormous population of reedbed and aquatic invertebrates, amphibians, fish and mammals.

These figures are hypothetical and based on existing knowledge of the habitat size requirement/home range of each species. Other factors, such as appropriate management, food supply, geographical location will influence the actual numbers which would occupy an area of new reed, eg seven marsh harrier nests in 120 ha of reed at one UK site.

Table 1: A hypothetical comparison of natural expansion and creation of reedbeds

● A 20-ha reedbed (447 m x 447 m) expanding at 5% per annum (along its 1,790-m edge based on a growth rate of 5 m/annum) would take 14 years to double in size to 40 ha.

● A 40-ha reedbed could be established and support bitterns within 2–5 years (provided there is a good food supply and appropriate water quality and quantity).

Table 2: Reedbeds for bitterns

To increase the number of booming bitterns from their 1994 level of 16 to the RSPB's and EN's target of 100 by the year 2020 the following would need to be achieved:

● the rehabilitation and enhancement of existing UK reedbeds has the potential to support 32 additional 'boomers'

● the creation of a further 1,040 ha of suitable reedbed habitat has the potential to support an additional 52 'boomers'

Data from RSPB 1994

Table 3: Reedbeds for thatching

It was estimated that 423,000 bundles of domestic reed were used by thatchers in England in 1989. An additional 1.5 million bundles were imported (Bateman *et al* 1990). For domestic reed production to satisfy the demand of UK thatchers, the following would need to be achieved:

● the rehabilitation and enhancement of 1,500 ha of existing reedbed to produce single wale reed or 3,000 ha for double wale

or,

● the creation of an additional 1,500 ha of single wale reedbeds or 3,000 ha of double wale

Figures calculated on basis of yields of 1,000 bundles/ha which represents an average of good single wale and average double wale yields.

3.1.1 Criteria for site selection for reedbed creation

Reedbeds may be created on virtually any type of land but the following are commonly chosen:

- unused/disused industrial land, eg Haverton Hole, Teesside (Plate 1)

- arable land and improved pasture (including former wetland areas), eg Hickling, Norfolk (Plate 2)

- disused mining or gravel workings, eg East Chevington, Northumberland (Plate 3).

Ideally, the land should possess the characteristics listed in Table 4. Other factors which need to be considered when selecting a site have been described in Part 1. However, several including size, location and physical characteristics are particularly important and are examined further.

a) Site size and location

Reedbeds of all sizes are valuable for wildlife. However, certain key species require minimum areas because of their ecological requirements (see Table 23 in Part 2). As a general rule, larger reedbeds tend to support more species since there will be a greater range of habitats present. Nevertheless, these are only general guidelines since in particularly favourable circumstances, bitterns have been known to nest in reed areas as small as 2.5 ha. Smaller reedbeds may support wintering bitterns and bearded tits, breeding sedge warblers and reed buntings as well as important plants and invertebrates.

Many species of reedbed animals and plants are not able to disperse themselves easily. The creation of new reedbeds close to existing ones is therefore preferable. These could potentially provide seed, rhizomes or cuttings with which to establish the new reedbed. Less mobile animals, particularly invertebrates, should soon colonise the new area if adjacent to an existing reedbed. Nevertheless, small reedbeds around the countryside may

C Hawke (RSPB)

C Hawke (RSPB)

Ian Douglas

The size of a reedbed is not critical although in general a larger reedbed will provide more benefits than a small reedbed. A reedbed may be created on a range of land-types and should ideally be created close to an existing reedbed and/or a market for cut reed.

▲ **Plate 1 The reedbed at Haverton Hole, Teeside was created on unused industrial land.**

◀**Plate 2 The commercial reedbeds at Hickling were created on drained marshland.**

◀**Plate 3 The reedbed at East Chevington, Northumberland was created by planting reed on a disused, open cast coal mine after major land forming.**

Table 4: Characteristics of land required for reedbed creation

- A reliable, adequate water supply (sufficient to maintain a flow and up to 30-cm surface depth in summer)

- Some control of water levels, eg existing ditches, sluices, bunds

- No potential to flood neighbouring land (unless avoidable by land forming etc)

- Free from saline intrusion

- A level or very shallow gradient

- An existing vigorous reed source to facilitate establishing reed across whole site

- Access for management

provide valuable 'stepping stones' for wildlife to disperse along thus facilitating colonisation of more distant new areas. Reedbeds created as part of a larger wetland complex will often have greater wildlife value, although an isolated reedbed can provide an important oasis in areas with otherwise little valuable habitat.

Large areas of newly created reedbed will require management to ensure that neglect and succession to woodland does not occur. Sustainable management by commercial cutting for thatching and other purposes is a means by which this could be achieved. Location of new reedbeds close to the markets for thatching reed should therefore be considered. Costs are reduced, thus maintaining competitiveness with imported reed. The south-west of England is an example where few commercial reedbeds exist and yet it remains one of the largest markets for thatching reed.

A reedbed where it is intended to harvest reed on a commercial basis for thatching will also depend on a range of factors, particularly the availability of labour for harvesting. Many cutters operate several small beds throughout the winter. This gives added value to small reedbeds of less than 1 ha. Also, cutters usually harvest reed to supplement their income, ie they are not totally reliant on it for their livelihood. Thus, there is no recommended minimum size but a total area of 10 ha could support one or two cutters for the season.

b) Physical and chemical characteristics

A basic topographical and hydrological study of a site and the immediate surrounding land should be carried out to assess the feasibility of the reedbed creation scheme before starting any work (Section 1.2). Where a site is hydrologically isolated from adjacent areas, perhaps due to bunding or topography, preflooding the site may provide valuable information, including:

● water distribution across the site

● where to locate additional/new bunds, dams, ditches and sluices, etc

● what further land forming may be required

● points where leakage may occur

● an indication of optimal locations for reed planting.

It may also assist with settling of the soil and inhibit unwanted plants (depending on timing and duration).

At Malltraeth in Gwynedd, preflooding was undertaken to determine the low and high points of the ground after initial land forming. This confirmed the findings of an earlier topographical study (Moralee pers comm).

Reedbed creation costs will vary according to the scale of the project. Capital costs for land forming and vegetation establishment should be taken into consideration at the planning stage. This section focuses on engineering operations, eg land forming, bund and ditch construction and on vegetation establishment techniques used in reedbed creation. Part 3 is completed by an overview of the design and wildlife value of reedbeds as water treatment systems.

3.2 Land Forming and Construction

3.2.1 Land forming

To create the ideal hydrological environment major earthworks may be required. This should also present opportunities to construct bunds and ditches and to install sluices.

Land forming involves shaping the surface of the ground and is often combined with the construction of bunds, ditches and grips/foot-drains. Earth moving may provide material for bunds and other structures as may ditch construction.

Major land forming requires the use of heavy machinery because of the quantities of soil that need to be moved. This may pose difficulties on soft peat soils which will need to be dry to support vehicles. On sites which have not been flooded for many years peat shrinkage may have occurred and formed a firmer surface on which machinery may operate. Preflooding may be unwise in such conditions and delay access to the site. Clay soils provide a firmer base for machinery to operate on and in general should not cause too many problems when dry. Work is usually carried out in late summer (August/September) when the ground is driest. Wide-tracked machinery or working on mats can overcome the problems of working on soft ground at most times of the year, although much depends on the experience of the driver. This will also make the going slower and add to costs.

a) Shaping the surface

The starting condition of the surface and the desired end-point will determine the approach. Land forming may not be necessary on an existing flat surface unless variations in surface height are required to produce variation in water depth. This will

be of added benefit to wildlife. Wherever feasible, the natural topography of the land should be retained. This should keep earth-moving to a minimum, thereby reducing costs.

Creating a level surface

A very rough surface may require some levelling such as at Ham Wall in Somerset (Case Study 13), an area of abandoned peat diggings with many old trenches and pits. Here, the natural topography had been considerably disrupted and so a bulldozer was used to infill the diggings and generally level-off the site to form a gently undulating surface (Street pers comm).

At East Chevington (**Case Study 12**) in Northumberland, a former opencast coal mine, land forming required the shifting of thousands of tonnes of clay and top soil to provide a graded, clay bed with a ridge and furrow system.

Creating ridge and furrow

This is a system of alternating high and low land traditionally used on wet grazing pastures to provide livestock with drier areas to graze and refuge from flooding (see section 2.1). If already in place on unploughed pasture, it can be used to give a variety of land form and water depth. Ridge and furrow systems may be created on flat fields using a digger or by deep ploughing and rolling. It should be designed to enable effective water distribution across the site taking into account natural variations in topography, etc (Figure 2).

Figure 2 Example ridge and furrow system which could be incorporated at the land forming stage. A maximum vertical drop of 1 m is recommended. Anything greater will prevent reed encroaching into the furrows and produce steep slopes. By spacing the crowns farther apart, greater depths and slopes can be achieved if required, which will produce small ditches or grips where reed had difficulty in growing.

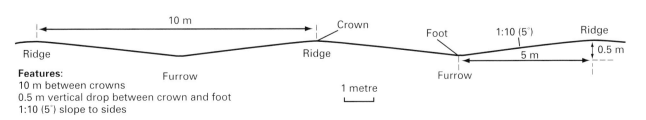

Features:
10 m between crowns
0.5 m vertical drop between crown and foot
1:10 (5°) slope to sides

Commercial cutting of reed is straightforward on shallowly graded ridge and furrow systems. However, the quality of reed may vary between ridges and furrows, a feature which may be considered undesirable for thatching material.

For ease of operating cutting equipment, ridge and furrow should be spaced at a minimum of 10 m between crowns (Figure 2), although some existing systems on pasture may be as little as 5 m. However, much will depend on the objectives and cutting equipment used. The use of very large equipment such as a Seiga harvester may be impractical on anything other than a flat bed. Ridge and furrow represents a working compromise between the requirement of a flat bed for optimal cutting performance and the variation of land form for increased wildlife value and water distribution. An alternative would be to have both features in one site (Figure 3). Because of the added cost of incorporating ridge and furrow into a site it is probably only appropriate where surplus spoil can be used or where the benefits it may offer are considered appropriate for the objectives.

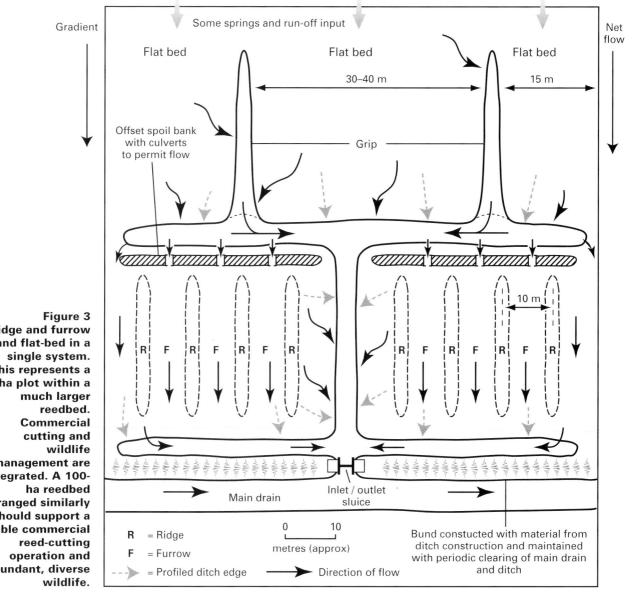

Figure 3
Ridge and furrow and flat-bed in a single system. This represents a 1 ha plot within a much larger reedbed. Commercial cutting and wildlife management are integrated. A 100-ha reedbed arranged similarly should support a viable commercial reed-cutting operation and abundant, diverse wildlife.

Creating an uneven land surface

Creating a gently graded and varied surface on a flat field can be achieved easily during other land forming operations, in particular ditch and bund construction, which will provide surplus spoil that can be spread in a carefully planned, but uneven design. The aim is to create a diverse range of water depths: permanently dry to permanently wet; open shallow flashes; narrow deeper strips, etc. This approach is of maximum benefit to wildlife. The addition of large pools and meres should also be included at the land forming stage and may be incorporated into the formation of an uneven surface (see also section 2.2.4 b). Spoil from excavation will be available for spreading to vary a flat surface or to create islands and other features.

However, an uneven surface may pose management difficulties. Where cutting is not a commercial priority and wheeled equipment is unable to operate, this can be achieved with brush cutters or hand scythes. On clay soils, draw-down may not completely remove surface water on uneven ground. The resulting pools will act as reservoirs for aquatic wildlife during the winter management months. It may not be possible to cut these patches which could be left undisturbed or cut only in dry years, ie irregular long rotations.

3.2.2 Constructing bunds/dams and ditches

The construction of bunds and dams is often necessary when creating reedbeds. Bunds may be used to isolate a site to prevent raised water levels from flooding neighbouring land. They can also be used to divide a site into smaller compartments or units to enable more effective water management. Principles to consider in the design of bunds and dams are described in section 2.2.1. Table 5 considers a number of additional factors which should be considered when constructing bunds. For example, in areas where there is limited existing access, flat-topped bunds can provide new access routes.

The construction of new ditches is often required. On large sites in particular this facilitates the distribution and control of water. Material from ditch construction may also be used for construction of bunds and dams (Plate 4). Section 2.2.3d describes how existing ditches may be reprofiled to maximise wildlife benefit. Such principles should also be applied to the construction of new ditches.

Table 5: Additional factors to consider when constructing a new bund

- Provision should be made during bund construction for the addition of sluices, culverts, pipes, etc.

- Large bunds can be constructed with a berm to provide shallow water for aquatic wildlife and feeding birds.

- After construction, bunds may settle by as much as one-third in height.

Bunds may be used to retain water. Clay is more suitable than peat as it is less permeable. Ditches facilitate water level control and distribution and may be designed to maximise their benefits to wildlife.

Plate 4 At Malltraeth, Gwynedd the clay soil was excavated to create an enclosing bund with a ditch running along the inside.

C Hawke (RSPB)

a) Bunds

Boundary bunds need to be of sufficient height to contain winter levels of water. On large sites a spillway may be required to prevent water over-topping and/or rupturing bunds. The construction of bunds may also require planning permission (Part 1 and Appendix 3). Internal bunds can be very small, separating small areas on a 'paddy-field' system such as created at Rutland Water (Case Study 15) where the clay bunds are little more than 30–40 cm high and 40–50 cm wide at the base.

Bunds need to be impermeable to retain water, hence clay is more suitable than peat. Well compacted peat bunds will retain water to a degree but seepage usually occurs. At Ham Wall in Somerset, the peat overlies clay and was excavated to one side so that clay could be dug out for constructing a bund (Plate 5). The peat was used to cap the bund or to back-fill the resulting borrow pit (**Case Study 13**). A suggested guideline procedure for constructing a simple bund is given in Table 6. Figures 4 and 5 give examples of simple and boundary bund profiles.

Plate 5 At Ham Wall, Somerset the peat top-soil was scraped away to reveal the clay beneath (fore ground) which was used to construct the core of the enclosing bund (right).

Figure 4 An example of a simple bund profile and the ditch created in providing the required material.

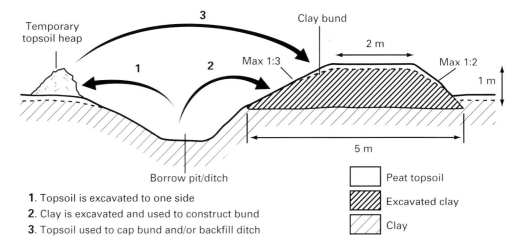

1. Topsoil is excavated to one side
2. Clay is excavated and used to construct bund
3. Topsoil used to cap bund and/or backfill ditch

Figure 5 Example of a large, boundary bund with a keyed-in keel. (see also Case Study 13, Ham Wall).

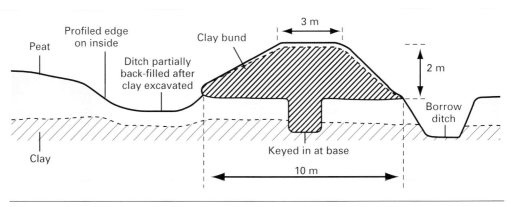

Table 6: Guidelines for simple bund construction

- Remove a linear strip of vegetation and top soil down to subsoil level, sufficiently wide to accommodate the keyed-in base of the bund and provide an area for source material, preferably clay.

- Excavate source material and use to construct the bund to desired height and profile. Usually, the source material is taken from the inside of the area being bunded, thus providing a ditch in the process.

- The top soil is used to cap the bund providing a substrate for terrestrial wildlife to occupy (alternatively it may be used to back-fill to create a shallower ditch or for other land forming).

Adapted from Burgess and Hirons 1990

b) Ditches

Points to consider when constructing ditches:

- Ditches should be provided with a shallow graded edge to one or both sides to increase their wildlife value. A maximum of 30° is recommended, and within the range 5–15° is optimal. (Provision may need to be made for boats, eg moorings or one side steeper).

- Ideally, ditches should be spaced at 30–50 m apart on peat soils so that draw-down from the water-retentive soil is complete. Less ditching may be required on clay soils but the greater the number the better for wildlife.

▼ **Figure 6 Main ditch profiles with wildlife benefit.**

a) Standard profile boundary bund plus ditch with profiled edge.

b) Berm on inside slope of outer bund.

c) Profiled to base of near edge.

d) Profiled to base of bund.

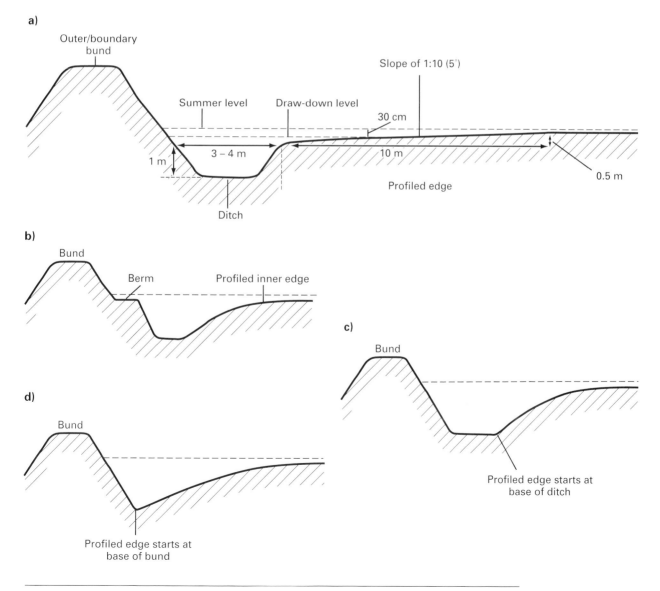

a)

b)

c)

d)

- Grips should be added between ditches to facilitate draw-down, improve water distribution and flow, and to provide additional habitat for wildlife (eg Figure 7c).

Suggested profiles and dimensions of ditches are given in Figures 6a-d and 7a-c. In order to construct internal ditches without bunds (Figure 7a), the excavated material can be spread across the surface on either side of the ditch. Alternatively, bunds could be offset (Figure 7b) providing an edge to both sides of the ditch. Ditch edges wherever possible should be provided with at least one shallow battered side as illustrated in Figure 6a.

Small ditches and grips/foot-drains can be constructed using a ditching machine as used by the Norfolk Wildlife Trust at Hickling and other sites. Grips can be

created using a rotary ditcher, which replaces conventional flail-heads on tractor-mounted machines. Many old grips and ditches were originally dug and maintained by hand, an option on small sites or where sufficient labour is available. However, the vast majority of ditch construction is done by mechanical excavators, usually tracked Hy-mac types or JCB types where ground conditions permit.

Existing ditches can be modified or incorporated into the design as illustrated in Figure 8.

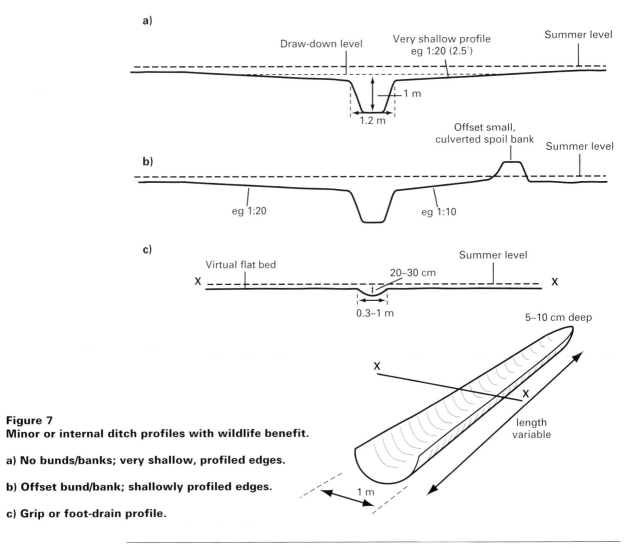

Figure 7
Minor or internal ditch profiles with wildlife benefit.

a) No bunds/banks; very shallow, profiled edges.

b) Offset bund/bank; shallowly profiled edges.

c) Grip or foot-drain profile.

a)

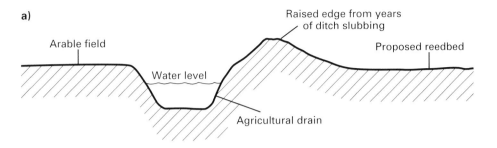

Arable field

Raised edge from years of ditch slubbing

Proposed reedbed

Water level

Agricultural drain

b)

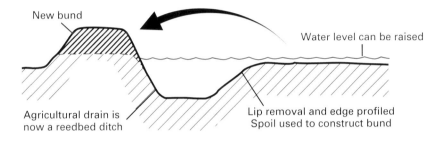

New bund

Water level can be raised

Agricultural drain is now a reedbed ditch

Lip removal and edge profiled
Spoil used to construct bund

c)

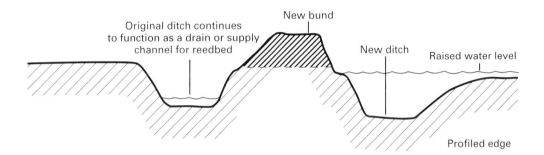

Original ditch continues to function as a drain or supply channel for reedbed

New bund

New ditch

Raised water level

Profiled edge

Figure 8
Two options for incorporating an existing agricultural ditch into a new reedbed.

a) Existing supply ditch

b) Option One: New bund created on arable field edge to incorporate ditch into new reedbed.

c) Option Two: Raised edge added to or new keyed-in bund constructed in its place, using spoil from newly constructed ditch.

3.2.3 Installation of water control structures

The many types of water control structures used on reedbeds have been described in section 2.2.1 c. It should be feasible prior to construction to determine how many and which types of structure might be needed. The type of structure will depend on the way in which water is supplied to the site, eg a tidally influenced river may require a large, robust penstock sluice with non-return flaps to convey quickly large quantities of water on or off the site. Drop-board sluices may be more appropriate for sites with a continual input of water or a diffuse supply (ie springs etc) enabling a flow across the site to be maintained. They also enable fine control over levels to be achieved when used in conjunction with an extensive network of ditches. Flexipipes are inexpensive and easy to maintain and operate. They are commonly used on internal bunds to facilitate the draw-down of individual hydrological units (Plates 6a and 6b).

The numbers and sizes of structures will depend on the degree of flexibility needed for water management and on the quantities of water to be moved around. Figure 9a and b illustrate how, starting with a drained field, an area may be hydrologically isolated by bunding, etc, and created into a functioning reedbed by the addition of ditches and sluices.

Choice of water control structures will depend on the water regime and the influence of seasonal variations. Cost may also be a factor.

Figure 9
Starting with a flat field and ending up with a reedbed.

a) Featureless, flat field with ditching already in place. This example is commonplace in lowland England in particular. It lends itself to modification for the creation of a reedbed.

b) After land forming: ditches, bunds, grips and sluices have been added to create a two-unit reedbed.

a)

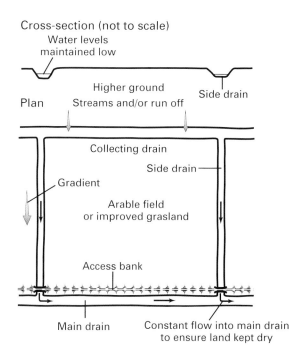

Cross-section (not to scale)
Water levels maintained low

Plan

Higher ground
Streams and/or run off

Side drain

Collecting drain

Side drain

Gradient

Arable field
or improved grasland

Access bank

Main drain

Constant flow into main drain
to ensure land kept dry

b)

Cross-section (not to scale)

New boundary bund

Minor internal ditch

New main
internal ditch

Plan

Spring fed and / or run off

Minor internal ditches
(profiled) and grips

Main inlet sluice

30 m   50 m

Reedbed 1

Flexipipe

Secondary
outlet sluice

Flexipipe   50 m   Flexipipe

New boundary
bund constructed
with material
from ditch
excavation

Secondary
inlet
sluice

Reedbed 2

Main internal ditch

Main drainage channel

Main outlet sluice

Outlet structures should be placed at the lowest point (as assessed by topographical survey or preflooding). The height of the outlet structure should be set to retain winter/spring levels with the facility to adjust downwards for draw-down in autumn. Where possible, provision should be made to allow for a gradual increase of the water levels as the reedbed ages as a result of the accumulation of litter and/or silt. At East Chevington in Northumberland (Case Study 12) the site has been designed to allow for a 1-m increase in water levels as the reedbed matures.

In most situations, the installation of control devices need not be expensive. Simple structures such as a basic drop-board sluice will often suffice. On a system where large quantities of water need to be moved, more elaborate structures may be required, eg concrete structures with penstock mechanisms. These latter structures can be expensive and should be considered at the planning stage. Factors influencing the choice of structures are highlighted in section 2.2.1 c.

Plate 6a During bund and ditch construction, water level control structures may be installed. A flexipipe is shown being installed at Malltraeth, Gwynedd.

D Rees (RSPB)

6b Three flexipipes after installation through the new bund at Malltraeth, Gwynedd.

D Rees (RSPB)

3.3 Vegetation Establishment

Several techniques are commonly used for establishing reed (and other wetland plants in some instances). These include:

- Expansion
  - 'natural' expansion (section 3.3.2 a)
  - layering (section 3.3.2 b)

- Planting
  - seeding (aerial, drilling, hand) (section 3.3.3 a)

- pot-grown plants (commercial and home-grown) (section 3.3.3 b)
- rhizomes (soil transfer, cuttings, turfs) (section 3.3.3 c)
- stem cuttings (section 3.3.3 d)

Table 7 gives a selection of sites where reed has been established in the UK. See also the map of sites in the UK where creation and management techniques have been undertaken (Appendix 4).

Table 7: Some example sites where reed has been established

Site Name	Location/Org.	Land Type/Soil	Technique	Function	Year 1	Reed Area
Hickling	Norfolk/NWTa	pasture/peat	expansion	thatching	ca 1970	ca 8 ha
Whitlingham	Norfolk/BA,AW	pasture/peat	rhizomes & pot-grown	wildlife & thatching	1993	2 ha
Ham Wall	Somerset/RSPB, SCC, EN	disused peat workings	pot-grown & seeds	wildlife & thatching	1995	16 ha
Gt Westhay	Somerset/STNC	disused peat workings	rhizomes	wildlife	1987	> 10 ha
Woolhampton	Berkshire/Priv.	disused mineral/ gravel	rhizomes	wildlife	ca 1991	> 5 ha
Llyn Coed Y Dinas	Montgomery/ MWT	disused mineral/ gravel	rhizomes	wildlife	1993	1 ha
E Chevington	Northumberland/ NWTb	disused mining/ clay	pot-grown & others	wildlife	1994	39 ha
Rutland Water	Leicestershire/ L&RTNC	pasture/clay	rhizomes/ turfs	wildlife	ca 1980 1995	1 ha ca 1 ha
W'field Pill	Pembrokeshire/ DWT	tidal/mud	stem cuttings	wildlife	ca 1990	0.25 ha
Billingham	Cleveland/ICI	unused indust.	pot-grown	WTS	1991	5 ha
Llanwern	Gwent/BS	pasture/clay	pot-grown	WTS	1987	18 ha

Key:

EN	= English Nature	STNC	= Somerset Trust for Nature Conservation
WTS	= water treatment system	MWT	= Montgomeryshire Wildlife Trust
NWTa	= Norfolk Wildlife Trust	L&RTNC	= Leicestershire and Rutland Trust for Nature Conservation
NWTb	= Northumberland Wildlife Trust	ICI	= Imperial Chemical Industries
BA	= Broads Authority	BS	= British Steel
AW	= Anglian Water	DWT	= Dyfed Wildlife Trust
RSPB	= Royal Society for the Protection of Birds	SCC	= Somerset County Council

3.3.1 Bed preparation

The extent to which the bed will require preparation prior to seeding or planting will depend on the technique used, soil type and general condition of the bed to begin with.

Successful establishment of reed can be achieved on most soil types. Haslam (1972) indicated that reed grows best in finer soils such as clays and silts. However, peat soils for example are not considered ideal for establishing reed (Ekstam 1992) and coarser soils such as gravels and sands are also less favoured by reed. The addition of top soil on heavy clays or gravels has been used to improve the situation but problems may arise with the importation of unwanted plants in the soil's seed bank, such as rushes and sweet-grass, as occurred at Pinkhill Meadows in Oxfordshire.

A potential problem with peat soils that have undergone prolonged oxidation as a result of drainage and drying out, is that on rewetting the pH may drop rapidly. This occurred on Marazion Marsh in Cornwall where the pH fell to 3.0 immediately after flooding, although the effect was temporary (Flumm pers comm). It may be necessary on such sites to 'deacidify' the soil by flooding prior to planting until the pH rises again to above 5.0.

There are two major considerations in bed preparation:

● control of competing vegetation

● water level control.

a) Control of competing vegetation

Competition from unwanted plants is the most important factor in establishing a reedbed. Projects where reed development has been poorest have usually been due to problems with control of unwanted plants (see section 3.4).

Stripping away litter or vegetation is easily achieved during the land forming phase of creation. The spoil from such activity is often used in bund construction or even to make deep water areas more shallow, eg Rutland Water (Case Study 15) and Far Ings (Case Study 3).

Where no land forming is required, such as the reflooding of drained pasture, the use of herbicides (eg Roundup), rotovation, ploughing and flooding may be considered. Herbicides may be necessary to eliminate vigorous plants such as canary-grass or sweet-grass but are usually only practical or economic on small sites of less than 2 ha. Roundup was used successfully at Whitlingham in Norfolk to remove dominant reed sweet-grass prior to planting with pot-grown seedlings (Case Study 14).

Disturbance of the soil by rotovation or ploughing may bring the seed bank to the surface and while rotovation breaks up the roots to the detriment of most plants, rushes are known to benefit, each rhizome fragment establishing itself as a new plant. For this reason, anything other than deep ploughing is not advised on soils where rushes are present, unless followed by deep, prolonged flooding or desiccation. Spring flooding after ploughing or rotovation will reduce most other unwanted plants, especially on arable sites that have developed a considerable terrestrial plant seed bank. Beware of drained marshes, however, which once supported wetland plants whose seeds may persist in the soil for many years and would benefit greatly from shallow flooding. Knowledge of previous land use should be sought in such circumstances.

Prolonged flooding, sometimes through three or more growing seasons, may also be used to control unwanted plants.

b) Control of water levels

In order to encourage the establishment of reeds and to discourage other plants, water levels need to be carefully balanced. Young plants are vulnerable both to lack of water and to drowning. In general, start with a damp soil achieved either through draw-down after flooding or when the water table is at or very near the surface. Once reed seed has germinated or shoots have developed, shallow flooding is advisable, always ensuring the top third of the shoots is above water. This ensures the rhizome and roots receive oxygen through the aerial parts above water. Plants grown in 5 cm depth of water were double the weight of those grown where the water was 15 cm below the soil surface (Parr 1987).

Such fine control is more easily achieved on flat beds. On undulating ground there will be deep and shallow areas, which is why care should be taken when choosing exactly where to plant or sow (see 3.3.3 b). Planting or sowing on a pre-prepared, fine ridge and furrow system, eg 1 m between crowns, will ensure that many of the seedlings/seeds are at a suitable water depth.

3.3.2 Creation by expansion

a) 'Natural' expansion

The simplest and cheapest method for creating a reedbed is to flood shallowly an area of low-lying land that already has fringing reed (Plate 7) and allow the reed to spread into the flooded area unaided. This technique has been commonly practised for many years, often on areas that were previously drained to allow grazing, thus the ditches and sluices were already in place.

An additional 1 ha of reedbed was created at Salthouse in Norfolk by digging a new ditch across a grazing meadow to join two existing ditches. Grazing was prevented and the reed left to colonise the new area on its own (Figure 10).

Plate 7 Reed may spread quickly from ditches such as these at Dunwich in Suffolk, if the water levels are raised and the pastures flooded.

Raising water levels and/or the cessation of grazing may allow natural expansion. 'Layering' may be used to increase the rate of expansion but it is labour intensive and practicable only on small areas.

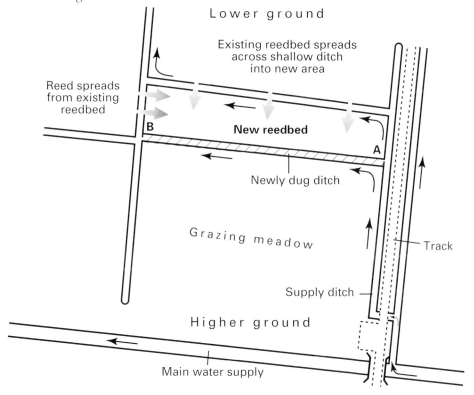

**Figure 10
A reedbed can be extended by encouraging 'natural' expansion, as was undertaken on a small area at Salthouse, Norfolk. A new ditch was constructed from point A to B connecting two existing ditches. Reed was allowed to encroach across and from the shallow ditches and colonise the new, 1-ha extension.**

At Cors Erddreiniog in Gwynedd, existing reed was encouraged to spread by ceasing summer grazing and raising the water levels. This creates an area of reed now in excess of 10 ha. A similar approach was adopted at Leighton Moss in Lancashire; raised water levels permitted reed to expand outwards in all directions, adding significantly to the total wet reed area of the reserve.

At Hickling in Norfolk an area of derelict grazing marsh was bunded and flooded allowing marginal reed to colonise. It took about five years to produce a closed stand of harvestable reed, now covering some 50 ha. Bunding was necessary to contain water and prevent flooding of neighbouring land. The bunding was constructed with material from clearing existing ditches and the excavation of new ones.

Expansion can also be encouraged by preparing an area adjacent to an existing reedbed for reed to grow into (Plate 8). Usually, this accompanies efforts to lower the ground level and increase surface water depth. A scraped surface allows competing vegetation to be removed. This can be used to construct bunds if required. This kind of approach has been utilised at Rutland Water in Leicestershire in combination with planting (Case Study 15) and throughout the Broadland fens in association with scrub removal.

The rate at which expansion occurs will vary greatly, from 1–10 m in one year along the leading edge (see Table 1), faster in exceptional circumstances. The leading edge of a dense reedbed tends to grow more slowly. On unflooded but damp soils, especially clay, reed will produce side shoots, which grow rapidly along the surface, producing a new vertical shoot at each node (Plate 9). The factors most affecting the rate of expansion are probably weather (temperature) and water depth.

b) Layering

This technique is rarely used as it is quite labour intensive but has been employed at Rutland Water with good effect (Appleton pers comm). It is probably best used to hasten a slowly encroaching reed edge and is claimed to be an efficient method for thickening up a sparse stand of reed (Ekstam *et al* 1992).

The technique, as illustrated in Figure 11, involves bending a growing shoot down and burying most of the stem in soil. This enables new roots and shoots to develop from the buried nodes within a few weeks. This can be done in May or June, usually no later than July, when the shoots are tall but still actively growing.

Layering is probably most appropriate for edges of open water where the water level drops in early summer and the desire is to encourage the reed to spread towards the open water. It is only practicable on small areas or where a large workforce is available.

Plate 8 A digger was used at Rutland Water, Leicestershire to excavate an area for adjacent reed to expand into.

T Appleton

Plate 9 On clays and silts in particular, reed may produce lateral shoots which spread across the surface. New vertical shoots are produced at each node.

C Hawke (RSPB)

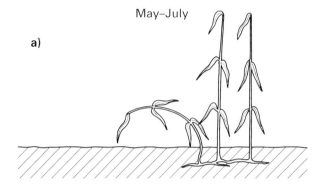

May–July

a)

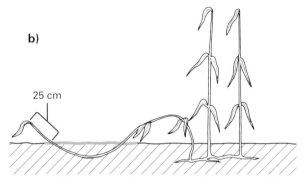

b)

25 cm

5–7 weeks later

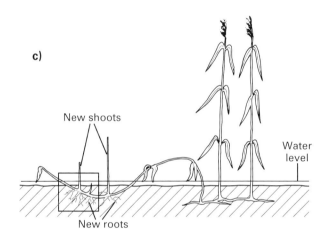

c)

New shoots

New roots

Water level

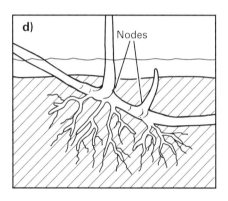

d)

Nodes

Figure 11   The technique of 'Layering'.

a) A single tall shoot is gently bent over towards the ground. The ground should be wet but not flooded.

b) At the point where the shoot easily contacts the ground a slot some 10 cm deep is cut into which the shoot is laid burying as many nodes as possible. The slot is closed over and gently heeled in. The terminal 25 cm of the shoot should remain above ground.

c) After 3–4 weeks, roots should develop. After another 2–3 weeks new shoots should sprout.

d) Enlargement of buried stem showing new shoots and roots arising from nodes.

3.3.3 Planting techniques

There are two main considerations when planting reed, whether by seeding, cuttings or as whole plants:

● source of material for planting

● where to plant in the site.

Source of material
In general, it is advisable to obtain seeds, rhizomes or shoots from another part of the site itself, from a nearby area of reed or from a site with similar growing conditions.

Reed should be obtained as locally as possible and from similar growing conditions. It is recommended that reed is not planted in water deeper than 5 cm.

Reed from a brackish source will possibly fail or grow more slowly if attempts are made to grow it in fresh water. Similar differences can occur with reed from peat soils grown on silts and clays. Frequently, the reed will 'recover' from its new environment but establishment may take longer and be less satisfactory than from reed from a similar area.

There is some debate over introducing 'non-native' reed to new sites in the UK. Because of the possibility of different genetic types behaving differently from UK reed, it is not worth risking introducing unsuitable varieties into the country when an abundant source of UK reed already exists. It is true that the origins of much UK reed is uncertain but unless it can be established that there are no differences between reed from different parts of the world it is best to err on the side of caution.

Successful establishment is more likely with reed that demonstrates characteristics of vigour, ie tall, green, rapid growth with large, seed-laden panicles. This is particularly important if the reed is to be cut for thatching, and it will also need to possess thatching qualities (BRGA leaflet – address Appendix 3). Much UK reed seems to have low seed productivity and germination rates may be very low (Self pers comm; McKee and Richard in prep). It is wise to use panicles with large numbers of seeds and test for viability (section 3.3.3a).

If a reedbed is known to have high infestation rates of 'reedbug', the reed-boring larvae of wainscot moths, it may be advisable to avoid using reed from the site, especially if the primary objective is to produce thatching reed. This suggests a high degree of susceptibility to the moths, and the use of shoots or rhizomes may transfer the moths to the new site. Nevertheless, the larvae of these moths are an important food source for birds and usually occur in isolated pockets or at low densities, rarely causing a problem on all but the smallest of commercially cut reedbeds. Many species are widespread and common and are likely

Figure 12 Contour planting.

a) Cross-section showing planting zones in shallow areas.

b) Plan showing planting zones on shallow crowns of ridge and furrow-type surface.

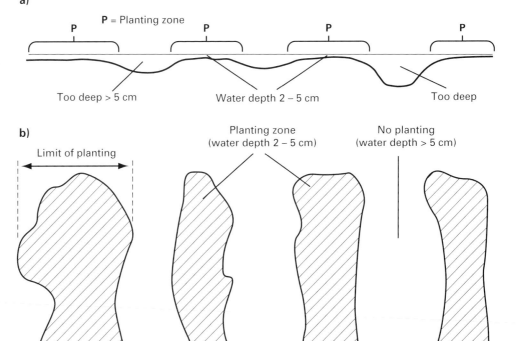

a)

P = Planting zone

Too deep > 5 cm   Water depth 2 – 5 cm   Too deep

b)

Limit of planting

Planting zone (water depth 2 – 5 cm)   No planting (water depth > 5 cm)

No planting (water depth > 5 cm)

to occur in most reedbeds anyway, or will quite quickly find their way there if near by. Others, eg the Fenn's wainscot and the white-mantled wainscot are very rare and restricted in their distribution such that they require special consideration.

Where to plant in the site

The shape of the surface of the ground will influence the success of establishment unless care is taken over where to place seeds or plants. The problem arises on undulating ground. The lower areas will contain deeper water, and reed planted in the depressions will fail or struggle to grow. By flooding the site prior to planting, to a depth where the highest points are covered by 2–5 cm of water, the shallowest areas on the site will become apparent. Using canes, these areas can then be marked out for planting after draw-down. This technique, known as contour planting is illustrated in Figure 12 a and b. Any anomalous high-points revealed by the preflooding can be re-formed after draw-down (see 3.2).

Table 8: Separating viable seed from panicles

1 Collect a sample of 10 panicles in November–December (the seed should have matured and the panicles should be dry).
2 Use scissors to cut a single panicle into small pieces, directly into a kitchen blender.
3 Add about 80 ml tap water.
4 Operate blender for a few seconds (5 x 5 seconds) until separation is evident.
5 Pour through a coarse sieve to remove panicle debris, into a large, round bowl. Stir slowly. The seed will settle to the bottom.
6 Pour off the water or draw off the seed with a pipette or large syringe.
7 Tip or place seed onto a filter paper and dry at room temperature.
8 Count seeds.
9 Repeat for 10 panicles and calculate the mean number of viable seeds per panicle.

a) Seeding

The number of seeds in each reed panicle varies throughout the plant's geographical range, from year to year and within a single site. Cold and wet weather can delay flowering and result in very poor seed sets (Ekstam *et al* 1992). Seed numbers can range from as low as 5 per panicle, eg at Malltraeth on Anglesey, to 285 as recorded from Tay, in 1994/95 (Self pers comm). However, up to 2,300 seeds in a panicle have been recorded from Strumpshaw Fen in Norfolk in the past and 3,500 in a panicle from reeds in Sweden. The viability of seed varies greatly too and germination rates and subsequent seedling survival in natural habitats in the UK is poor (Haslam 1971) . However, germination can be as high as 100% from seed grown in a controlled, protected environment, eg propagators (Parr 1987). It is advisable, therefore, to ascertain the seed densities from the seed source, which can be easily done by the method described in Table 8.

If facilities are available, the germination rate of a seed source can be tested by planting seeds in potting compost and incubating at 28–30 °C by day and 15–17 °C by night, with a 12-hour split (Parr 1987). Damp filter paper or sand can be used instead of potting compost and often produces better results (Self pers comm). The seeds may germinate in as little as 36 hours. This should give a more accurate indication of the likely success rate of establishment from a particular seed source.

Having established the number of seeds per panicle from the seed source, the number of panicles required to sow an area can be calculated. It is not necessary to extract the seeds from the panicles for sowing as this is achieved by spreading chopped panicles. Panicles can be collected in winter and stored dry and cold until the spring, usually with no discernible reduction in germination rate.

Aerial seeding

Huge areas of the Dutch polders were seeded with reed in 1957 and 1968 to claim the land for agriculture and other uses (van der Toorn and Hemminga 1994). Between 14–30 May 1968, a total area of 40,800 ha

The seed density of the source material should be determined before sowing. Sowing may be done by light aircraft or by hand. Hand sowing is impracticable on large areas.

was aerially sown by light aircraft. Whole shoots were mechanically harvested from 250 ha of reed, representing 28,886 kg of reed panicles containing approximately 6,000 viable seeds/m^2. To aid dispersion, the panicles were chopped into stem pieces about 6 cm long and stored in sacks in a warehouse for 1–2 years. Under these conditions, seed viability decreased from 75% to 44% in a year.

Prior to sowing the land was pumped relatively dry, leaving surface-wet mud. Small aeroplanes fitted with modified Swath Master sowing apparatus were used, handling 24 kg of seed material at a time. Seed material was sown at the rate of 0.48 kg/ha (approximately 60,000–100,000 seeds). Between 7–500 plants/100 m^2 were established within three months of sowing. A closed stand of reed was achieved within three years.

Aerial sowing is expensive and only cost-effective on very large areas.

Table 9: Suggested procedure for hand sowing

1 Collect 10 panicles and test as described in the working example below.

2 If viable seed count is low (< 100) more panicles/m^2 will be required.

3 If viable seed count is high (> 100) use at least one panicle/m^2 to be sown.

4 If an abundant supply of panicles is easily available, use as many panicles/m^2 as practicable to increase take (bearing in mind that germination rate may be as low as 10% and seedling survival is also not guaranteed).

5 Cut panicles into pieces using scissors or similar.

6 Distribute buckets containing cut panicles amongst operators and sprinkle cut panicle material evenly across area to be sown.

Working example of hand sowing procedure:

- Panicle test (Table 8) revealed seed count of 145 viable seeds per panicle.

- To increase take, will use 2 panicles/m^2.

- Area to be sown is 1 ha (10,000 m^2).

- With 10 operators = 1,000 m^2 each.

- Each operator chops up 2,000 panicles (say 200 at a time to sow 100 m^2).

- Each operator evenly spreads chopped panicles across 10 x 100 m^2 areas.

Hand sowing

By comparison with aerial sowing, the quantity of seeds required to establish more than one plant/m^2 can be reduced considerably if sowing is carried out on a smaller scale (Ekstam *et al* 1992). Hand sowing is feasible on small sites. As a guideline, the procedure as detailed in Table 9 may be followed. The soil should be wet but not flooded so the seeds adhere to the surface film.

Important factors to consider when hand sowing:

- Sow in still wind conditions.

- Ensure soil is saturated, ie surface wet but not flooded.

- Preferably, sow on a flat, vegetation-free bed or on ridges of specially prepared, fine ridge and furrow. Avoid sowing on low points or depressions.

- Sow during April or May when day time temperatures are in the range 10–25 °C and nights are frost-free.

It is recommended to sow at 20–125 viable seeds/m^2 on bare, wet soil. Once the shoots have grown, flood to 2-cm depth, usually about 5–6 weeks after germination. In good conditions, germination can occur within 3–4 days. Rainfall can wash the seeds away and inhibit germination and will always be a risk. Any other flooding should be avoided until the seedlings are well on their way and have reached a height of 10–20 cm, when the bed may be flooded to a depth of 5 cm (Parr 1987).

The conversion of large areas of greenfield land into reedbeds by hand seeding is not practicable. The adoption of a tractor broadcasting method in the UK on current arable land is considered severely limited by anticipated weed competition (Staniforth 1989). Even spraying with herbicide prior to seeding is unlikely to reduce competition significantly in the first few weeks of development. The seed bank in arable soil, even after 10 years of cultivation, remains considerable. It may be that intermittent flooding out of emerging plants over three or four years may be a necessary precursor to sowing.

Drilling

To overcome the problem of competition from vigorous plants, consideration may be given to drilling the seeds directly into the soil with specially designed equipment. This would have the advantage of planting in rows, permitting band-spraying between to control over 70% of competing plants. Precision drills can handle seed as small as 1.2 mm, too large for reed seed which is less than 1 mm. Conventional drills could be used, by mixing the seed with sand to limit the rate of seed discharge (Staniforth 1989). Reed seed should not be drilled more than its own diameter into the soil, ie > 1 mm.

However, the small size of seed and mechanical problems of separating it from the panicles have meant there has been no development in this area to date but it may become a viable option in the future.

b) Pot-grown reeds

The use of pot-grown plants increases the success of establishing a reedbed and has been used widely both in water treatment systems and for wildlife. Growing the plants from seed in a controlled, protected environment and planting them out as established plants, puts them in a better position to compete with other plants and survive adverse weather. Individual plants are grown from seed in pots, cluster trays or plug tubes, usually under glass to protect from frost.

Commercial production

A small number of nurseries specialise in growing reed on a large scale for individual creation schemes (Addresses in Appendix 3). The cost of buying commercially grown seedlings will depend on the supplier, bulk-buying and whether a planting service is also required. In 1995, the cost per seedling varied from 29–70p. The source of seed used by nurseries varies and it would be wise to check its origins before proceeding to ensure similar growing conditions are met. Alternatively, the nursery may be supplied with the seed from a known source as was undertaken for the planting project at Whitlingham in Norfolk (**Case Study 14**). The advantages of nursery produced plants is that seed supply, assessment of viability,

germination rates and growing is done by experts with good equipment, with a guarantee that required numbers of plants will be supplied. This can make a scheme expensive but the larger the scale the lower the cost per hectare so it is often the most cost-effective way of creating a reedbed. Smaller scale projects might consider home-grown pot-plants but well resourced projects, such as water treatment systems, nearly always use commercially produced plants. An unpublished RSPB survey of reedbed creation conducted in 1993 identified 22 projects which utilised pot-grown plants of which 18 used commercially produced plants.

Home-grown plants

This is a much cheaper alternative for small-scale projects but is labour intensive and not frequently undertaken. The Northumberland Wildlife Trust have experimented with growing plants in an open nursery on the creation site at East Chevington (Case Study 12). Seed or chopped panicle is sprinkled into soil-filled pots (usually 2 l) and placed in a small bunded area flooded to 2–10 cm. They are left to grow uncovered and planted out when about 20+ cm high, at any time of the year. The nursery needed to be fenced against rabbits (Douglas pers comm). Granular fertiliser has been used experimentally to improve the rate of growth of plants in pots but is probably not required if a vigorous stock of reed is used or if the soil is nutrient-rich.

The Wildfowl & Wetlands Trust have considerable experience and success at growing reed in pots with seed obtained from a variety of local sources (Worrall and Peberdy 1994).

Planting by hand

This is usually done by making a hole (usually with a dibber) of sufficient size to receive the contents of the potted plant. The pot is inverted and the soil extruded onto the palm of the hand taking care not to damage the seedling. The whole thing is then placed in the hole and gently heeled in (Plates 10a and 10b). The more care that is taken at this stage, the increased likelihood of an individual plant establishing.

Although expensive, planting pot-grown reeds is often the most cost-effective method of reedbed establishment. Planting by hand is labour intensive and planting by machine will be needed for large areas.

Plate 10a A dibber is used to create a suitably sized hole ready for planting pot-grown reed plugs at East Chevington, Northumberland. Note the seedlings are being planted in shallow water.

10b The planted reed plug is then firmed-in by hand.

a)

b)

Ian Douglas

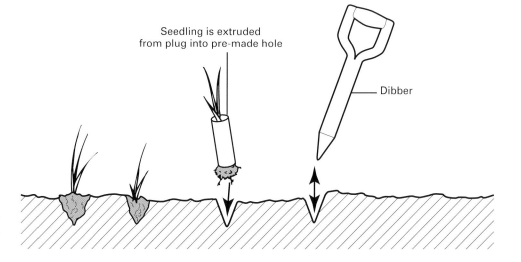

Seedling is extruded from plug into pre-made hole

Dibber

Figure 13 Use of a dibber to plant seedlings grown as plugs.

Commercially produced, cylindrical plugs are planted using a dibber of the correct size, usually supplied by the nursery (Figure 13). The dibber makes a hole into which the plug is placed. Plugs usually contain one seedling each, which ensures an even spacing of plants. The use of a dibber on hard, clay soils may require considerable force and may be much easier on damp soils. Alternatively, a small hand auger may be useful for making suitable holes for planting on clay soils and avoids compacting the sides, which inhibits root expansion.

Individual seedlings, whether in plugs or pots, are planted at 1 m spacing or 4/m² for full cover within one year. Pots containing clusters of seedlings, such as produced at East Chevington, will spread more rapidly in all directions and are spaced at about 3-m intervals (Douglas pers comm).

Planting may be undertaken at any time of the year but the best time is in April/May, as early as possible after frosts have ceased.

Later planting at Whitlingham gave a poor take and the seedlings struggled to compete with dominants such as reed sweet-grass (Andrews pers comm).

Water levels immediately below the surface are sufficient to maintain plantings, although water depths of as much as 5 cm are considered optimal (Parr 1987). Plants should not be submerged but the surface should not be allowed to dry out since this can reduce establishment.

Planting by machine
In order for large-scale, commercially viable, sustainable reedbeds to be created, mechanisation of reed propagation and 'planting out', will be necessary. Because reed is perennial and, once established, it grows vegetatively from the rhizomes, it can be repeatedly harvested without the need to replant (unlike annual cereal crops). A machine for planting might only be required once by a land owner, making purchase on a co-operative basis or hire a more feasible approach.

Modular systems for growing plants from seeds are well developed in the horticultural industry and could be adapted for use with reed seed. Similarly, small-scale, manual, two-row transplanters could be used to plant out seedlings in the field.

c) Rhizomes

Establishing a reedbed by planting rhizomes can be a highly effective method to use. The rhizome is the perennial stock of the plant and its growth is the dominant mode of stand expansion (Ekstam *et al* 1992). However, establishment using rhizomes is not always successful because the quality of the rhizomes will influence the take (Parr 1987). In addition, handling may cause damage.

The main techniques for planting rhizomes are:

- spreading soil containing rhizomes

- planting turfs

- planting cuttings

- planting cuttings with shoots attached.

Spreading soil containing rhizomes
This could be described as a rough and ready technique for establishing a reedbed and has been used with some success on several sites. It usually involves the excavation of the 'top soil' of an existing reedbed, usually about 30–50 cm depth to ensure the rhizomes are present and protected by a 'wrapping' of soil. The most common source of soil with rhizomes is from ditch clearing work and has been used in small areas quite extensively by the NRA, eg where reed has been planted for river bank protection.

At Hauxley in Northumberland, several small patches of reed were established by depositing lorry loads of soil with rhizomes into bays excavated along the edges of the open water. The reeds quickly established and spread in all directions such that Hauxley now supplies reed for other small establishment projects in the area (Douglas pers comm).

In 1991, the Teesside Development Corporation began work on creating a large reedbed at Haverton Hill using soil with rhizomes transported from The Broads. Using a digger, the material was excavated from Ward Marsh at Ranworth and loaded into a lorry. The spoil was spread across the prepared area of about 2 ha by a bulldozer. Initially, the reed grew well but was not maintained possibly because the soil dried out. Nevertheless, by 1994 the margins of open water had been fully colonised by the reed along with reedmace and yellow iris, presumably brought in with the soil (Smith pers comm).

At Rutland Water in Leicestershire (**Case Study 15**), a reedbed was created by transferring soil with rhizomes into shallow trenches excavated in the furrows of a ridge and furrow system. By 1995, more than 1 ha was well established and work began to extend the reed.

The following points should be considered when using soil with rhizomes to establish a reedbed:

- Spread the soil at least 25 cm deep across the site.

- Ensure the soil is moist, but not saturated. Spreading the soil over a shallowly flooded area might suffice, or raising water levels after work is completed would be better, permitting finer control as the new soil absorbs water.

- Avoid drying out of the soil.

- Ideally, minimise the amount of manipulation of the soil containing rhizomes and store for no longer than about a week, although several months of storage prior to spreading has produced good results.

- Excavation and spreading is best carried out from November–February before new shoots have begun to develop. Excavate to just below the rhizome depth (a series of test digs may be necessary to establish how deep).

There are four main techniques for planting rhizomes. They have varying degrees of success and cost. Planting turfs has a high success rate and requires least aftercare.

An interesting bonus to using soil from a site is that it will also contain litter and soil invertebrates, which will be able to colonise the new site as it develops.

Plants of nature conservation value may also be brought in but those which compete with reed in the early stages of establishment may also be introduced and can cause problems.

Because of the volume of material involved with this method (2,500 m³ soil is required to spread to a depth of 25 cm over 1 ha), it may be necessary therefore, to pre-excavate the area into which the soil is to be spread so that the required water depth can be achieved. If spoil is required for bund construction, this will be less of a problem, but the shifting and transporting of large volumes of material makes this an expensive technique for establishing a reedbed unless done very locally and on a small scale. Table 10 compares the costs of local and long distance transportation and establishment costs.

Potential problems with this technique are that many rhizomes are damaged, they may not be planted in the optimal position and unburied portions may be exposed to frost.

Planting turfs
This technique is a variation of spreading soil with rhizomes. Clumps of rhizome mat are excavated to reduce damage to the rhizomes by a proportion of the rhizome mat remaining intact. It has been effectively used in creating reedbeds for water treatment systems and for wildlife. The main advantage compared with spreading soil with rhizomes is that there is less material to transport. The success of this technique can be attributed to the high number of undamaged rhizomes, an intact rhizome mat and aeration of rhizomes through retained aerial parts. In addition, the rhizomes are not exposed to frost.

On a small scale, turfs can be dug from a reedbed with a spade but for large-scale projects the use of a digger with a bucket that can cut turfs of at least 1 m x 1 m is usually used. The same implement is used to dig the hole in which the turf is to be planted (Plate 11). Bucket size is not important and merely affects the time taken to do the work and the rate at which the reedbed will achieve full cover.

Plate 11 A digger at Rutland Water, Leicestershire making a hole in which to plant a reed turf which has just been dug from the adjacent reedbed. The area was previously prepared by stripping off the vegetation and lowering the surface. Note the turf is being planted in shallow water.

T Appleton

Table 10: Costs in 1993 of preparing a new 1 ha reedbed using soil with rhizomes

Procedure	m³ (£)	1,000m³* (£)	2,500m³* (£)
Stripping soil with rhizome	1.20	1,200	2,500
Spreading soil with rhizome	1.35	1,350	3,375
Transporting < 800 m	0.80	800	2,000
(total for very local	3.35	3,350	7,875)
Transporting < 5 km	3.80	3,800	9,500
(total for local	6.35	6,350	15,375)
Transporting > 100 km	20.00	20,000	50,000
(total for long distance	22.55	22,550	55,875)

* 1,000 m³ = spreading to depth of 10 cm over 1 ha
* 2,500 m³ = spreading to depth of 25 cm over 1 ha
Adapted from Ward 1993

Larger turfs should achieve full cover more quickly than smaller ones but the use of smaller turfs more closely spaced will produce more growing reed edge of value to bitterns.

Both spade and mechanical digger techniques have been used with good results at Druridge Bay in Northumberland where reedbeds have been created at Hauxley and East Chevington (Case Study 12). So successful was the establishment of reed at Hauxley that large turfs (cut with a large bucket and placed in a trailer or pick-up truck) are occasionally sold to create small water treatment systems for individual houses, farms and other establishments.

In 1995, work began at Rutland Water, Lecicestershire (Case Study 15) to increase the size of the existing reedbed by planting turfs in a prepared area adjacent using material from the original created reedbed.

At Malltraeth in Gwynedd, recent work involved the cutting of turfs by a digger from the existing, naturally expanding reedbed to create an area of adjoining reedbed. The turfs were planted at variable spacings (10–30 m) to create a reedbed with maximum expanding reed edge to benefit bitterns and other wildlife. The area had been prepared by scraping and bunding, and flooding for several months before planting began. The turfs were planted in March 1995 and had visible shoots by May.

The spacing of plantings depends entirely on the size of the turfs and the desired rate of spread of the reeds. For most commercial applications full cover is required as quickly as possible whereas for wildlife a more slowly developing system will maximise the opportunities for a range of species to use the reedbed. Such design considerations are detailed in section 3.4. As a general guideline the following points may be considered:

- Larger turfs will contain more undamaged rhizomes.

- Larger turfs will establish a reedbed more quickly.

- Positioning 1-m^2 turfs at 10-m spacings (100 turfs/ha) should achieve full cover within one year's growth, depending on conditions.

- By spacing 1-m^2 turfs in size at 25 m apart (9 turfs/ha) full cover should be achieved in 3–5 years, depending on conditions.

- Water levels may be in the range of just below the surface to 50 cm deep provided the turfs have long, intact reed stems.

- Bed preparation is less critical as turfs can be planted directly into arable, pasture or rough vegetation provided water levels can then be raised quickly to suppress competing plants.

- When transported or temporarily stored, turfs should be not be stacked one on top of the other. In this way the aerial stems are not damaged (these supply oxygen to the rhizomes if soil is saturated or flooded).

- The work is best done in winter during draw-down of water levels.

Rhizome cuttings
This involves the planting of rhizome fragments usually collected from ditch clearing or digging out of an existing reed bed. Some commercial nurseries may supply cuttings (see Appendix 3 for addresses). It is a labour intensive technique but has been used widely for water treatment systems, eg Anglian Water's sewage treatment bed at Broxted (Coombes 1990) and for wildlife reedbeds, eg Woolhampton in Berkshire. The success of the technique has varied considerably although given the correct conditions and aftercare, should work well. The technique is illustrated in Figure 14. Points to consider include:

- Rhizomes should be dug up or collected in late winter, early spring, ie about March, before shoots sprout.

- Sections of undamaged rhizome with at least one internode, bearing either a lateral or terminal bud, should be used for planting. (Damaged rhizome may let in water and rot.)

**Figure 14
Technique for
planting rhizome
cuttings.**

**a) Dig up rhizomes
with a spade or
collect from spoil
heaps in early
spring (March)**

**b) Select rhizomes
with one
undamaged
internode and two
nodes with lateral
buds. Trim off
damaged surplus.
Rhizomes with a
terminal bud may
also be used.**

**c) Plant in
approximately
horizontal–45
degree angle so
that at least one
node is about 4
cm buried. Plant
in March–May at
about 4
cuttings/m².**

**d) Shallow flood
(2–5 cm) ensuring
cut end remains
above surface
water. Shoots
should appear in
May/June.**

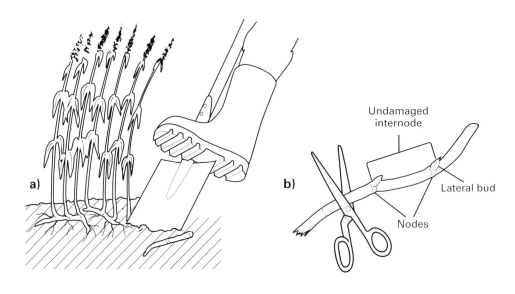

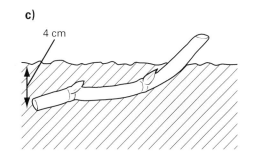

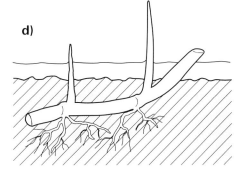

- Mineral soils and shallow flooding are the best conditions for planting.

- Rhizomes should be planted with one end raised above the water surface. (Total submersion may rot the rhizomes.)

- Better takes are achieved if planting is done in March/April.

- Expect a 20–25% reduction in take due to damage (Veber 1978).

- Planting density will depend upon the objective. As many as possible in a square metre will ensure full cover is achieved more quickly. The most commonly used range is 4–10.

- Planting in wet soil is recommended followed by shallow flooding. Water depths used have ranged from just below the surface to more than 50 cm surface depth, with good results.

In shallow water it was found that rhizome cuttings had a better chance of successfully developing if they were planted obliquely so that some of the cutting was above the water surface (Parr 1987).

At Pinkhill Meadows in Oxfordshire, rhizome cuttings were planted in trial plots prior to the main reedbed planting. The rhizomes were planted at approximately 5/m² and initially took well. The soil in which they were planted contained seeds of other wetland plants which grew rapidly and out-competed the reeds. At Woolhampton, the rhizomes were planted at 1/m² in waterlogged sand/gravel soil. The take was good especially in the depressions left by bulldozer tracks which retained 6–10 cm of water.

Planting cuttings with shoots attached
This is another labour intensive technique, which involves the digging up of actively growing shoots with rhizome attached. The method has been fully researched by Ekstam *et al* (1992) and is illustrated in Figure 15.

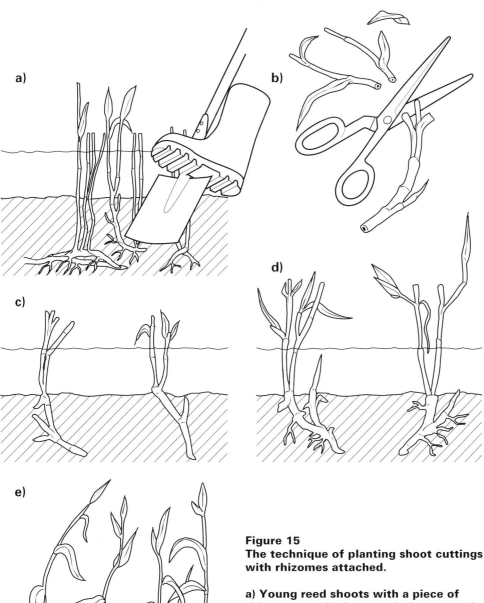

Figure 15
The technique of planting shoot cuttings with rhizomes attached.

a) Young reed shoots with a piece of rhizome attached are cut below ground surface in late May, early June.

b) Reduce the leaf area by trimming off upper portion.

c) Plant out immediately.

d) In July side shoots are formed at the nodes.

e) New shoot buds for the next growing season are formed from rhizomes in August.

Points to consider include:

- Use rhizomes 20–40 cm long, with shoots attached.

- Optimal planting period is May/June when the shoots are green with 2–4 leaves.

- Planting should be done immediately after digging up the rhizomes.

- Rhizomes with growing shoots are more tolerant of flooding (Parr 1987).

The technique has not been widely used to date, presumably because of the many limitations as summarised in Table 11. At Rutland Water in Leicestershire, rhizomes with buds and shoots attached were planted randomly (approximately 1 m apart) in wet mud or shallowly (< 10 cm) flooded mud in April of 1995. The rhizomes were collected from debris floating on the water after digging works by a Hymac. The take was variable.

d) Stem cuttings

This technique involves the cutting of a portion of a growing reed shoot and planting it in soft soil. If the conditions are right, it will produce roots and establish itself as a new plant from which new shoots will develop. Despite the take being relatively poor, usually around 40% (Peberdy pers comm), the method is quick and simple, enabling large numbers of shoots to be collected and planted out in a short space of time. At Greater Westhay in Somerset, takes of more than 70% were achieved with plantings in spring (Hancock pers comm).

Variations upon the basic technique have been used quite widely with equally varying degrees of success. More commonly, the last 20–50 cm of the stem is used (Ekstam *et al* 1992) although Bittman (1960) used shoots 80–120 cm long cut off below ground level. Parr (1987), used 25–40 cm cuttings with 1–6 nodes, noting that single node cuttings were rarely successful. Cuttings have been planted directly into wet soil or shallow-flooded soil, but Veber (1978), precultivated cuttings in nutrient water at 16–18 °C until roots developed

The use of stem cuttings is a simple and inexpensive technique for establishing a reedbed. However, it requires considerable labour input and may cause disturbance to breeding wildlife.

10–20 days later, and then planted them outside.

At Westfield Pill in Dyfed, stem cuttings were used to establish a new reedbed on isolated marine mud. A good take was achieved and the reedbed has spread well since planting. At Slimbridge, 60 cm apical cuttings were planted in shallow water at 10–15 stems/m^2 (Merritt 1994). The shoots were collected from a nearby reedbed by volunteers and planted immediately. Despite 60% failing to establish, those that did were sufficient to create the small area of reed required (Peberdy pers comm). Conversely, stem cuttings failed to take at all on a trial plot at Pinkhill Meadows possibly as a result of competition with other plants introduced in top soil.

Because of the variations used in this technique, Figure 16 presents a general guideline based on the most commonly used methods.

Other points to consider include:

- Take rate varies according to time of planting.

    cuttings planted in late April
    ▶ 40% take (Peberdy pers comm)

    cuttings planted in May
    ▶ 35% take

    cuttings planted in July
    ▶ 25% take

    cuttings planted in August
    ▶ 2% take   (Parr 1987)

- Nutrient-rich water and/or soil increase the success rate and takes may be poor on peat soils.

- Trimming the leafy part of the upper stem increased the success rate (Parr 1987).

Table 11: Summary of advantages and disadvantages of establishment techniques

Technique	Advantages	Disadvantages	Technical Points
Seeds:	• Easy to handle	• Low viability/germination. Precise water levels required. Rainfall damage. High weed susceptibility	• Very variable take depending on environmental factors (10–90%)
Aerial	• Large areas can be established quickly	• High costs. Only feasible on large flat open areas	• Sow on wet muddy surface • 60,000–100,000 seeds/ha • Sow in spring
Hand	• Sowing can be accurately targeted • High densities achievable on small areas	• Labour intensive	• Sow on wet soil • Sow at 20–125 seeds/m^2 • Sow along contours on undulating surface
Drilling	• Sowing precise, therefore low wastage • Enables large scale/ commercial establishment • Increased take	• High cost of equipment for one-off usage • Requires flat ground/ large areas	• Firm ground needed to operate tractor & drill • Set for shallow sowing depth
Pot-grown:	• Easy to handle • 70–100% take • Commercially available • Planting targetable	• Labour intensive • High costs	• Draw-down necessary • Plant along contours • Plant at 1-m spacing or 4/m^2 • Shallow flood
Rhizomes: In soil	• Simple technique • May import valuable invertebrates	• High cost of transport for bulky material • Establishment often poor • May import unwanted plants • Requires heavy machinery	• Spread soil to 10–25 cm depth • Keep soil moist • Flood shallow when shoots emerge (2–5 cm)
Turfs	• Less material to transport therefore lower costs • Good take, up to 100% • Timing & water levels not critical	• Requires heavy machinery	• Turfs must be planted, not placed on surface • Draw-down necessary • Avoid damaging aerial shoots
Cuttings	• Uses 'waste' rhizomes from dredgings	• Variable take, often poor • Labour intensive • Critical water level control	• Use undamaged rhizomes • Rhizomes should have 1 or 2 nodes • Plant 4 cm deep with one end exposed to air • Flood when shoots emerge
Cuttings & Shoots	• Tolerant of flooding • Good take, usually 100%	• Labour intensive • Precise technique • Done during bird nesting period	• Dig rhizomes of 20–40 cm and shoots • Plant immediately
Stem cuttings:	• Easy to collect • Simple technique	• Labour intensive • Done during bird nesting season • Take variable (up to 70%)	• May–June • Cut top 20+ cm (up to a maximum of 60 cm) • Plant immediately in soft mud with/without shallow water • Plant 10–15 stems/m^2 minimum

▶

Table 11 cont'd

Technique	Advantages	Disadvantages	Technical Points
Expansion: 'Natural' expansion	● Low costs ● Usually good take ● Natural development of animals and plants	● Can be slow over large areas ● Requires raising water levels ● Requires reed to be already present	
Layering expansion	● Low costs ● Thickens sparse reed ● Enhances rate of already present	● Labour intensive ● Only feasible on small areas ● Requires reed to be ● Disturbance to breeding wildlife	● Requires draw-down *or* exposed soil ● Carry out in summer when stems long but before panicle develops

Figure 16
The technique of stem cutting.

a) ● **In May, cut shoots of 20–50 cm length.**

   ● **Include 2–6 nodes if possible.**

   ● **Cut at an angle to produce 'quills'.**

NB: Longer shoots with more nodes may be used after May although the later it gets the lower the take (Parr 1987). Shoots may be harvested in large quantities using scythes or reciprocators but brushcutters are best avoided because they smash the ends.

b) ● **In very soft soils the 'quills' can be pushed into the ground or into a slot cut with a spade.**

   ● **Ensure at least two nodes are buried, more on longer cuttings, and that at least one node is above the surface of the water on flooded soils.**

   ● **Plant at 10–15 cuttings/m^2.**

   ● **New roots and side shoots should have developed by August.**

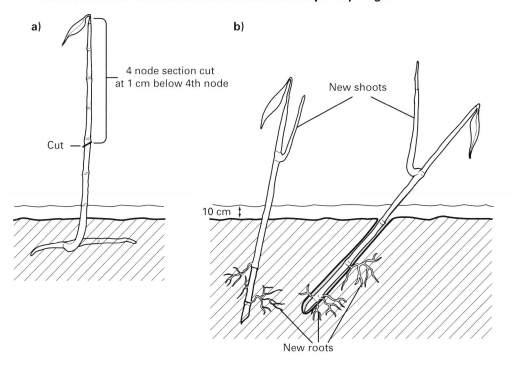

3.4 Aftercare

Whichever technique is used for planting reed, considerable aftercare to increase survival will be necessary. There are three main problems, two of which may need to be dealt with:

- competition from unwanted plants

- grazing from animals

- weather.

3.4.1 Unwanted plants

By far the greatest cause of failure or poor establishment of reed is competition from other plants. The usual methods for dealing with this are:

- controlled surface flooding (1–5 cm depth, at least top third of reed plants should be above the surface of the water)

- herbicides (see section 2.3.3)

- manual removal.

Shallow flooding is an effective method for controlling flood-intolerant plants such as rosebay willowherb, nettle and thistle which may persist in the soil's seed bank (see also section 3.3.1 a). If the site was previously marshland, shallow flooding may encourage plants such as reed sweet-grass, rushes and sedges at the expense of the newly planted reeds. Another potential problem with shallow flooding is that wave action produced by winds can damage seedlings.

The use of herbicides is another possible solution although great care must be taken to avoid contact with the reed seedlings. The use of a weed wiper system can resolve this. If herbicide spraying is anticipated, planting the reeds in rows spaced at least 1 m apart will facilitate operation of a knapsack sprayer (Figure 20 in Part 2), which should permit approximately 70% of unwanted plants to be controlled. The remainder would have to be dealt with manually.

At Rutland Water in Leicestershire frequent removal of competing plants by hand proved to be very effective and ensured the reedbed established well (Appleton pers comm). Again, such treatment is really only practicable on small sites.

3.4.2 Grazing animals

Tender reed shoots are eaten by many types of grazing animals. Deer, geese, rabbits and livestock have all caused problems on planted reed areas. Cattle will even eat older, tougher shoots. Possible solutions include:

- **Over-planting.** It may be possible to compensate for losses from grazing by planting more than would normally be required to establish a reedbed. This would prove expensive if commercially produced pot-grown plants were used, but if an abundant supply of seed,

rhizomes or cut stems is freely available, it could be an option.

- **Fencing.** Standard wire-mesh fencing could be erected against rabbits and deer which should allow sufficient time for the seedlings to establish. Temporary electric flexinets may also be used but problems with current shorting on wet vegetation can easily render them ineffective (Andrews pers comm). If invasion by livestock is likely to be a problem, the erection of proper stock fencing is advised.

- **Netting.** The use of nets to keep off grazing birds such as geese, coot and ducks is possible but highly impractical and not especially effective. Difficulty may also be experienced removing the nets once the shoots have begun to grow through them and their presence would make manual weed control virtually impossible.

- **Deep water.** The construction of marginal ditches as described in 3.2.2 b will act as deep water barriers to rabbits and if large enough, deer. If these animals are likely to be a problem in a particular area it is worth considering this at the design stage. Ditches 2 m wide x 1 m deep should be sufficient to keep out rabbits but deer are good swimmers and will only be deterred. Nevertheless, the larger the ditch, the greater the deterrent factor for deer, eg 3 m wide x 2 m deep.

- **Trees and tall vegetation.** Geese require quite large unobstructed approaches for flighting in and out of an area. Small plots, therefore, are less likely to receive attention from geese than large ones, and if there is an enclosing boundary of trees such as marginal carr woodland, geese may be inhibited from flighting in. Even tall soft vegetation can act as a deterrent. (At Minsmere reed is cut in small plots leaving uncut reed on all edges partly for this reason (Robinson pers comm)).

At Rutland Water in Leicestershire, new shoots on recently planted reed turfs suffered grazing by Canada geese in the spring of 1995. Those turfs situated close to a high bund were left untouched by the geese, presumably because of reduced visibility/increased predation risk.

3.4.3 Weather

Heavy rainfall can flatten seedlings and wash away seed. Late frosts may damage or kill young shoots (see section 2.3.2), but efforts to protect shoots using straw mulch usually only succeed in inhibiting shoot growth. In reality, planted reed is at the mercy of the weather. The use of turfs, rhizomes with shoots attached and stem cuttings will lessen the likelihood of weather associated problems. Drying out may also be a problem, however, so access to water through the summer is critical.

3.5 Water Treatment Systems

3.5.1 Background

Population growth and increased industrialisation have led to a marked increase in the amount of potentially polluting substances which need to be disposed of as safely as possible. Concern over the pollution of waterways and the oceans they eventually feed in to, has led to higher standards being required for the discharge of effluents.

Most domestic and industrial effluents require some treatment prior to discharge into the environment, but effective treatment systems can be very expensive. A summary of the stages of treatment of effluents is given by Merritt (1994). Some industrial effluents contain specific pollutants requiring special processes to remove them, such as incineration or recovery and recycling of by-products.

Because of increasing costs of treatment, related to more stringent regulations, low-cost treatment systems have been sought. The use of constructed wetlands, especially reedbed systems, has become popular because of their ability to break down many organic and some inorganic materials.

In the UK, virtually all the water service companies have constructed wetlands for treating sewage, both raw and pretreated. Most systems are small and have been designed to deal with point-source pollution such as:

- industrial processes effluents

- domestic sewage/drain water/storm flows

- agricultural effluents, eg dairy yard washings

- others, eg airport run-way run-off, collections of ornamental ducks.

Non-point source, or diffuse pollution, such as fertiliser run-off from arable farmland, waste-tip seepage, cannot be provided for so effectively, although a degree of indirect influence may come from natural wetlands that receive water enriched in this way. The absence of controls in such systems means that not all the polluted water will be treated. Nevertheless, reed-filled ditches, reed fringes on rivers and along the edges of some waste tips (eg Lodmoor in Dorset) undoubtedly benefit water quality in the environment.

The RSPB's project to create a large reedbed at Ham Wall in Somerset (Case Study 13) will examine the ability of the system to break down pollutants, particularly nutrients, simply by measuring the quality of the water before and after passing through the reedbed. This may give an indication of the effectiveness of such wetlands to clean water passively.

In the USA, wetlands have been constructed to deal with agricultural non-point source pollution from pig farms, crop run-off and livestock wastewater treatment. Most involve the use of constructed grasslands, ponds and emergent marshes (Hammer 1992). Similarly, in California, a combined marsh and forest system of some 37 ha has been constructed to make use of treated effluent, the primary purpose being for wildlife and recreational use (James and Bogaert 1989).

In the UK, wetlands have been constructed mostly to treat point-source pollution with only a handful of 'wetland' designs, the majority utilising pure reedbed treatment systems.

Reed and other wetland plants are able to break-down many pollutants in water. This has been used to treat effluents from a range of sources. A brief overview of the design and functioning is given.

The precise mechanism of how wetlands break down pollutants is unclear but probably involves a range of chemical and physical processes which will be influenced by temperature, acidity and other environmental and physical factors. Ways in which they function may include:

- The plants, leaf litter and soil provide attachment sites for bacteria and other micro-organisms involved in the break-down of pollutants.

- Oxygen is transferred from the atmosphere by the aerial parts of plants, through their roots and into the soil spaces. Bacteria that require oxygen (aerobic) utilise this source in the break-down of substances. In parts of the soil where oxygen is not present, live bacteria that do not require oxygen (anaerobic) to break down substances.

- The alternation of aerobic and anaerobic bacterial processes can efficiently break down many pollutants (Harvey pers comm).

- Some plants directly absorb/adsorb nutrients and metals.

- Certain soil fungi are capable of breaking down many synthetic chemicals such as lindane, PCBs, dioxins and chlorinated carbons (Hudson 1992).

- Soil particles (mineral and organic) act as filters of particulate matter, both physically and chemically.

- Suspended solids in surface flows are composted in the litter layer.

- The rhizomes of reeds grow vertically and horizontally opening up the soil to create pathways for water movement.

(Adapted from Merritt 1994 and Cooper *et al* 1990)

3.5.2 Combined systems and overland flow

Water treatment systems that utilise a mixture of vegetation types can effectively remove pollutants while providing a valuable area for wildlife. In addition, they have aesthetic and educational value.

Such a system has been constructed by the Wildfowl & Wetlands Trust at Slimbridge (**Case Study 16**) to clean up water contaminated with bird faeces and other pollutants from the wildfowl enclosures. It comprises an overland flow, cascade and pool system with a mixture of plant types. The cleaned effluent is channelled into a series of created features specifically for wildlife.

Overland flow systems are generally not favoured for industrial effluents because the surface water does not reach the root zone where the break-down of pollutants occurs (Cooper *et al* 1990). However, the Wildfowl & Wetlands Trust have had considerable success with their systems.

The advantages of overland flow are described by Merritt (1994) as:

- easier to construct; less demanding in terms of sediment requirements and a simpler in-flow structure

- potentially easier to maintain; surface flooding prevents colonisation by most unwanted plants

- more closely resembling a natural reedbed and therefore offers better quality wildlife habitat.

Yorkshire Water have experimented with using reedmace, reed canary-grass and reed sweet-grass, sometimes in combination with reed, with variable results in terms of efficiency of sewage treatment. Their overland flow systems were designed to work with 10 cm of surface water in combination with conventional treatment systems, but experienced problems during storm flows (Merritt 1994).

3.5.3 Reedbed water treatment systems

The majority of constructed reedbeds for water treatment systems are based on the original design by Kikuth (1970) and subsequently refined by the experiences of many organisations throughout Europe (Cooper 1990).

By 1990, some 500 systems had been built in western Europe and there have been many more since. Some early systems in Germany have been operating successfully for more than 20 years. One of the first to be constructed in the UK was at Acle in Norfolk by Anglian Water in 1985 (Coombes 1990). By 1989 there were at least 26 systems in the UK (Cooper *et al* 1990) with approximately 150 completed by 1995.

a) Types

There are two principal variations upon the basic theme, that of horizontal flow (Figure 17) and of vertical flow (Figure 18).

Figure 17 Horizontal flow water treatment reedbed. (Source: Cooper 1990; permission WRc)

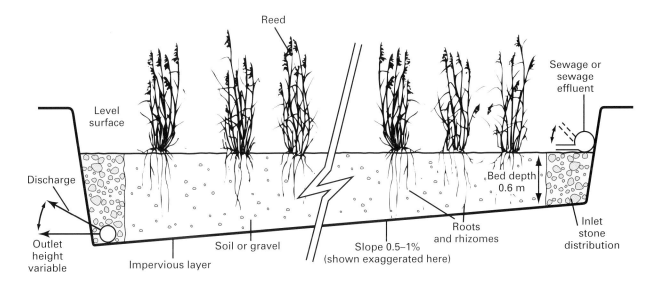

Figure 18 Vertical flow water treatment reedbed. (Source: Cooper 1990; permission WRc and Camphill Village Trust)

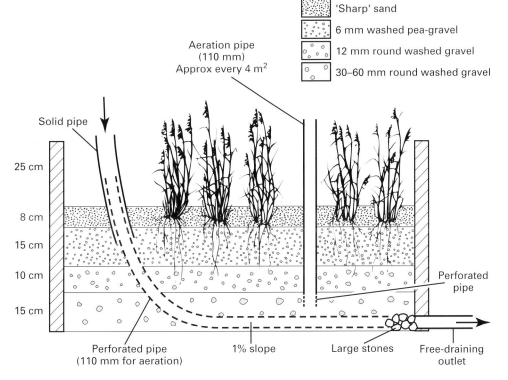

Horizontal flow

The process depends upon the passage of effluent horizontally through a bed of soil or gravel in which reed is growing (Cooper 1990). Variations upon this theme lie principally in:

● surface profiles (level or sloping bed)

● use of soil, gravel or other material

● inlet and outlet arrangements

● reed planting techniques.

Design criteria and construction are detailed in Cooper (1990). However, there are certain fundamental points to be considered. Most systems utilise effluent which has undergone some pretreatment and areas of reedbed generally equate to population equivalent (pe) values. For storm flow reedbeds Green (1994) recommends $0.5 \, m^2/pe$ and $1 \, m^2/pe$ for tertiary treatment (Green and Upton 1994). For settled sewage an area of $5 \, m^2/pe$ is recommended. It is usually necessary to line the bed with an impermeable plastic, eg Monarflex, high density polyethylene or other material such as puddled clay or bentonite clay (eg NaBento). Pot-grown seedlings have been widely used to establish the reedbed usually planted at a density of $4/m^2$ in May or June.

Vertical flow

The principle here is that the effluent is introduced to the system through a perforated pipe passing through the root zone and layers of graded gravel by gravity (Figure 18). On its way most of the suspended solids and organic matter are removed. One potential draw-back of the system is that effluent may by-pass the root zone and not be subjected to the same degree of treatment as that which does not. The use of vertical flow in combination with horizontal flow systems effects a more complete treatment, the construction and design of which is detailed by Cooper (1990).

A system developed in Australia is based on a vertical flow bed but utilises a reverse flow principle where effluent is introduced at the base and pushed up through the soil or gravel ensuring maximum exposure to the root zone of the reeds (Brett 1989). Figure 19 is a schematic representation of the system. A similar system has been employed by British Steel at Llanwern in Gwent where experimental beds are being developed to treat site-produced sewage and pretreated 0.5% ammonia liquor from the coking plant (Harvey pers comm). It is used in combination with standard horizontal flow beds, producing a total of 18 ha of reedbed.

Storm water systems

Periods of sudden high rainfall can produce large flows of storm water which may overload a sewage treatment works causing effluent of unsuitable quality to discharge into water courses. Storage tanks are usually used to hold storm water for treatment later on. Severn Trent Water have developed a reedbed system which deals with storm water events for sewage works serving small communities of not more than 2,000 people (Green 1994). Designs are similar to the tertiary reedbed systems described by Green and Upton (1994), being based on a horizontal flow system. A constructed reedbed of the required size in terms of pe is positioned in the sewage works so that it takes in storm flow water, usually after primary screening. The reedbed may be separate and for storm flow only or included in the system as an on-line tertiary treatment, treating storm flows when required.

Figure 19
Reverse flow, vertical water treatment reedbed. Pre-treated effluent is introduced at the base of the bed and passes upwards towards the outlet. This ensures that all the effluent is exposed to the root zone, thus maximising the break-down of pollutants.

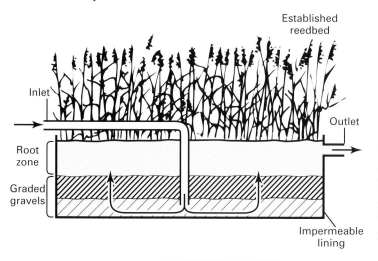

b) How effective are they?

Many parameters of effectiveness of reedbed treatment systems have been measured but the most important in ecological terms are:

- BOD (Biochemical Oxygen Demand)

- N (nitrogen, especially nitrate)

- P (phosphorus, especially phosphate).

Other pollutants such as metals, pathogenic bacteria and suspended solids may be assessed depending on the nature of the effluent being treated and the discharge limits being sought.

The results achieved have varied from site to site even where very similar systems have been used. Some values are given for Slimbridge (Case Study 16). ICI's treatment reedbed at Billingham (**Case Study 17**) is designed to operate at 95% reduction in pollutants. Cooper *et al* (1990) reviewed the then current situation in the UK and concluded that BOD and suspended solids were dealt with well but that P and N removal were barely significant. However, as the bacterial population adapted to the conditions, performance appeared to improve with time. It is conceivable that more natural reedbeds may perform better in this respect and a study of that at Ham Wall in Somerset (Case Study 13) is in progress. A reduction in performance may occur during winter when the reedbed is less active.

Adaptation or 'conditioning' of the reed may be necessary to establish an active system. Experimental work at Llanwern in Gwent has shown that initial exposure of the new reed to foul effluent such as coking ammonia can knock back the reed, which to all intents and purposes appears to have died. However, it quickly recovers, the regrowth being resistant to the effluent and able to break it down (Harvey pers comm).

Severn Trent Water use reedbed systems for tertiary treatment of domestic sewage from population centres of up to 2,000 as a matter of policy. By 1994, the Company had over 100 sewage works with reedbeds and the target by the year 2000 is 470

(Green pers comm). They have found that reedbeds are effective at polishing secondary effluents of widely varying quality comparable with the best conventional treatment plants (Green 1993). Performance data for five of the beds is given in Green and Upton (1994) which indicates BOD reductions of 77–88%, suspended solids reduction of up to 87%, total nitrogen reductions of 7–97% and phosphate reductions of 0–35%.

Hudson (1992), reported BOD, N and P reductions of 99%, 70% and 56% respectively for a system at Othfresen in Germany which has been in operation since 1974.

c) Advantages

There is little doubt that the main driving force behind the use of reedbeds for water treatment is one of cost. Cooper *et al* (1990) summarise the principal advantages as:

- low capital costs

- low maintenance costs

- simple construction design

- robust process able to withstand a wide range of operating conditions

- environmentally acceptable with potential for wildlife conservation

The main disadvantages are the large land area requirement and the lead-in time for reed establishment, typically three years although possibly longer for very difficult effluents (Hudson 1992).

With large projects such as ICI's Billingham reedbed and British Steel's Llanwern project the capital costs can be high, often comparable with conventional treatment systems (Smith pers comm). However, the experimental nature of the Llanwern project means that design modifications with time necessarily add to costs (Harvey pers comm). Green and Upton (1994), compared capital costs of constructing reedbeds with those of conventional modular sand filters for different population sizes and concluded that reedbeds are cheaper in both capital and running costs for populations of less than 2,000.

By way of comparison, ICI's Billingham reedbed equates to £400,000/ha whilst Severn Trent Water's tertiary beds range from £300,000–£1,000,000/ha. However, Severn Trent Water's beds rarely exceed 2,000 m^2 area, ie some £60,000–£200,000.

The life expectancy of reedbeds ranges from 20 years (Green and Upton 1994) to 100 years (Hudson 1992) although perpetuation could theoretically be achieved by rotational systems of two or more beds on a 30-year basis (Smith pers comm).

d) Wildlife benefits

Because of the relatively recent development of reedbed water treatment systems in the UK, their use by wildlife has not been studied in depth and may require more time for specific communities of plants and animals to colonise. However, records have been kept for ICI Billingham and are presented in Case Study 17. Casual bird surveys have been undertaken at British Steel's Llanwern site, which has an adjacent wetland, created when material for bunding the water treatment reedbed was excavated. This supports a range of common waterbirds. The reedbed itself supported breeding lapwings, yellow wagtails and redshank and feeding snipe and jack snipe when the reed was first planted. The reed is now well established and supports around 15 pairs each of reed warblers, sedge warblers and reed buntings, representing about a seven-fold increase on numbers previously present.

Both the above mentioned reedbeds are large, unlike the majority of other water treatment reedbeds, which tend to be less than 0.25 ha. This limits their potential value for wildlife generally as the range of habitats will be small and unsuitable for species with large home ranges, such as breeding bittern. In addition, most horizontal flow and vertical flow systems function best without surface water, and therefore lack the aquatic environment needed to establish some of the important food chains within a reedbed.

Nevertheless, small areas of dry reed will support a range of invertebrates and some birds, possibly small mammals too. An indication of the kinds of wildlife a 0.25-ha reedbed might support is given in Table 12, although a great deal will depend on the ability of these species to colonise and the nature of adjacent habitats.

Table 12: Wildlife that may be supported by a small, dry reedbed of 0.25 ha

- Up to 4 pairs of breeding reed warblers*

- 1 or 2 pairs of breeding reed buntings*

- 1 pair of breeding sedge warblers

- 1 pair of breeding wrens

- 1 feeding, possibly nesting pair of moorhens

- Feeding bearded tits in winter

- Breeding harvest mice

- Feeding, possibly breeding short-tailed voles

- A range of invertebrates (vital to support most of the above and some uncommon species may colonise if a population, nearby).

* Prefer presence or proximity of water

In order to enhance the wildlife value of water treatment reedbeds, they should be designed to replicate the features of existing natural reedbeds and include features such as those illustrated in Figure 20a and b which should not reduce the efficacy of the system. In addition, the following should be considered (Merritt 1994):

- large size - within the constraint of land availability and cost, 'oversizing' the reedbed should improve its efficiency in terms of water treatment and increase opportunities for wildlife and the inclusion of features that benefit wildlife.

- areas of open water within and adjacent to the reeds

- mixture of areas of dry and wet reedbed

- associated habitats, eg water, scrub, wet meadow adjacent.

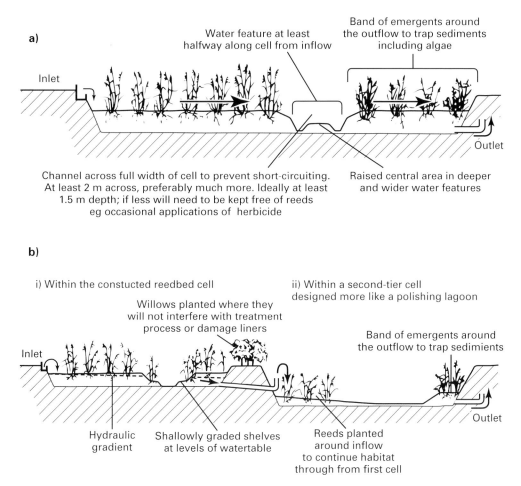

a)

Inlet

Water feature at least halfway along cell from inflow

Band of emergents around the outflow to trap sediments including algae

Outlet

Channel across full width of cell to prevent short-circuiting. At least 2 m across, preferably much more. Ideally at least 1.5 m depth; if less will need to be kept free of reeds eg occasional applications of herbicide

Raised central area in deeper and wider water features

b)

i) Within the constucted reedbed cell

ii) Within a second-tier cell designed more like a polishing lagoon

Willows planted where they will not interfere with treatment process or damage liners

Band of emergents around the outflow to trap sedimients

Inlet

Outlet

Hydraulic gradient

Shallowly graded shelves at levels of watertable

Reeds planted around inflow to continue habitat through from first cell

Figure 20
Examples of ways to modify water treatment reedbeds to enhance their value for wildlife. (Source: Merritt 1994; permission from WWT)

a) Overland flow system

b) Sub-surface flow system eg horizontal

Part 4
CASE STUDIES

Contents

A. MANAGEMENT AND REHABILITATION

B. CREATION

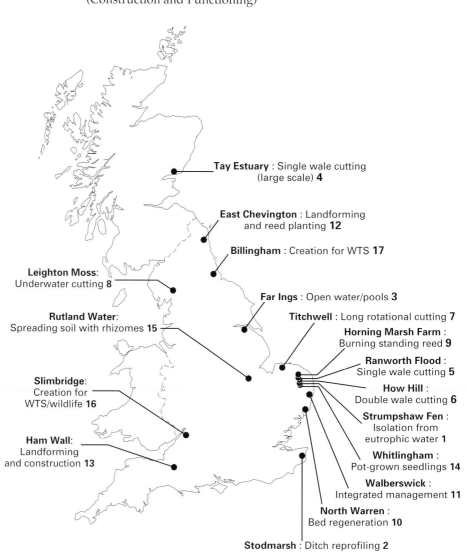

Strumpshaw Fen

(RSPB)

Location:	Strumpshaw, Norfolk OS 1:50,000 sheet No 134 GR TG 341066
Area:	197 ha total 82 ha reedbed

Objectives:
To maintain and enhance the quality of the reed and associated habitats for the benefit of wildlife

Techniques:
WATER QUALITY: ISOLATION FROM EUTROPHIC WATER (section 2.2.2 a) (Provision of an Alternative Supply)

Background

The fen lies in the River Yare floodplain. As with all the true Broads, Strumpshaw Broad resulted from peat digging in Medieval times. Subsequent rising sea levels caused extensive flooding, creating areas of open water with reedbed habitats closely associated. Regular inundation of the fen and Broad by the eutrophic and sediment-laden waters of the River Yare led to a gradual in-filling of the Broad and an alteration of the composition of plants and animals (Tickner *et al* 1991). The reed quality declined and the reedbeds became dry in summer.

So serious was the decline in wildlife value that isolation of the reserve from the polluted river and suction dredging of the Broad were seen as the best options for rehabilitation.

Isolation from Water Supply

- In 1978, a dam was constructed at the outflow of the Broad Dyke (Figure 1) by excavating 2,000 tonnes of silt from the river using a pontoon dredger. This prevented river water flowing up the dyke and onto the surrounding fen and Broad. A second small dam was built in the river embankment adjacent to the Sandy Wall (Figure 1).

- Following an increase in numbers and diversity of wildlife in the Broad, between 1979 and 1981 all remaining dykes leading from the river to the fen were dammed. The height of Broad Dyke dam was raised after settling had occurred. Following a levelling survey, low points along 700 m of the existing embankment were heightened using river dredgings.

- In 1979, a bund was constructed along the edge of the Lackford Run (Figure 1). This prevented nutrient enriched water entering the reedbed at high tides.

- In 1981 and 1982, spoil from dyke clearance was added to the embankments to raise them after initial settling. This was repeated in 1988. In 1983, installation of a drop-board sluice enabled effective water level control.

- In 1995, work was undertaken by the NRA further to upgrade the flood defence wall. This has enabled more water to be retained on the reedbed in winter

and reduced the frequency of over-topping by the River on surge tides.

By 1980, 120 ha had been isolated from the river in this block. Similar work on Surlingham Church Marsh and elsewhere on the reserve means that a total of 188 ha of fen and open water has been isolated by 1995.

Provision of Alternative Supply

- Subsequent to isolation from the river, summer water levels within the reedbed fell by 1 m, exacerbated by localised groundwater abstraction for domestic water supply.

- A hydrological study commissioned in 1987 to assess the impact of abstraction on the reedbed revealed it caused a 27% deficit in water requirements.

- The use of river water to compensate for the deficit was considered undesirable because of the concentration of nutrients. However, in winter when the river is in flood and dilution of nutrients is greatest, water is taken onto the fen (Tickner *et al* 1991). Levels are maintained as high as possible throughout the winter to minimise the summer deficit.

- A borehole was sunk in 1987 by Anglian Water adjacent to the reedbed and low-nutrient groundwater was abstracted according to the regime shown in Table 1. The water was used to compensate for the summer deficit.

Wildlife Benefits

A combination of improved water quality and reedbed management has had significant wildlife benefits as summarised in Table 2.

Table 1: Water regime at Strumpshaw Fen

- High winter and spring levels of 25–50 cm.

- Gradual lowering of levels by evapotranspiration in early summer.

- Supplemented with borehole water throughout summer to maintain shallow surface levels (usually May–August/September).

- After reedcutting, raise levels in autumn/winter.

Pumping borehole water at > 30 l/s draws in saline fossil water, which is undesirable. Hence, the continued use of winter flooding with river water. This provides only a short-term solution to the summer deficit problem because the location of the borehole further depletes the supply for the site.

Table 3: Dyke flora recovery on Strumpshaw: the presence of pollution tolerant (T) and intolerant (I) aquatic plants

Species	1976	1979	1980	1986	1990
Yellow water-lily	T	T	T	T	T
Common water starwort	T	T	T	T	-
Filamentous algae	T	-	-	T	T
Fennel pondweed	T	-	-	T	-
Rigid hornwort		T	T	T	T
Common duckweed			T	T	T
Canadian pondweed		TI	TI	TI	-
Curled pondweed		TI	TI	TI	-
Frogbit		TI	TI	TI	-
Horned pondweed		TI	TI	TI	-
Spiked water milfoil			TI	TI	TI
Amphibious bistort			TI	TI	TI
Cowbane				TI	TI
Sweet flag				TI	TI
Common water crowfoot		I	I	I	-
Stoneworts		I	I	I	-
Greater bladderwort			I	I	I
Ivy-leaved duckweed			I	I	I
Small pondweed				I	I
Branched bur-reed				I	-
Water starwort (*Callitriche palustris*)					I
Water starwort (*C platycarpa*)					I
White water-lily					I
Water dock					I
Greater spearwort					I
Lesser reedmace					I

(Adapted from Tickner *et al* 1991.)

Table 2: Summary of wildlife benefits since isolation from the river

Wildlife	Comments
Aquatic plants	Increased from 4 to 17 species (see Figure 2).
Reed	Increased in quantity and vigour.
Marsh pea	Increased numbers, distribution and sets viable seed.
Milk parsley	Increased numbers and distribution.
Meadow rue	Increased on fen areas.
Fenn's wainscot moth} Flame wainscot moth } Rush wainscot moth }	Generally benefited from improved quality of reedbed habitats.
Marsh carpet moth	Benefits from increased meadow rue.
Swallowtail butterfly	Benefits from increased milk parsley. Sightings of adults increased from about three per year in the 1970s to 45+ per day in the 1990s.
Dragonflies	Increased from six to 18 species with 10 species thought to breed.
Bittern	Regularly overwinters. Occasional 'boomers' but breeding not proven up to 1995.
Bearded tits	Up to 100 winter (feed on increased reed seed production). Breeding since 1978 with about 10 pairs annually.
Marsh harrier	First bred 1980, now up to three pairs annually.
Savi's warbler Cetti's warbler Reed warbler	Bred in three out of 15 years. First bred 1974, up to 10 males by 1994. Greatly increased numbers of these and all insect-eating, reedbed birds.
Eel	Recruitment reduced by isolation. 1994–96, 3,000 4 g eels/year were successfully introduced.
Other fish and amphibians	Roach, bream, rudd, perch, tench and pike now present. Amphibians recolonised quickly, but not attained pre-1950 numbers.

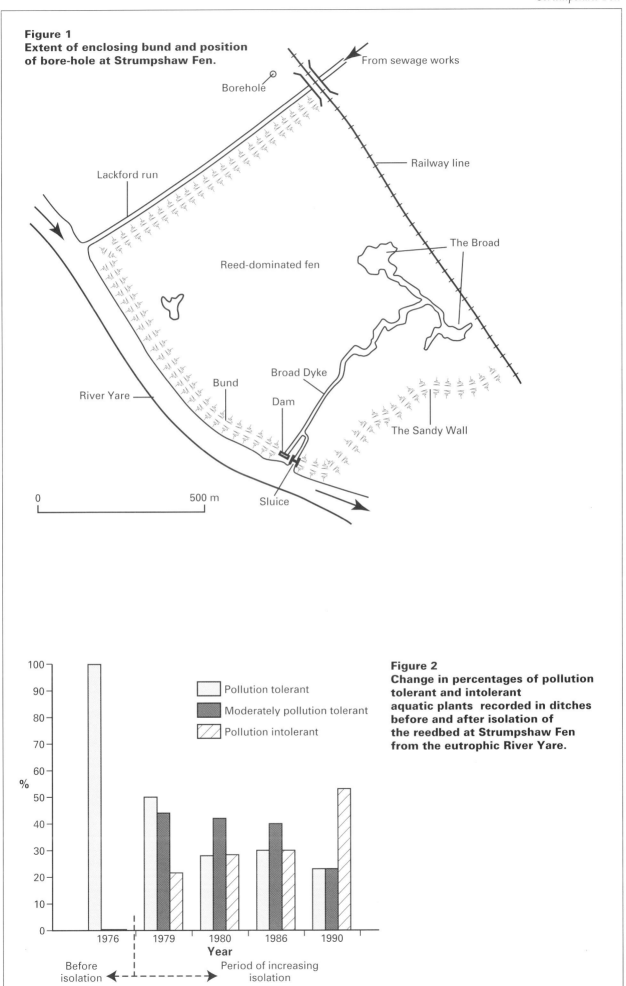

Figure 1
Extent of enclosing bund and position of bore-hole at Strumpshaw Fen.

Borehole

From sewage works

Railway line

Lackford run

The Broad

Reed-dominated fen

Broad Dyke

Bund

Dam

The Sandy Wall

River Yare

Sluice

0   500 m

Figure 2
Change in percentages of pollution tolerant and intolerant aquatic plants recorded in ditches before and after isolation of the reedbed at Strumpshaw Fen from the eutrophic River Yare.

Pollution tolerant

Moderately pollution tolerant

Pollution intolerant

%

Year

1976   1979   1980   1986   1990

Before isolation

Period of increasing isolation

Stodmarsh

Case Study 2

(**English Nature**)

Location:	Stodmarsh, Kent
	OS 1:50,000 sheet No 179
	GR TR 2261
Area:	166 ha total
	77 ha reedbed

Objectives:
To manage and enhance the wildlife value of the site. To improve the ditches as a feeding habitat for bitterns.

Techniques:
DITCH REPROFILING (section 2.2.3 d)
Rotational Cutting (section 2.3.1 a)

Background

Originally a drained floodplain now largely protected by a flood wall on the River Great Stour. Chislet Colliery opened at the beginning of this century and coal was mined until 1968. The mining operation caused subsidence, which lowered the land causing water-logging and creation of marshland. Reed encroached from the river edge and ditches to produce a wetland of reedbeds with open water and ditches.

In 1985, an additional clay bund was constructed to join with the old Lampen Wall so that an area of approximately 35 ha of reedbed has been enclosed where control over water levels is achievable. Summer levels here are in the range of 7–30 cm. Scrub invasion has been checked by removal and raised water levels and a programme of 10–15 year rotational cutting on fixed blocks throughout the site reduces litter accumulation on a proportion of the reedbed and maintains reed quality. The ditches are mostly wide and deep with steep sides yet support good flora and fauna; the site boasts 15 species of dragonfly. Nevertheless, the ditch profiles were not considered ideal for feeding bitterns, birds which once bred on the site, and in 1994 work began on a programme of reprofiling using funds from EN's Bittern Recovery Programme. Plate 1 shows a typical ditch before reprofiling.

Ditch Reprofiling

- Draw-down commenced early, in August, permitting access for the work to start before winter set in. Draw-down was complete so there was no surface water on the bed.

- The digger tracked over the standing reed, which acted as a mat preventing it from becoming bogged down on soft ground. In addition, an assistant walked ahead of the machine initially to identify difficult terrain in advance.

- The digger removed the old ditch-spoil lip and scraped back a 10-m wide corridor of material along 1,230 m of ditch edge. This produced a graded edge of about 1:30. Figure 1 shows the profile and plan of the design.

- Small 'ponds' were created every 50 m to enhance the wildlife value.

- In addition, 1,300 m of ditch edge was given a shallow edge by old spoil removal and slight grading, mostly on banks opposite to the work described above. No scraped corridor was added. This would be suitable for digger access for future ditch management work.

- Spoil from excavation work was used to construct off-set banks about 10 m in from the ditch edge (Plate 2). The banks were provided with frequent gaps to allow the free passage of water and fish (Figure 1d and Plate 3).

- The four blocks managed in this way were cut and burned and will be subject to a three-year rotational cutting programme.

- Some of the newly created reed margins will be cut biennially to provide a varied vegetation structure and the 'ponds' will be maintained as open water.

Wildlife Benefits

- The shallowly profiled ditch edges should provide encroaching reed margins suitable for breeding fish and feeding bitterns.

- The shallow water on the ditch margins will also provide habitat for aquatic invertebrates, many of which are an important food source for bearded tits which breed already, bitterns, reed warblers and Cetti's warblers.

- Both aquatic and emergent plants, including the nationally important marsh sow-thistle, should benefit greatly from provision of shallow ditch margins. In turn, the invertebrates associated with these will also benefit.

Figure 1
Ditch reprofiling at Stodmarsh NNR.

a) **Section through ditch before reprofiling**

b) **Section through reprofiled ditch**

c) **Plan of reprofiling programme**

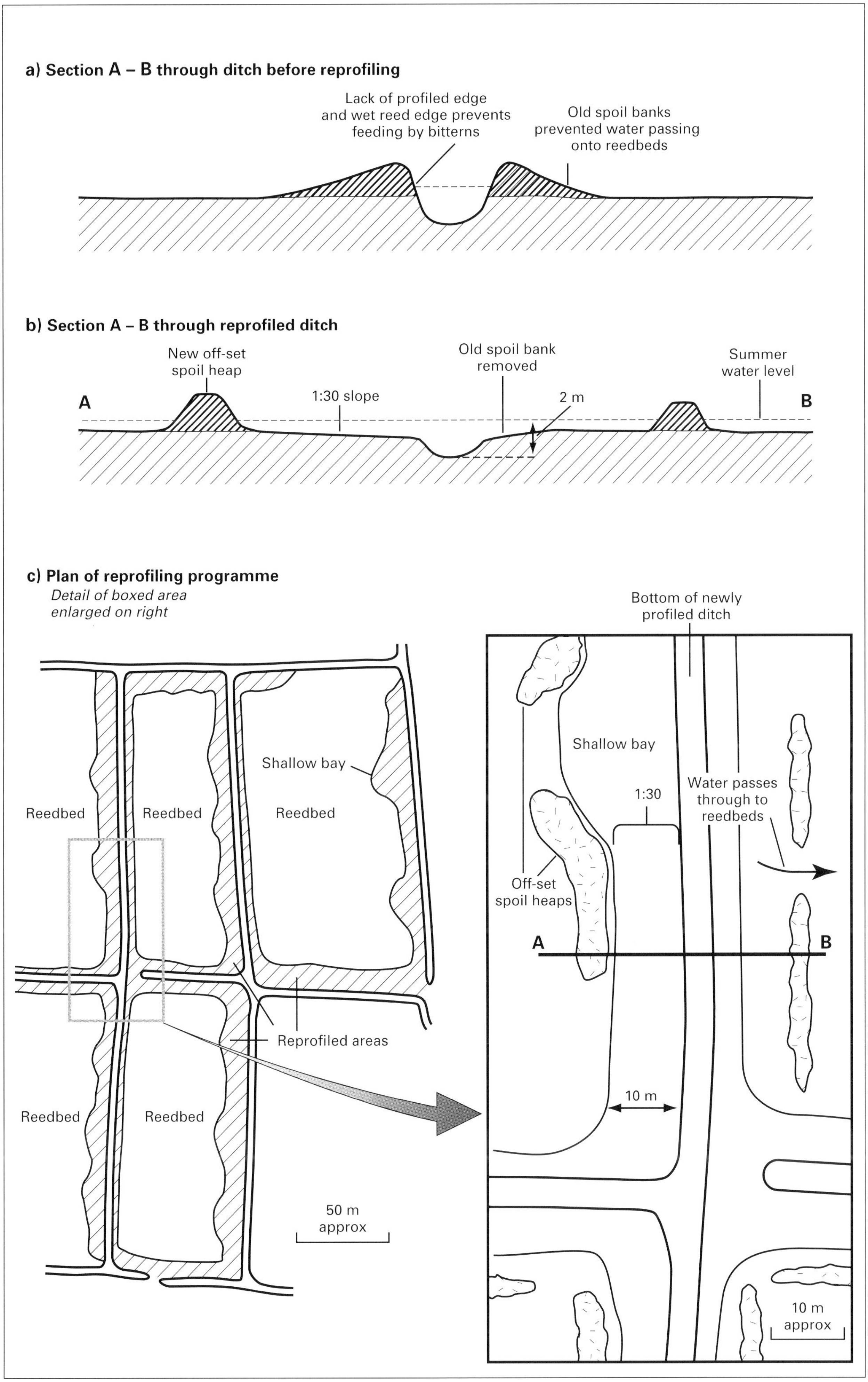

a) Section A – B through ditch before reprofiling

Lack of profiled edge
and wet reed edge prevents
feeding by bitterns

Old spoil banks
prevented water passing
onto reedbeds

b) Section A – B through reprofiled ditch

New off-set
spoil heap

Old spoil bank
removed

Summer
water level

A

1:30 slope

2 m

B

c) Plan of reprofiling programme
*Detail of boxed area
enlarged on right*

Reedbed

Reedbed

Shallow bay

Reedbed

Reedbed

Reedbed

Reprofiled areas

50 m
approx

Bottom of newly
profiled ditch

Shallow bay

1:30

Water passes
through to
reedbeds

Off-set
spoil heaps

A

B

10 m

10 m
approx

Table 1: Machinery and costings

A digger and driver were contracted to do the work. A Case Poclain, tracked machine with a 6-m jib and 1-m bucket was used:

- Hourly rate was £17.25.

- A nine-hour day was usually worked.

- Mean cost was £1.38/m ditch edge worked.

- 80 m of reprofiled edge, scraped corridor and ponds could be done in a day which equated to £1.94/m. (Total 1,230m = £2,386)

- 220 m of reprofiled edge (old spoil removal) was achieved in a day equating to £0.70/m. (Total 1,300m = £910)

- In addition, transport charges were £200.

- Total cost works out at about £3,500.

NB: Costings are approximate and exclude VAT.

P Burnham

Plate 1 Steep sided ditch before reprofiling

P Burnham

Plate 3 Ditch reprofiled on both sides, showing gaps left in spoil banks to enable water to flow onto the reedbed (shown after cutting) ▼

Plate 2 Ditch reprofiled on one side (left) with offset spoil banks. ▲

P Burnham

Far Ings

(Lincolnshire Trust for Nature Conservation)

Case Study 3

Location:	Barton-upon-Humber, Humberside OS 1:50,000 sheet No 112 GR TA 009231
Area:	Reedbed 7 ha Open Water 4 ha

Objectives:
Rehabilitation of the existing areas of reed to benefit the wildlife in general and to provide conditions associated with reedbed specialists such as bittern and bearded tit.

Techniques:
CREATION OF OPEN WATER (section 2.2.4 b)
Scrub Removal (section 2.3.5)
Double Wale Cutting (section 2.3.1 a)

Background

The reserve forms a part of the Barton and Barrow Clay Pits SSSI, which extends to a total of 149 ha of which 41 ha is reedbed. The pits are a series of old clay workings stretching for 8 km along the south bank of the River Humber. When the pits were abandoned early this century, they flooded naturally and were partially colonised by reed. Many years of neglect and dereliction followed until legal protection was granted in 1968. Now 10 of the 35 pits are nature reserves. The remaining pits have a variety of uses including coarse fishing, water sports and wildfowling (Kirby 1994).

The reserve is primarily rainfall fed, supplemented by artesian groundwater. Sluices at the outlets enable water level control. There is some seepage of salt water under the flood defence wall.

The aim to create a sustainable reedbed system throughout the SSSI is being led by the Lincolnshire Trust's 'Operation Bittern' which centres on implementing a management programme of rehabilitation of the degraded reedbeds by raising water levels, rotational reed cutting or burning, and pool creation (Grooby 1994). A major component of the rehabilitation programme has been the creation of shallow, interconnected pools designed to maximise reed/water edge to encourage breeding and wintering bitterns (Plate 3). Scrub removal by cutting and by winching (Figure 2) has also been carried out.

Creation of Pools

- Between 1993 and 1995, over 1,000 m of chains of pools were created (see Table 1) with the assistance of the NRA. Work began on digging more pools on other pits in the SSSI in 1994 with financial assistance from English Nature and the co-operation of owners.

- Pool creation was undertaken by the NRA contractors in January and February of each year after water levels had been drawn-down.

- As much of the reserve is deep water, heavy machinery can operate safely only from the causeways left in place from the clay workings' railway lines. This largely limits pool creation to reed adjacent to causeways.

- Scrub was coppiced along the causeways to enable digger access and reduce shading of the reedbed.

- A tracked, long-reach (15 m) digger with a wide bucket was used to excavate pools by removing 0.5–1 m of litter/soil (Plate 1). The aim was to achieve an adequate depth to maintain shallow water above the rhizomes in summer.

- Where feasible, spoil was dropped into deep water areas on the opposite side of the causeway to produce shallow marginal areas. Otherwise, spoil was used to consolidate the causeways.

- Pools of varying sizes were created as scalloped margins to the reedbed the largest approximately 30 m long by 5–8 m wide (Figure 1 and Plate 2 and 3).

Wildlife Benefits

- Reed rapidly encroached on the extensive marginal areas of the pools. This provided feeding and in some cases nesting habitat for shoveler, pochard, great crested and little grebes, mute swan, coot and mallard. The sheltered bays attract small fish and should provide feeding habitat for bittern. In addition, the pools are intended to provide feeding sites for bearded tit, a species which already breeds on the reserve.

- Regenerating the reed by cutting, burning and excavation has produced up to an eleven-fold increase in panicle weight. Bearded tits have been noted feeding on these during winter. An area cut double wale produces reed of thatching quality.

- The raising of water levels together with rotational cutting and burning should provide wet reedbed habitat for breeding bitterns. Bitterns last bred on the SSSI in 1979 and have wintered intermittently since then. One individual remained from November 1993–May 1994.

- Raised water levels and improved flow through the site has reduced the influence of saline seepage through/under the flood defence wall.

- The reserve supports important reedbed moths such as the silky wainscot, the fen wainscot and the brown-veined wainscot. Rotational cutting and burning together with non-intervention areas will ensure the survival of these species by improving and maintaining suitable habitat for both the adults and their stem-boring larvae.

Table 1: Estimated quantities of habitat feature produced by pool creation at Far Ings

Total length of chains of pools created	1,330 m
Total length of water/reed edge created	2,394 m
Total area of shallow water created	1.5 ha

Figure 1
Plan of Far Ings showing newly excavated reed margins to create shallow, open water (pools) with encroaching reed at the edges.

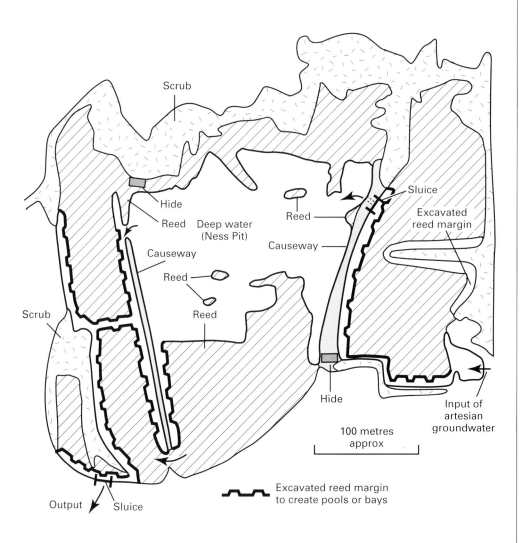

Plate 1 Long reach hydraulic digger excavating shallow pools along reedbed margin. The tractor and trailer transported spoil away where it was tipped into deep water areas to make them shallower.

Plate 2 A chain of 'bittern pools' on West Pit.

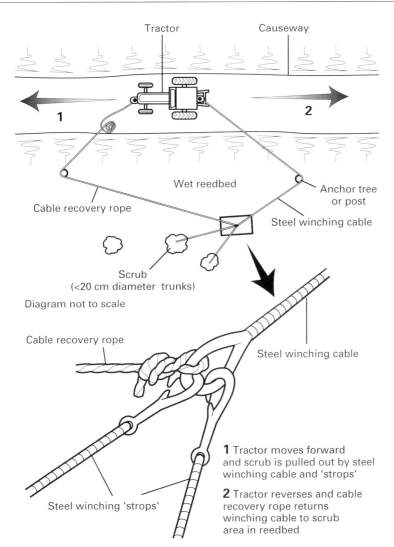

Figure 2
Winching method used at Far Ings to remove small and medium scrub from the wet reedbed.

Tractor

Causeway

1

2

Wet reedbed

Anchor tree or post

Cable recovery rope

Steel winching cable

Scrub
(<20 cm diameter trunks)

Diagram not to scale

Cable recovery rope

Steel winching cable

1 Tractor moves forward and scrub is pulled out by steel winching cable and 'strops'

2 Tractor reverses and cable recovery rope returns winching cable to scrub area in reedbed

Steel winching 'strops'

Plate 3 Aerial view taken in 1995 of chains of pools on the nature reserve.

Geoff Trinder

Inner Tay

(Private and Tayreed Company)

Location:	Tayside, Fife
	OS 1:50,000 sheet No 53
	GR NO 260 220
Area:	410 ha

Objectives:
Commercial cutting of reed for thatching and the maintenance of wildlife interest

Techniques:
SINGLE WALE CUTTING – Large Scale (section 2.3.1 a)
Burning Standing Reed (section 2.3.4 b)
Rotational Cutting (section 2.3.1 a)

Background

The reedbeds on the Tay are thought to date back to the 1800s when prisoners from the Napoleonic War were drafted in to plant the reed to protect the mudflats from erosion. Reed has been cut for thatching for many years but ceased for 30 years after World War II. Commercial cutting began in 1974 and is now a thriving commercial operation undertaken by the Tayreed Company.

The reedbed is tidal, the lower third is inundated on a twice daily basis, the upper reedbed floods only on spring high tides. However, the freshwater flows of the River Tay mix with tidal waters in the estuary producing at most, brackish water on the reedbed itself. A small amount of spring-line seepage occurs, plus field drains either run directly onto the bed or are channelled across to open water in ditches. One or two becks outfall into the estuary across the reedbed.

There are many private landowners with which Tayreed Company negotiate annual leases for cutting and pay a royalty for each bundle. There is no water management on the reedbeds and cutting and burning are the only reedbed management techniques practised. Reed which would normally be cut but fails to attain high quality in any one season is burned standing in early spring. This includes areas damaged by starling roosts. A series of plots are cut on a six-year rotation (in agreement with a landowner and SNH) by the Tayreed Company for the benefit of wildlife.

Single Wale Cutting (Large Scale)

- Cutting commences once the lower leaves have dropped generally December–14 April (the later breeding season this far north enables management to continue later in spring).

- High tides and wet weather make cutting impossible. The amount cut each year will be dependent on these factors.

- Prior to cutting, the bed is cleared of large tidal debris which might otherwise damage the cutting equipment.

- Each year, approximately the same areas are cut single wale leaving uncut strips along creek and channel edges plus a 10-m wide strip along the landward edge is left uncut as agreed with SNH. Areas of consistently poorer reed are left uncut (Plate 3).

- A Seiga Harvester cuts and bundles the reed (Plate 1).

- The machine leaves the reedbed when full to offload onto a trailer or stacking area then returns to continue work (offloading and stacking takes one hour).

- Thus, in an eight-hour working day, four loads of 500 bundles may be harvested and stacked.

- Bundles are stacked on dry ground, alternating top-to-toe and covered with a tarpaulin or 'thatched' by a pitched roof of reed bundles. A strimmer is used to remove long ends.

- On days when cutting is impossible or orders are required, the bundles are cut open and fed into the cleaning and trimming machine (Plate 2) which reties bundles at the finish.

- The new bundles are stacked top-to-toe in a baling basket mounted on a fork-lift truck (Plate 2). A bale contains 80 bundles and is tied with a steel strap.

- Bales are fork-lifted onto a trailer or flat-bed lorry for transportation.

Wildlife and Commercial Benefits

- Large tracts of reed stubble attract feeding waders and wildfowl. Snipe and lapwing nest but the latter inevitably fails as the reed regrows (Moyes 1990).

- The majority of nesting bird territories are in the uncut areas, especially the 10-m strip along the landward edge. Sedge warblers and water rails benefit greatly, their nest sites tending to be close to the cut/uncut boundary. 600–1,000 sedge warbler territories were recorded in study areas plus 22 pairs of water rail in a 13-ha study plot (Moyes pers comm).

- Ringing studies recorded 18 breeding pairs of bearded tit in 1994. The majority of the area they nested in had been burned off the previous year. There is some evidence to suggest that they also select nest sites adjacent to the Seiga's regular tracking route where reed growth is inhibited. The colony as a whole occupies one of the wettest parts of the Tay reedbeds.

- Marsh harriers breed, mostly in the unmanaged sections of reedbed. Bitterns have been recorded in winter and one was heard booming in July of 1993. Roe deer and otters are recorded occasionally.

- Single wale cutting of 20–30% of the total reed area ensures there is minimal litter build up on these sections. This produces consistently high quality thatching reed which requires little cleaning. Yields (Table 1) are comparable to double wale, freshwater beds.

Plate 1 The Seiga cutter in operation. Note the reed bundles are carried on the cargo rig.

Plate 2 The bundles are fed into a dressing machine which reties them before being baled.

Table 1: The Tayreed Company, yields and prices for single wale cutting

- Employs three full-time staff all year.

- Exports reed to Ireland, Holland and USA.

- Produces some 20% of the UK thatching reed output.

- Usually harvests 70,000–100,000 bundles each year.*

- Yields of up to 1,250 bundles/ha are obtained.*

- Sells at £1.40–£1.70** a bundle (net of losses ***), depending on quantity and delivery.

- Pays a royalty to landowners of 10%/bundle sold (not cut).***

- Offers a complete service to thatchers, delivered to the job.

*   This equates to 56–80 ha per annum, ie about 20% of the total area

**   1995 prices

***   15–20% of harvest is lost in waste from cleaning which reduces the final yield. Landowners have no management costs or overheads.

Plate 3 Large areas are cut single wale but uncut areas are retained. Note the narrow strip on the far right which is always left uncut.

Ranworth Flood

Case Study 5

(PRIVATE)

Location:	South Walsham, Norfolk OS 1:50,000 sheet No 134 GR TG 3614 3714
Area:	40 ha commercial reedbed 60 ha non-commercial reedbed

Objectives:
To produce an annual crop of reed suitable for sale for thatching while retaining the wildlife interest of the site.

Techniques:
SINGLE WALE CUTTING (section 2.3.1 a)
Water Management (section 2.2)

Background

This area of Broadland was originally drained for grazing and probably left to flood in the 1920s to benefit the duck shoot. Reed encroached and was subsequently commercially cut. 60 ha of the marsh is reed-dominated fen with alder and scrub. This area is subject to tidally influenced natural flooding. Small patches of reed and sedge are cut occasionally when suitable for thatching. The area supports nine species of sedges and many mosses and ferns including the rare crested buckler fern. A bunded, 40-ha area is commercially cut for thatching reed (Figure 1). Eutrophic water from the River Bure supplies this area via a simple sluice and ditch system. Surface water is maintained on the commercial beds throughout the spring and summer. Ditches are cleared when necessary. Four hectares of open water is maintained for the benefit of wildlife. The site has produced reed of a consistently thatchable quality for many years.

Single Wale Cutting

- Draw-down starts in October by removing the upper boards of the outlet sluice. The rate is slow because of the high water retention of peat soil.

- As much as possible is cut single wale. Reed unsuitable for thatching, on very soft ground, on ditch edges and the margins of open water are left uncut. In practice, only 60% of the total area is cut annually.

- Uncut areas of poorer quality reed may be burned in spring to encourage an improved regrowth for the following winter's cut.

- A range of cutting equipment is used, including Olympia harvester, reciprocator mowers and scythes (on small, inaccessible areas).

- Reed bundles are transported off the beds either by ATV and trailer or by boat to the main collecting point where they are stacked on dry land.

- The reedbed is re-flooded as soon as cutting has been completed. Levels are raised slowly by installing boards in the outlet sluice to achieve the required depth. The rate of input can be similarly controlled using a reverse, non-return flap, drop-board sluice.

Benefits

- A harvest of cut reed is produced each year and sold for thatching (Table 1).

- Reed buntings, bearded tits and wrens use the single wale beds in winter and are believed to breed in uncut patches and adjacent habitats.

- Marsh harriers breed in summer in uncut areas and hunt the marshes in winter.

- The maintenance of associated habitats such as ditches and open water greatly benefits fish populations and wintering wildfowl.

- The reedbeds support a large population of grass snakes, frogs and toads.

Table 1: Yields and prices for single wale cutting

- Up to 60% of the 40-ha commercial reedbed is cut each year.

- The yield averages 750–1,000 bundles/ha.

- Total output depends on weather. Potential of 40,000 bundles never realised. Flooding in 1994 meant only 10,000 bundles harvested. In a good year, 24,000 bundles is usual maximum,

- The reed is sold standing to contractors at a royalty of 15% of the selling price per bundle. The royalty may be waived in areas with poorer quality reed.

- 1994/95 selling price to thatchers was £1.60 + VAT per bundle.

- The landowner is responsible for all capital costs/improvements.

NB: These figures are highly variable depending on proportion of crop harvestable in each year, demand and market price.

Figure 1
Plan of Ranworth Flood showing bunds, ditches, grips and position of sluices.

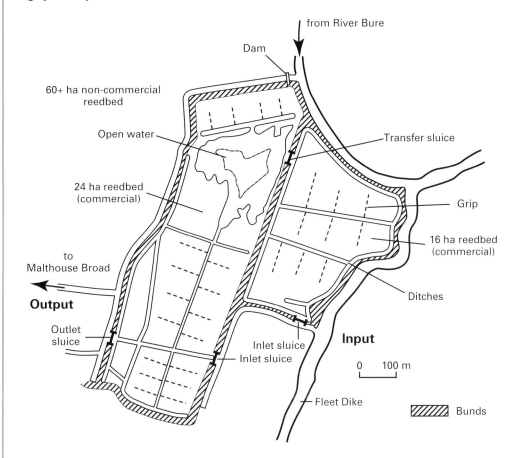

from River Bure

Dam

60+ ha non-commercial reedbed

Open water

Transfer sluice

24 ha reedbed (commercial)

Grip

16 ha reedbed (commercial)

to Malthouse Broad

Output

Ditches

Outlet sluice

Inlet sluice
Inlet sluice

Input

0   100 m

Fleet Dike

Bunds

How Hill

(Broads Authority)

Location:	How Hill, Norfolk OS 1:50,000 sheet No 134 GR TG 368189
Area:	40 ha

Objectives:
To produce a commercial crop of reed for thatching while retaining the wildlife value of the reedbed.

Techniques:
DOUBLE WALE (section 2.3.1.a)
Ditch Management (section 2.2.3)

Background

The reedbeds at How Hill lie in the River Ant floodplain. The river's flood-bank protects the reedbeds from constant inundation but high tides in spring and winter frequently cause flooding. This may influence exactly when and how much reed may be cut in any one year. Reed has been harvested for many years and for several years has been cut double wale. Ditches and grips are periodically cleared to facilitate a flow of water on and off the reedbed.

Double Wale

- Reed is cut any time between November and March when conditions permit.

- In any one winter, no more than 50% of the reed area is cut and usually only about 12% (5 ha) is cut.

- Reed is cut using a hand-scythe (Plate 1) or reciprocator mower.

- The reed is bundled, cleaned, dressed and tied by hand.

- The reed bundles are stacked on the river bank to be later transported from the reedbed by boat (Plate 2).

- Reed debris and some litter is raked at the end of harvesting and burned.

Benefits

- Reed of consistently good thatching quality is produced.

- In an average year approximately 4,000 bundles of reed are harvested.

- The accumulation of litter is greatly reduced.

- Scrub invasion is prevented.

- Bearded tits and reed warblers use the standing reed for both breeding and feeding.

- Harvest mice also build their nests in the standing reed.

- Marsh harriers breed annually.

- The standing reed provides a wintering refuge for invertebrates, including the Fenn's wainscot moth.

- By leaving an area uncut each year, biennial and short-lived perennial plants such as cowbane and greater spearwort are able to set seed and spread. Another, milk parsley, also thrives and is important as the food plant for the caterpillar of the swallowtail butterfly.

Plate 1 Cutting reed with a hand scythe.

Plate 2 Double wale bundles stacked on the river bank awaiting transportation by boat.

Titchwell Marsh

(RSPB)

Location:	Titchwell, Norfolk OS 1:50,000 sheet No 132 GR TF 749436
Area:	13 ha intertidal reedbed 11 ha freshwater reedbed

Objectives:
To manage the freshwater reedbed for the benefit of bitterns and other reedbed wildlife.

Techniques:
LONG ROTATIONAL CUTTING
(section 2.3.1 a)

Open Water Creation (section 2.2.4 c)

Background

Situated on the North Norfolk coast, Titchwell was subject to regular tidal influence when acquired by the RSPB in 1973. The sea walls, which had been constructed years earlier to permit grazing, had long since been destroyed by surge tides. Most of the 24 ha of reedbed was flooded with sea water during spring tides but was otherwise dry. In the 1970s, a 10-ha section of the tidal reedbed was isolated from the sea by building a 3-m high, clay sea wall. In 1983, an inner low bund was constructed around the 10 ha to allow the water levels to be independent of adjacent marshes creating more than 1 km of ditches in the process. The reedbed is now fresh water, being fed by springs from the higher landward side (Sills 1988).

The creation of a series of 'inverted pools', where the upper organic layer is exchanged with the underlying mineral soil using a digger (section 2.2.4 c), has added wildlife value in the form of temporary, shallow water to the freshwater reedbed. This technique has been partially combined with experimental, rotational cutting on a five-, eight- and 10-year basis (Figure 1).

Long Rotational Cutting

- With all rotations, reed was cut and, together with as much litter as possible, was raked and burned off in heaps.

- **Five-year**. An experimental, five-year programme was initiated in 1987 in association with the creation of small inverted pools (Figure 1). The small plot size of 10 x 10 m was because cutting was done by hand. This technique meant that each year 0.08 ha of reed was cut in addition to the 4-m wide access and viewing swathe. Each small plot adjoined a similar sized area of open water with encroaching reed, ie an inverted pool.

After one complete cycle of five years this system was abandoned because of the small scale and the acquisition of a reciprocator mower permitting larger areas to be cut. (By 1995, the inverted pools had not yet achieved a full cover of reed and were still used by bearded tits for feeding).

- **Eight-year.** An eight-year rotation was established on the eastern half of the freshwater reedbed in 1989. Each plot was 12 m x either 190 m or 220 m long, ie approximately 0.25 ha (Figure 1). Hides were erected

on the sea wall overlooking the plots to monitor usage by nesting bearded tits. The amount of accumulated litter was assessed in each plot after cutting and the vigour of the newly grown reed was measured by stem density and height.

- **Ten-year.** A 10-year rotation was established in 1991 adjacent to the previously cut five-year rotational system (Figure 1). Plot sizes were 30 m x 40 m and 30 m x 20 m and close enough to a footpath to watch nesting bearded tits. This landward area is the driest part of the reedbed because of the sloping topography of the land, the wetter part being the northern half of the reedbed.

Wildlife Benefits

- Bittern – while the reedbed was tidal no bitterns were recorded breeding. Within one year of having isolated 10 ha of freshwater reedbed, a booming male was recorded (1980). Thereafter, one pair bred each year until 1989. Since isolation, the eel population of the site has aged such that the average weight exceeded 60 g, ie too big for bitterns to eat. In 1994, a three-year reintroduction of eels started by stocking with 3,000 fingerlings weighing 4 g each. Other fish and amphibian populations are small. In addition, the inverted pools provide secluded, encroaching reed edge for bitterns to feed in although there is no evidence that they have done so.

- Marsh harriers – colonised Titchwell in 1980, one year after isolation, and usually two pairs breed annually. Observations showed that during the incubation phase virtually all prey items taken by the adults were from the freshwater reedbed (Sills 1988). Cutting a small proportion of the total reed area each year does not appear to affect breeding marsh harrier density (Burgess and Evans 1989).

- Bearded tits – breed in both tidal and freshwater reedbeds, the reserve supporting usually about 20 pairs. The provision of a freshwater reedbed, cut reed areas and small pools has provided bearded tits with additional feeding habitat. Hide observations revealed birds feeding on chironomid flies emerging from the shallow water and settling on reed stems around the inverted pools or on new reed in the most recently cut areas. Although the study is still in progress, early results from the eight-year rotation plots suggest that nesting bearded tits prefer plots with two years of growth after cutting. In other words, deep litter formed over many years is not a prerequisite for bearded tit breeding, which suggests that rotations could be shorter, say four years, and still support a breeding population (Sills pers comm).

● Invertebrates – the freshwater reedbed with associated ditches and pools has provided habitat for a diversity of aquatic and semiaquatic invertebrates.

Figure 1
The rotational cutting programme at Titchwell Marsh.

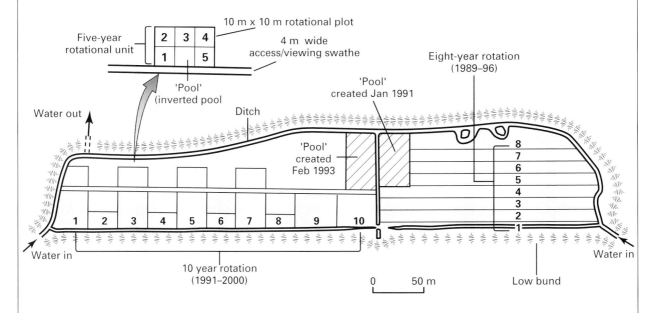

Table 1: Breeding birds associated with reedbeds before and after isolation from tidal incursion

Species	Before (1973–79)	After (1980–86)	Post 1990
Bittern	0	1	1
Mallard	0	several	several
Marsh harrier	0	1–3	1–3
Water rail	0	1+	1+
Bearded tit	ca 5	ca 20	15–20

NB: The fact that post 1990 figures almost mirror those of the period immediately after isolation is indicative that the habitat has remained unchanged, partly a result of reed management and partly because of the small time-scale involved. Other factors, eg weather or natural population fluctuations, have caused variations in numbers annually. (From Becker and Sills 1988.)

Leighton Moss

(RSPB)

Location:	Silverdale, Lancs. OS 1:50,000 sheet No 97 GR SD 482 750
Area:	134.5 ha total 79 ha reedswamp/fen

Objectives:
To maintain and increase reed-fringed open water for wetland birds, otters and aquatic invertebrates.

Techniques:
UNDERWATER CUTTING (section 2.3.1 c)
Summer Cutting (section 2.3.1 c)
Water Level Control (section 2.2.1)

Background

Leighton Moss is a valley fen with shallow, eutrophic meres succeeding through reedswamp and fen to scrub and carr. A combination of management techniques has been employed over many years to prevent reed from encroaching into open water. Dalapon was sprayed to control reed at the reed/water interface. This expensive method was gradually replaced as the technique of underwater cutting was developed. Maintaining a high spring and early summer water level also prevents encroachment and improves the effectiveness of underwater cutting.

Underwater Cutting

- First underwater cut is early, usually July with regrowth cut again in August and September. These cut areas are kept wet throughout the growing season. Areas that dry out in summer are cut only once in September.

- A reciprocator mower (Honda 660) will cut underwater and permit one operator to cut up to 0.5 ha/day. Reciprocating scrub cutters are used in very wet areas allowing up to 0.25 ha/day to be cut by one operator depending on regrowth.

- In year one of treatment areas are cut in winter and debris is burned. Summer cut regrowth is left to decay.

- As plant diversity increases, selected high value species such as sedges and spike-rush are left uncut to provide seed for winter wildfowl.

Wildlife Benefits

- A total of 1.25 ha of shallow, open has been created and managed with underwater cutting. Up to 5 ha is cut annually in summer.

- In summer-cut areas the plant diversity has increased from almost total dominance by reed to up to 10 regular species and a further 13 occasional (Table 1). These areas are grazed by deer, and birds such as greylag geese and wigeon, and provide nest sites for lapwing and snipe, and in tussocky areas for coot, mallard and shoveler. Bitterns regularly fish the wetter areas, especially where mare's-tail and sedge are dominant.

- Wintering wildfowl use these areas, feeding on the abundant seed supply.

- The water/reed interface created by these techniques is used by bittern for feeding and by coot, greylag, moorhen, shoveler, pochard and tufted duck for nesting.

- Otters regularly use the open water and reed margins (Plate 1).

- Many invertebrates benefit from the increase in plant diversity and open, shallow water.

Table 1: Plants which have benefited from underwater cutting

Marsh yellow-cress
Purple-loosestrife
Water pepper
Great water dock
Water forget-me-not
Water-mint
Common skullcap
Marsh bedstraw
Trifid bur-marigold
Marsh cudweed
Water plantain
Branched bur-reed
Common spike-rush
Marsh foxtail
Bottle sedge
Cyperus sedge

Plate 1 Otters are well established in the reedbed where they hunt fish in the ditches and open water areas.

Plate 2 Trifid bur-marigold – a plant that grows in summer-cut areas. It has benefited from underwater cutting at Leighton Moss.

**Figure 1
Underwater cutting with a reciprocator mower.**

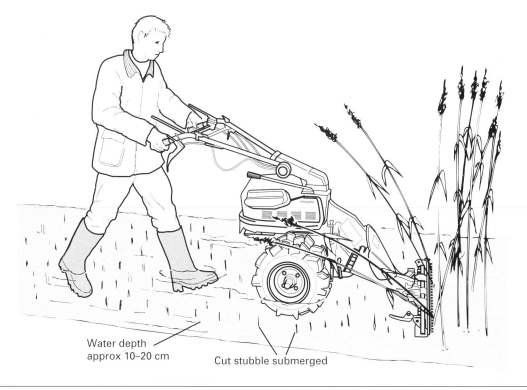

Water depth approx 10–20 cm

Cut stubble submerged

Horning Marsh Farm

(Broads Authority and Suffolk Water Company)

Location:	Horning, Norfolk OS 1:50,000 sheet No 134 GR IG 350 163
Area:	40 ha

Objectives:
Rehabilitation by scrub control and subsequent burning management; commercial cutting of reed and sedge.

Techniques:
BURNING STANDING REED (section 2.3.4 b)
Scrub Removal by Cutting (section 2.3.5)
Saw-sedge Harvesting (section 2.3.1)

Background

Historically, the site was dug for peat and has the ditches and grips that were constructed to drain the area for this activity. Subsequently, the area developed a reed-dominated, open fen vegetation from which reed, sedge and bedding litter were probably harvested. An absence of cutting management for many years led to scrub invasion, especially by bog myrtle. A management agreement between the Broads Authority and Suffolk Water Company, who own the site, meant that in 1989 a programme of scrub clearance began, which re-established large areas of open fen. Clearance continues at the margins but bog myrtle has re-grown to some extent in the previously cleared areas, despite treatment with Amcide.

The open fen is managed by rotational burning, which suppresses scrub reinvasion and maintains reed quality.

Saw-sedge is harvested in July on a three- or four-year rotation and sold for thatching. Reed cutting is not yet practicable because of the large number of scrub stumps which remain unrotted.

Burning Standing Reed

- Burning is done on a wet but not flooded bed, between December and February.

- A 3-m wide fire-break is cut on all sides of the area to be burned using either brushcutters with tri-star blades or a reciprocator mower.

- No more than one-third of the total open fen area is burned in any one year, ie a three-year rotation, although in very wet winters burning may not be feasible.

- No more than 1 ha is set on fire at any one time.

- A pump is used to extract water from the ditch to dowse the fire-break before and during burning to prevent loss of control.

- The reed cut along the fire-break is burnt on a bonfire. Burning reed from the bonfire is used to set alight the area to be burned. Forks are used to place burning reed at the base of the standing reed at one corner or along the edge of the plot (Plate 1).

- The burn is initiated at the side which is being hit by the wind, ie burn WITH THE WIND. This assists the burn, making it move quickly through the reed and ensures the burn is light and minimises scorching the litter layer.

- Burning is only undertaken in light winds of no more than Force 2 (slight movement in the tops of trees).

Wildlife and Commercial Benefits

- Reduces litter accumulation and produces a straighter, more vigorous reed and cleaner bundles at harvesting.

- The burn removes re-seeded or regrown scrub maintaining the important open fen habitat.

- The technique leaves unburnt stubble and litter sufficient for over-wintering stem-boring moth larvae and other invertebrates to survive.

- The three-year rotation permits biennial and perennial plants such as milk parsley to develop and drop seed and improves the survival rate of important invertebrates. In addition, at least two-thirds of the reed remains standing for use by other reedbed wildlife, and acts as a reservoir for recolonisation of the burned plot.

Broads Authority

Plate 1 Burning standing reed 'with the wind'.

North Warren

(RSPB)

Location:	Aldeburgh, Suffolk
	OS 1:50,000 sheet No 156
	GR TM 460594
Area:	205 ha total
	23 ha reedbed

Objectives:
Rehabilitation of a degraded reedbed by scrub removal and bed regeneration for the benefit of reedbed wildlife.

Techniques:
BED REGENERATION (section 2.3.6)
Ditch Construction (section 3.2.2 b)
Scrub Removal (section 2.3.5)

Background

Situated near the Suffolk coast, the reedbed was known to have been cut single wale until about 1954. In the late 1970s it continued to support species such as bittern, bearded tit and garganey. Gradually, scrub invaded as succession continued unchecked and these key species were lost. The reedbed dried out and nettle and bramble colonised from the margins.

The water supply is from the Hundred River via two sluices plus some input from several springs. Levels are low in winter because the NRA run-off down stream is a flood prevention measure. This, however, facilitates management work. Levels are higher in summer as a boating lake downstream holds back water, resulting in patchy wetness on the reedbed. Any effort to raise water levels further would flood neighbouring land. Consequently, bed regeneration by excavation was necessary to rehabilitate the reedbed. The construction of bunds, additional ditches (up to 2,000 m) and two sluices has facilitated water level control.

Regeneration by Excavation

- Scrub was cut using chainsaws and the brash burned in advance of excavation work. Reed was not cut or burned in advance.

- A tracked Hitachi FH200LC digger with a large bucket (1.7 m^3) and 10-m reach was contracted. The soil is thin peat over silts and clay providing a firm base to operate on. Softer, wet areas necessitated mats.

- Work was conducted in four phases of 7, 6, 5 and 5 ha during the winters of 1993–96 (Figure 1a).

- The digger excavated to a depth of 30 cm across the bed. Some scrub, scrub stumps and root-plates were removed at the same time and piled by the digger to be burned later (Plate 1). Pools created by root-plate removal were left in place. The result was to produce a lower, wet surface (Plate 2).

- Excavated material and spoil from ditch construction (Plate 2) and reprofiling was used to construct a boundary bund. Surplus material was transported off the reedbed using a 10-tonne dumper truck.

- When shoots emerged in the spring, water levels were gradually increased to a maximun depth of 30 cm, ensuring the growing shoots were never submerged.

- A rotational cutting programme is undertaken on the regenerated reedbed to maintain reed quality and habitat structure.

Wildlife Benefits

- The 7-ha (1993) plot on silt produced a patchy regrowth the following spring of about 40% cover. The 6-ha (1994) plot, however, was on peat and attained full reed cover within one growing season. The 'new' reed was more vigorous (taller, thicker and denser) than before and quickly outcompeted unwanted plants.

- The new ditches, reprofiled existing ditches and pools created by root-plate extraction will provide reed-edge habitat for feeding bitterns and other wildlife including aquatic invertebrates and plants.

- The increased reedbed wetness and improved reed quality will have nesting potential for bitterns, bearded tits and marsh harriers, all of which use the site in winter/on passage. Other reedbed birds should also benefit, as should fish, amphibians and small mammals such as water shrew and harvest mouse. Two otters were reported in the reedbed in 1995.

- Reedbed invertebrates such as wainscot moths, especially the nationally rare white-mantled wainscot, which occurs locally, may colonise in the future.

Table 1: Cost of reedbed regeneration at North Warren RSPB nature reserve

Machinery hire and labour	Cost (£ per day)
Digger + driver	250 (£25 per hour)
Mats (8 × £8)	64
Dumper truck (self drive)	120
Maximum cost	434

Cost of Job
In March 1994, it took approximately 23 days to regenerate 6 ha of reedbed including ditch creation, scrub clearance, spoil movements.
Including machinery hire, total cost was: £10,000
Therefore, cost per hectare £ 1,667

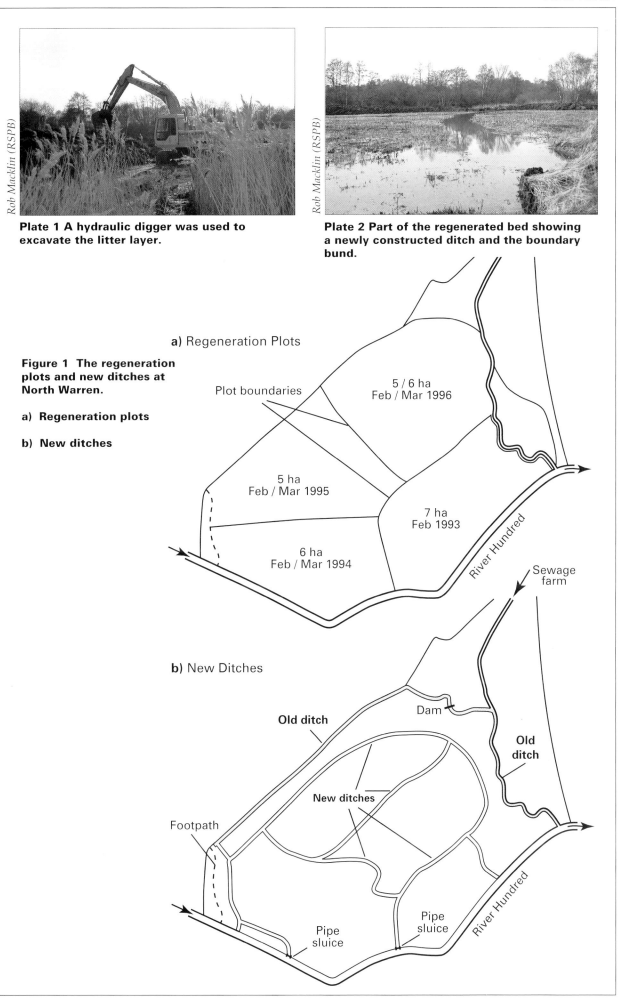

Plate 1 A hydraulic digger was used to excavate the litter layer.

Rob Macklin (RSPB)

Plate 2 Part of the regenerated bed showing a newly constructed ditch and the boundary bund.

Rob Macklin (RSPB)

Figure 1 The regeneration plots and new ditches at North Warren.

a) **Regeneration plots**

b) **New ditches**

a) Regeneration Plots

Plot boundaries

5 / 6 ha
Feb / Mar 1996

5 ha
Feb / Mar 1995

7 ha
Feb 1993

6 ha
Feb / Mar 1994

River Hundred

Sewage farm

b) New Ditches

Old ditch

Dam

Old ditch

New ditches

Footpath

Pipe sluice

Pipe sluice

River Hundred

Walberswick Marshes

Case Study 11

(English Nature and Private)

Location:	Walberswick, Suffolk
	OS 1:50,000 sheet No 156
	GR TM 475 733
Area:	240 ha reedbed

Objectives:

To manage this nationally important reedbed for its special wildlife value while producing an annual harvest of cut reed for thatching.

Techniques:

INTEGRATED MANAGEMENT:
  WATER MANAGEMENT (section 2.2)
  OPEN WATER (section 2.2.4)
  SINGLE WALE CUTTING (section 2.3.1)
  LONG ROTATIONAL CUTTING (section 2.3.1)
  SUMMER CUTTING (section 2.3.1)
  SCRUB AND CARR (section 2.3.5)
  (NON-INTERVENTION)

Background

The freshwater reedbeds at Walberswick developed when grazing ceased and the land was left to flood as a defence against enemy invasion during the World War II. A system of ditches was already in place therefore, and the site receives a constant flow of spring water and run-off from the higher ground that almost entirely encloses it. At its eastern end there is a shingle bank, which is maintained by the NRA and affords some protection from high tides. The site has been a nature reserve since 1972 and has been managed both for its wildlife value and as a source of commercial reed for thatching. Part of the reedbed is managed privately.

Optimal management of a reedbed requires more than one technique. The integration of a range of best-practice techniques ensures that commercial and wildlife value is maintained. At Walberswick, a programme of management has evolved that achieves this aim. The techniques and their benefits have been described separately for clarity but should be considered synergistic.

Water Management

- The reedbed has been divided into three major compartments or units by enclosing areas inside bunds constructed from excavating ditches on site over the past 16 years. Each compartment has a cross-bund to allow finer control of water levels.

- The construction of a sea wall/large bund in 1993–95 has isolated some 75% of the total reed area. The bund was constructed from material excavated on either side which has created 1–1.5 ha of open water with an estimated 15,000 m of reed edge (Plate 1).

- The ditch network is managed on a rotational clearing system of 8–15 years. This work is done by mechanical excavator which removes only accumulated plant material (ie not soil) which is distributed over the reedbed to avoid the build up of raised ditch edges. Where soil has to be removed too, the soil is placed on ditch edges and culverted pipes installed to permit water flow. Ditches are maintained at an average

depth of 1.5 m with edges graded at about 20–30 degrees where possible.

- Water is distributed between units and water levels controlled by a series of different sluice mechanisms, mostly of the angled pipe type. Plate 2 shows a sluice being installed through the new bund.

Benefits

- The division into hydrological units permits selective draw-down enabling management to be carried out in one unit without affecting the others.

- The use of sluices in combination with hydrological units enables different water regimes to be managed in each compartment although some are maintained to be similar. This provides subtly different reedbed habitats within one site.

- The maintenance of wet, freshwater reedbed provides suitable habitat for a range of animals and plants and maintains reed quality of benefit to wildlife and for thatching.

- The sea wall/bund prevents further incursions by the sea, thus protecting a large area of freshwater reedbed from periodic catastrophic change. Such events are detrimental to reed quality and wildlife, which may take years to recover.

- Periodic clearing of ditches on a rotation maximises their potential to support wildlife such as pond weeds, frogbit and bog St John's wort, black-tailed skimmer and white-faced darter dragonflies, common and great crested newts, and aquatic invertebrates.

- The provision of graded edges to the ditches and the absence of a raised edge provides fish and amphibians with suitable breeding habitat and facilitates feeding by birds such as bittern, heron, water rail and moorhen.

Open Water

- In addition to ditches, the reedbed has approximately 5 ha of open water with some 8,000 m of reed edge. The depth varies from very shallow (approx 5 cm) to quite deep (approx 1 m) in places.

- Some 1–2 ha of this was created by spraying reed with Dalapon in summer, 4–16 years ago.

- After the initial spraying, the dead reed was cut and burned.

- The re-encroaching reed edge was controlled by re-spraying with Dalapon about every 3–5 years.

- Additional, small areas of open water were created by excavating the ground to produce an undulating surface on which the reed re-encroached in 'ribbons' (comparable to an irregular ridge and furrow).

Benefits

- The shallower areas support a range of aquatic plants including mare's tail which quickly dominates but is used as cover for feeding bitterns.

- Common waterbirds breed at the reed/water edge and in intermittent years the rare garganey has bred.

- Avocets have bred on the reed 'ribbon' areas.

- Marsh harriers hunt over the open water and adjacent reedbed.

Single Wale Cutting

- Each year 15–30 ha of reed is cut and sold for thatching.

- The reed is sold as a standing crop to local reedcutters who pay a royalty of 32p/bundle (1995). This yields about £4,000/annum income for the reserve.

- The reed is cut in fixed plots of varying size (eg 0.4–2.5 ha) as shown in Figure 1.

- Some reed is cut single wale for five years when an alternative plot is burned standing ready to start a fresh five-year cycle the following winter. The previously cut plot is rested for five years, then is similarly burned off ready to begin another fresh single wale cutting programme (Figure 1).

- The reed is cut using an Olympia harvester and transported off the reedbed by a John Deere ATV with a modified deck.

- The reed is cleaned and dressed (Part 2, Plate 24b) on dry land and stacked away from the reedbed for later collection.

- An average yield of 750 bundles/ha means that approximately 13,000–17,000 bundles are cut each year.

Benefits

- An annual crop of straight, thatching quality reed is produced.

- Single wale cutting produces a high density of thinner stemmed reeds which many thatchers favour as they pack down more tightly.

- Each year, the cutting programme provides an additional 6,000–8,000 m of wet reed edge providing feeding areas for bittern and other birds as well as shallow water for fish and amphibians.

- The newly grown reed produces seed-laden panicles exploited by feeding bearded tits in late summer and winter.

Long Rotational Cutting

- A series of plots of varying size are cut on a 20–25-year rotation.

- Cutting is done in winter using a Bucher petrol reciprocator.

- Cut reed is raked into piles and burned off.

- Each year, 0–5 ha (usually 1–3 ha) is cut in this way.

Benefits

- Prevents long-term litter accumulation on 40% of the reedbed.

- Allows biennial and perennial plants to set seed prior to cutting.

- Allows invertebrates which overwinter in reed stems to complete cycles in interim years and recolonise from adjacent areas after cutting.

- Maintains reed vigour providing nesting sites for birds and mammals and seed-laden panicles for seed-eating wildlife.

- Provides temporary, open, shallow water in a secluded location for feeding birds like bitterns.

Summer Cutting

- Annual mowing in August/September of fixed plots (7–9 ha) is done using a Bucher reciprocator and rake attachment.

- About 40% of the cut vegetation is usually stacked into 'habitat' piles at the margins of the plots. The remainder is taken off-site and burned or given away as hay.

- The plots are largely on the drier edges of the reedbed, which support a greater range of plants than the wetter reedbed areas (Figure 1).

- Some of this management programme has been in place for 10 years.

Benefits

- Summer cutting has enhanced the already rich plant life of these plots, which now support marsh orchids, bogbean, marsh louse-wort, bog pimpernel, sneezewort, ragged-robin and up to eight species of Sphagnum mosses.

- The vegetation structure that has resulted from this management is shorter and more diverse, and has produced a habitat type that supports a great range of invertebrates such as spiders, beetles and craneflies (more than 100 species recorded). In addition, the cut plots are used by feeding and breeding snipe, redshank and lapwing.

- When flooded in winter, the cut plots provide temporary open water and feeding habitat for bitterns, water rails and wintering wildfowl.

- The piles of cut vegetation are utilised by breeding grass snakes which occur in the reedbed, and provide overwintering sites for invertebrates to escape rising winter water levels.

Scrub and Carr Management

- About 15% of the reedbed area contains scrub and carr.

- In the 1960s and 70s a great deal of scrub was cut and removed from the western end of the reedbed but the raised water levels from improved water management has kept reinvasion to a minimum.

- The alder carr woodland at the western end of the reserve is very wet and is managed largely by non-intervention. The system is presently self-perpetuating in that once trees attain a certain height they are no longer able to maintain their anchorage and fall over in the boggy ground. Selected large trees are ring-barked and die *in situ*.

Benefits

- Scattered clumps of scrub dotted throughout the reedbed are of value to invertebrates, as perches for marsh harriers and for feeding and nesting for birds such as sedge warbler, Savi's warbler and reed bunting.

- The fallen trees create water-filled holes in the ground which support invertebrates and are gradually colonised by plants.

- The dead, ring-barked trees provide valuable lookout perches for harriers and other birds.

- The carr understorey supports many *Sphagnum* moss species, cotton-grass and marsh violets and a great diversity of invertebrates.

- The carr woodland canopy provides nesting for many common birds including woodpeckers, redstart and wood warbler in some years. It supports a large biomass of invertebrates.

Non-intervention

- Approximately 40% of the reedbed area is unmanaged, apart from periodic burning off after damage due to sea incursion and starling roosts.

- These areas are characterised by some dry areas because of the litter build up over the years but mostly by wet reedbed where cutting or burning is not feasible.

Benefits

- Supports cowbane, milk parsley, marsh sow-thistle and hemp-agrimony.

- Used by nesting birds, including bearded tit, marsh harrier, Savi's, reed, grasshopper and sedge warblers. Also, reed bunting, wren and water rail and up to 11 pairs of Cetti's warbler until the hard winter of 1985.

- Used by nesting harvest mice.

- Probably benefits overwintering stem-boring larvae of white-mantled wainscot, Fenn's wainscot and reed leopard moth. Would benefit a wide range of reed litter invertebrates.

Summary

At Walberswick NNR several management techniques have been combined to produce a range of benefits. Division of the reedbed into hydrological units benefits the habitat overall and hence all reedbed species and reed quality. Similarly, isolation from the influence of the sea by construction of a sea wall/bund protects the reedbed. In the process, a series of shallow pools with reed edge was created. Other techniques which have created open water and reed/water edge include rotational ditch clearing, ditch reprofiling, spraying reed with herbicide, excavating 'ribbons' and reed cutting (single wale, long rotations and summer cutting).This has benefited aquatic plants and animals and birds such as bittern, heron, moorhen and bearded tit. Fallen trees in the carr woodland produce temporary pools of benefit to many species of plant and invertebrate.

Reed quality has been maintained by rotational cutting programmes, notably single wale for thatching reed and longer rotations. This reduces litter accumulation which reduces succession and prolongs the life of the reedbed. Similarly, scrub removal sets back succession enabling reed quality to be maintained. Longer rotations in particular benefit tall plants by enabling biennials and perennials to set seed. In addition, many invertebrates are able to complete their life cycles and recolonise recently cut or burned areas.

By reducing competition from reed, summer cutting increases the diversity of plants and invertebrates. Habitat 'piles' created with cuttings benefit invertebrates and grass snakes.

The retention of some scrub in the reedbed and maintenance of marginal carr woodland benefits many plants, invertebrates and birds.

Areas of unmanaged reedbed benefit tall plants, bearded tits, sedge warblers, reed warblers, marsh harriers, harvest mice and both reed-litter and reed-stem dwelling invertebrates.

C Hawke (RSPB)

Plate 1 Part of the new bund/sea wall which was created by excavating soil from the reedbed on either side creating a series of shallow pools (left) and increased reed edge.

C Hawke (RSPB)

Plate 2 A sluice pipe being installed through the new bund.

Figure 1
Plan of reedbed at Walberswick showing the different management techniques undertaken.

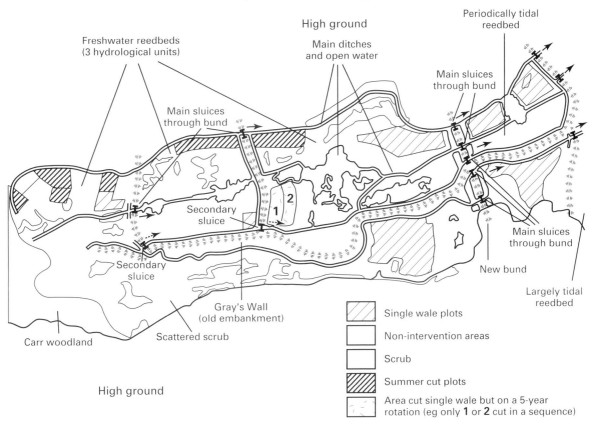

East Chevington

Case Study 12

(Northumberland Wildlife Trust/British Coal
Opencast/ADAS/Northumberland County
Council)

Location:	Druridge Bay, Northumberland OS 1:50,000 sheet No 81 GR NZ 270 990
Area:	69 ha total 39 ha reedbed

Objectives:
To create reedbed and associated habitats from
a former opencast coal site for the benefit of
wildlife and visitors.

Techniques:
CREATION:
LAND FORMING (section 3.2.1)
VEGETATION ESTABLISHMENT (section 3.3)
WATER MANAGEMENT (section 2.2)

Background

The site was originally farmland and included about
8 ha of reed, which originated from Hickling, Norfolk
over 75 years ago and was cut for thatching haystacks.
The area was subsequently opencast mined for coal for
about 15 years until 1993. Initial proposals to
relandscape the site to a nature reserve included the
creation of 50 ha of contiguous reedbed with a range of
associated habitats. Site access constraints resulted in a
revision of the plans to create two reedbeds of 30 and 9
ha respectively (Figure 1).

An assessment of the site revealed small pockets of reed
remaining, which will act as a source of both reed and
associated wildlife, plus dyer's greenweed, lesser
butterfly orchid, peregrines on territory and a large
population of eels. There is a plentiful supply of water
throughout the year.

Land Forming

The work was undertaken by British Coal Opencast
using heavy plant, commenced in 1994 and involved:

- moving thousands of tonnes of soil within site. No
  spoil was taken off site but used for land forming
  (Plate 1).

- laying a 10-m thick clay base with a subsoil and
  topsoil overlay.

- preparing two main areas; one of 9 ha, the other 30 ha
  (plus other smaller areas), the boundaries following
  natural contours of the land where possible.

- land forming the surface into a ridge and furrow
  system of varying depth with submerged islands and
  a low bund to divide the larger bed into two.

Vegetation Establishment

- Reed was planted by hand over the period 1994–96
  and followed the completion of land forming work.

- Nursery trials were conducted on a range of growing
  methods and showed that seed-grown pot plants and
  spade turfs of rhizomes were easiest to handle.

- Reed was primarily from local sources.

- Seed was sown in 2-l pots and multi-trays and grown
  on in the nursery. Seedlings were planted at 1-m
  spacing (10,000 /ha) or 2-m spacing.

- Reed turfs were cut and planted using spades or a
  digger (Plate 2). Turfs cut in spring established more
  successfully. Plantings were at 10-m spacing (100/ha).

Water Management

- Water input to the smaller bed is from Chevington
  Burn via a sluice and outfalls to sea through a second
  sluice. The flow down the Burn is influenced by a
  control valve at Red Row directing water either to the
  reedbed or to the Country Park lake which lies on the
  northern boundary of the larger reedbed.

- The larger bed receives its water from the lake via a
  23-cm pipe-sluice and exits over a weir eventually
  outfalling at the same point as the smaller bed.

- The larger bed is further divided into two
  hydrological units permitting finer control of levels.
  The smaller bed will be brackish influenced by
  permitting some tidal inflow.

Wildlife Benefits

- The reedbeds provide good invertebrate habitat
  especially with the mix of reedmace, bulrush and sea-
  club rush already established. Six moths new to the
  county have been recorded.

- The large eel population and extensive wet reedbed
  may attract bitterns. The conditions are suitable for
  colonisation by bearded tits and marsh harriers; the
  latter were recorded using the site in 1995.

- Otters are relatively common in the area. It is planned
  to provide artificial holts to encourage their
  establishment on the reedbed.

- Other benefits will be recreational and educational for
  visitors, giving them access via footpaths and
  bridleways plus the use of four viewing hides.

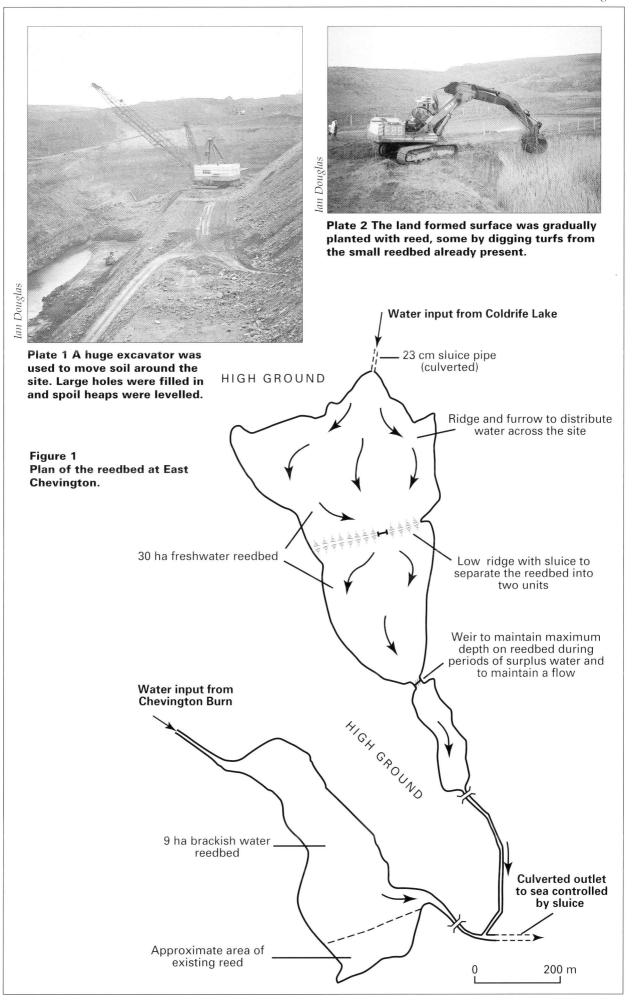

Plate 1 A huge excavator was used to move soil around the site. Large holes were filled in and spoil heaps were levelled.

Plate 2 The land formed surface was gradually planted with reed, some by digging turfs from the small reedbed already present.

**Figure 1
Plan of the reedbed at East Chevington.**

Water input from Coldrife Lake

23 cm sluice pipe (culverted)

HIGH GROUND

Ridge and furrow to distribute water across the site

30 ha freshwater reedbed

Low ridge with sluice to separate the reedbed into two units

Weir to maintain maximum depth on reedbed during periods of surplus water and to maintain a flow

Water input from Chevington Burn

HIGH GROUND

9 ha brackish water reedbed

Culverted outlet to sea controlled by sluice

Approximate area of existing reed

0   200 m

173

Ham Wall

Case Study 13

(RSPB/SCC/EN)

Location:	Street, Somerset
	OS 1:50,000 sheet No 182
	GR ST 460400
Area:	140 ha (proposed)
	16.5 ha (phase 1)

Objectives :
- To create a large reedbed on an expired peat workings for the benefit of wildlife.
- To carry out experimental investigations into reedbed establishment.
- To demonstrate the ability of large reedbeds to remove accumulated nutrients from water contaminated by diffuse agricultural land drainage and sewage treatment works discharges.

Techniques:
LAND FORMING AND CONSTRUCTION (section 3.2)
INSTALLATION OF WATER CONTROL STRUCTURES (section 3.2.3)

Background
Peat extraction in the Somerset Levels has left a large area of derelict land at a lower level than its surroundings. An ambitious scheme to create a reedbed on one such area, Ham Wall, is being undertaken by Somerset County Council, the RSPB and English Nature, backed by European Union Life funding. The ultimate aim is to create a 140-ha reedbed comprised of six hydrological units but initially work has focused on one experimental 16-ha area between the Glastonbury Canal and Ham Wall Rhyne. To maintain complete draw-down of water levels it was necessary to pump continuously while work was undertaken. Prior to work commencing, a levelling and hydrological survey was undertaken. Subsequently, a large bund was constructed to enclose the 16-ha site to enable control over water levels. Work began in the spring of 1995 to establish reed by planting, mostly pot-grown seedlings, but other techniques were also experimented with.

Land Forming
- Because of the previous land use of peat digging, the ground surface height varied abruptly, rising or dropping by as much as 1 m in places.

- A bulldozer (D53P low ground pressure hydraulic tilt) was used to reduce abrupt undulation to gentle undulation across the 16-ha plot (Plate 1).

- This was followed by power harrowing and disc harrowing to level the surface further.

Bund and Ditch Construction
- Work began in July 1994 to construct a 1,400-m bund around the 16-ha site. Plate 2 shows the bund being built and a view of its profile. Figure 1b gives cross-sectional dimensions and Figure 1a shows the extent.

- Underlying clay was excavated to form the impervious bund which was keyed into the clay sub soil at its base to prevent water seeping through the peat beneath (Figure 1b).

- The clay for bunds was compacted in layers and a peat cap, 0.3 m thick, was added to facilitate colonisation by plants.

- A large borrow pit resulted from the excavation work, which was partially refilled with peat from land forming and ditch construction. The borrow pit was up to 20 m wide but finished up at a maximum of 10 m wide after infilling (see below).

- To enable effective water movement throughout the site, a series of large and small ditches were excavated as shown in Figure 1a and 1c.

- Spoil from the ditches was not placed on the ditch edges but instead was transported by tractor and trailer and used for constucting the bund and to infill some of the borrow pit.

Installation of Water Control Structures
- Dams with flexipipe sluices were installed at the appropriate points (Figure 1a) at the same time as ditch excavation.

- In addition, a double drop-board sluice with a flow-rate controlling pipe was installed at the outlet point (Figure 1a).

- A mobile, 15-cm diesel pump controls water input from the supply ditch.

- A spillway was incorporated in the bund, 20 m long and set at 1.7 m AOD to ensure a maximum water depth of 1.2 m during flood conditions.

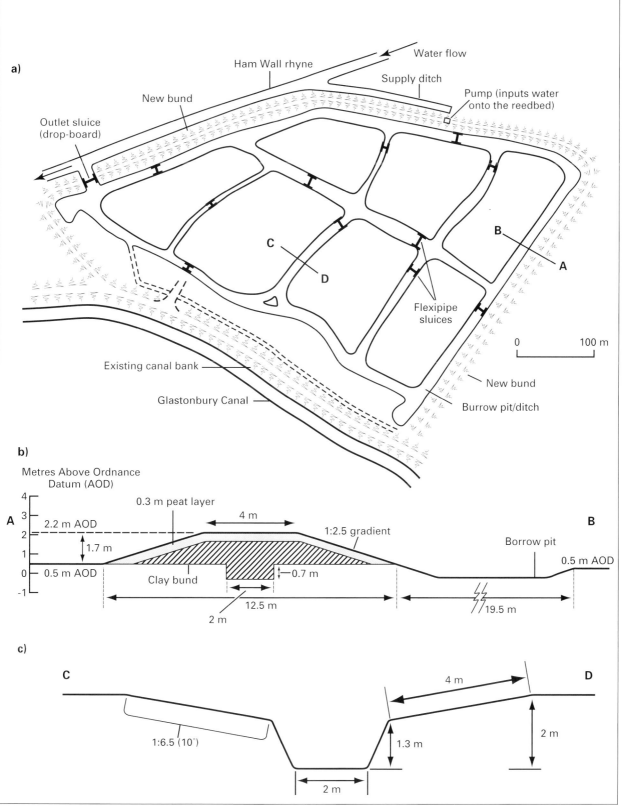

Figure 1
Plan of the Ham Wall reedbed creation project:
Phase 1 Land forming.

a) New bunds, ditches and sluices.

b) Profile of the boundary bund and borrow ditch.

c) Profile of main internal ditches (totalling 1,300 m in length) with 10 degree sloping edges.

Table 1: Summary of costs of land forming and construction work

Task		Cost (£)
Levelling: 16 ha of land surface was reformed.		
● Bulldozer hire at £27/hour		2,756
● Power harrowing at £20/hour		680
	Total	3,436
	(£/ha	215)
Bund construction:		
● Hire of two hydraulic diggers to construct 1,400 m		17,176
● Consultant engineers		8,342
● Drop-board sluice construction		1,060
	Total	26,578
	(£/m	19)
Ditch construction: 1,300 m of new ditches were constructed		
● Hydraulic digger hire at £14/hour (including flexipipe sluice construction)		3,801
● Two tractors and trailers at £11/hour to transport spoil		5,093
● Bulldozing excess spoil into borrow pit (£16/hour)		904
● 140 m of 250 mm flexipipe		490
● Miscellaneous		100
	Total	10,408
	(£/m	8)
	Grand total	40,422
	(£/ha	2,526)

Sally Mills (RSPB)

Plate 1 A bulldozer was used to land-form the surface.

C Hawke (RSPB)

Plate 2 Diggers were used to extract the clay soil to construct the bund and to place a peat capping over the clay.

Whitlingham Marshes

Case Study 14

(Broads Authority and Anglian Water)

Location: Whitlingham, Norfolk
OS 1:50,000 sheet No 134
GR TG 284075

Area: 2 ha reedbed

Objectives:
To create a reedbed for wildlife benefit and to produce reed for thatching

Techniques:
PLANTING WITH POT-GROWN SEEDLINGS (section 3.3.3 b)
Control of Water Levels (section 2.2.1)
Bed Preparation (section 3.3.1)

Background

Whitlingham is situated in the River Yare floodplain immediately south of Norwich. It was previously an area of grazing marshes and/or hay meadows, which when abandoned, quickly developed a swamp of reed sweet-grass, reed canary- grass, pond sedge and reedmace. In association with the owners Anglian Water, work began in 1987 to establish a reedbed on a 2.5-ha plot on the site. The overgrown ditches and grips were cleared using a low ground-pressure digger and a sluice was installed (Woodcock 1994). The vegetation was cut and burned and soil with rhizomes from a reedbed in the Broads which produced good thatching quality reed, was spread manually over the plot. Unfortunately, vigorous regrowth of reed sweet-grass outcompeted the new reed shoots and so an alternative approach using pot-grown seedlings was adopted.

Winter water levels are kept high other than to draw-down in late January for management work (principally double wale cutting for thatch). Summer levels are kept as high as possible but vary with rainfall and tides. It is a single hydrological unit with water on and water off at the same point.

Planting with Pot-grown Seedlings

● Complete draw down was achieved in late January by opening the non-return flap on the outlet side for three days.

● The plot was blanket-sprayed with glyphosate (Roundup) using a knapsack sprayer (section 2.3.3) when the reed sweet-grass shoots were growing in early spring.

● When signs of withering and browning were evident, the plot was flooded to inhibit any late emerging plants that had escaped the herbicide treatment.

● A few days prior to planting, complete draw-down was undertaken.

● 20,300 pot-grown seedlings were purchased from Yarningdale Nurseries (address in Appendix 3) who had grown them in plugs from seed provided by the Broads Authority (Plate 1). An additional 3,000 seedlings were used. The seed had been collected the previous winter from Turf Fen, a site known to produce high quality thatching reed.

● A workforce armed with trays of reed seedling plugs and dibbers, planted seedlings at 1-m spacing along lines marked out with string (Plate 2). It took several days to plant all the seedlings.

● Shallow flooding (5 cm) was undertaken as soon as possible after planting.

● Planting was done rather late, in July, because of the spraying and flooding treatment needed to eliminate competing plants in spring. Nevertheless, the overall take was good and near total cover was achieved by the end of 1994.

● Because one side of the plot was not protected by a ditch, rabbits accessed and grazed the newly planted reed along one edge. Electrified flexinetting was used to keep them out but wet vegetation created a short-circuit, rendering it ineffective. The rabbit grazed area became dominated by rushes and reed canary-grass.

● The reed was well established by the end of the first season (Plate 3). The plot was cut in winter 1994/95 to encourage a regrowth of straight, vigorous reed. It is planned to harvest the reed on a double wale basis thereafter.

Wildlife and Commercial Benefits

● The reedbed has added habitat variety to an area previously dominated by one type, ie reed sweet-grass

● Both reed and sedge warblers now breed.

● Bearded tits were recorded feeding on the reed seed-heads in 1995.

● Double wale cutting will ensure there is always standing reed in spring for nesting warblers, reed buntings, bearded tits and harvest mice and for invertebrates to colonise from nearby sites along the Yare valley.

● Double wale cutting will yield up to 1,000 bundles of cut reed each year for thatching.

Plate 1 Commercially produced pot-grown seedlings ready for planting.

Table 1 Costs of project

Item	£
• 20,300 seedlings at 42p + VAT each	10,018
• Digger hire for ditch clearing } Sluice + installation } Miscellaneous }	4,982
Total 15,000 (£/ha 6,000)	

Plate 2 The seedlings were planted at 1 m intervals in straight lines using dibbers and trowels.

Plate 3 The reedbed in its first winter after planting.

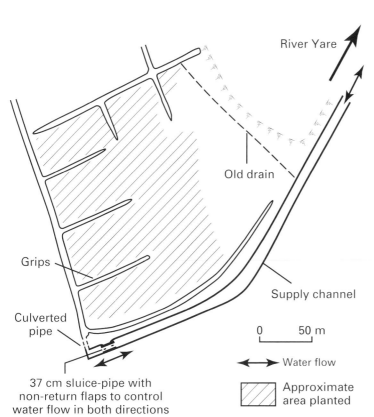

River Yare

Old drain

Grips

Supply channel

Culverted pipe

37 cm sluice-pipe with non-return flaps to control water flow in both directions

0   50 m

◄—► Water flow

Approximate area planted

**Figure 1
Plan of the creation plot at Whitlingham showing the approximate area planted with reed seedlings. Ditches, grips and the position of the sluice are also shown.**

Rutland Water

Case Study 15

(Leicestershire and Rutland Trust for Nature Conservation and Anglian Water)

Location:	Oakham, Leicestershire OS 1:50,000 sheet No 141 GR SK 885 082
Area:	1 ha existing created reedbed 0.5–0.75 ha planted 1995 (potential to expand to 5 ha)

Objectives:
To create and expand reedbed for wildlife.

Techniques:
SPREADING SOIL WITH RHIZOMES
(section 3.3.3 c)
PLANTING TURFS (3.3.3 c)
Layering (3.3.2 b)
Rhizome cuttings (3.3.3 c)

Background

Construction of a major water supply reservoir resulted in the loss of 2–3 ha of wetland habitat. To compensate, nearby pasture where grazing had ceased was identified as suitable for reedbed creation. The new reedbed was created in 1976 by transferring some of the reed from the former wetland to the new location. Reed is now established and presently covers about 1 ha (Plate 3). In 1995, work began on expanding this area to increase the total reed area to at least 6 ha. This has involved land forming and bund construction and planting with reed turfs and rhizome cuttings. Expansion was encouraged in the original planting using the technique of layering.

Spreading Soil With Rhizomes

- A digger with a narrow bucket was used to scrape seven areas approximately 0.5 m x 10 m x 0.3 m deep, in the furrows of the pasture on the margin of the water.

- The same digger was used to excavate soil with rhizomes from the former wetland which was transferred in a tractor and trailer to the scraped furrows (Plate 1).

- The soil and rhizomes were bedded and heeled in manually using shovels and feet.

- Unwanted plants were removed manually from around the growing reed annually for five years after planting.

- The water supply to the reedbed is tertiary treated sewage effluent which flows continually.

- A system of dykes with small earth dams was installed to carry water to each furrow.

- Plate 2 shows the reed growing in one of the furrows a year after planting.

Planting Turfs

- Land forming was undertaken prior to planting. Spoil was used to create small bunds and 'paddy-field' style units. Surplus spoil was pushed into the deep-water margin to create a shallower area for the reed to spread in to. An area of about 1 ha was prepared.

- A digger with a 1-m bucket was used to excavate holes (1 m x 1 m x 0.3 m) in which to plant the turfs.

- Turfs were excavated (1 m x 1 m x 0.3 m) from the adjacent reedbed originally created using soil with rhizomes.

- The turfs were placed in the excavated holes by the digger and heeled in with the bucket. Turfs were planted at approximately 6-m spacing.

- Flooding was undertaken immediately afterwards but reed stems were not submerged.

- The land forming and planting was carried out in winter.

Wildlife Benefits

A Constant Effort Site ringing programme has monitored breeding populations of birds in the reedbed and the willow coppice adjacent.

- Breeding reed warblers have increased from zero to 35+ pairs.

- Reed buntings (breeding and 100+ wintering), sedge warbler (breeding and passage) and water rails (11 present winter 1994/95) regularly use the habitat.

- Bearded tits have used the reedbed in winter.

- Moth monitoring revealed several species specific to reedbeds in particular the twin-spotted wainscot, which occurs at a 70% infestation rate.

T Appleton

Plate 1 Soil with rhizomes was excavated from the nearby reedbed and loaded into a dumper truck for transportation to the creation site. The soil was tipped into the trenches excavated in the furrows

Table 1: Approximate cost for about 20 days' work

- Digger + driver hire £24/hour
- Total cost of expansion work £4,500

Includes land forming, turf cutting and planting, ditch and bund construction.

Figure 1
Plan of phase 2: Reedbed extension by land forming, planting and 'natural' expansion.

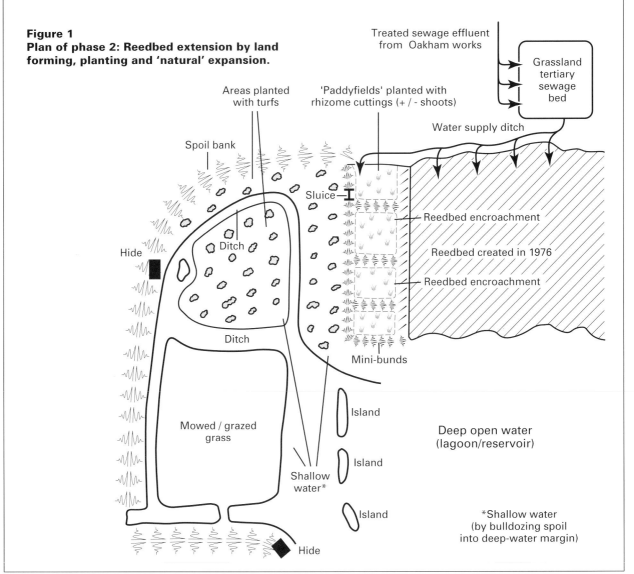

*Shallow water (by bulldozing spoil into deep-water margin)

Plate 2 New reed shoots growing in one of the furrows one year later.

Plate 3 Part of the reedbed in 1995 showing an area which had been recently cut (left) and an uncut area (right).

Figure 2
Schematic drawing of ridge and furrow planting system.

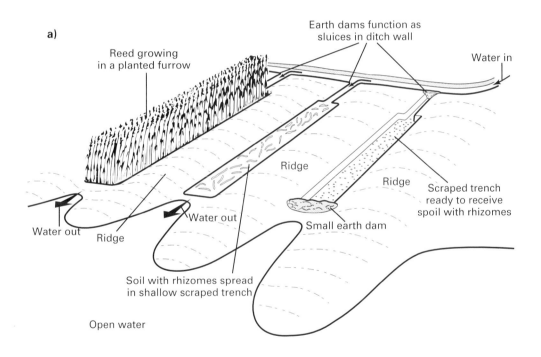

a)

Reed growing in a planted furrow

Earth dams function as sluices in ditch wall

Water in

Ridge

Ridge

Scraped trench ready to receive spoil with rhizomes

Water out

Small earth dam

Water out   Ridge

Soil with rhizomes spread in shallow scraped trench

Open water

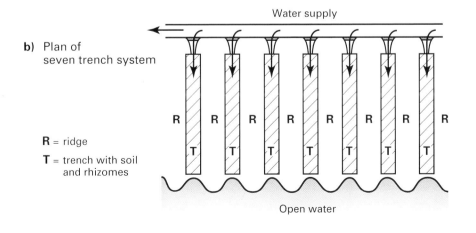

Water supply

b) Plan of seven trench system

R   R   R   R   R   R   R   R

T   T   T   T   T   T   T

R = ridge

T = trench with soil and rhizomes

Open water

Slimbridge

Case Study 16

(Wildfowl & Wetlands Trust)

Location: Slimbridge, Gloucestershire
OS 1:50,000 sheet No 162
GR SO 722 048

Area: 1.5 ha

Objectives:
To create an environmentally appropriate, wetland water treatment system of benefit to wildlife and with amenity and educational value.

Techniques:
CREATION
(Water Treatment System - Overland Flow):
SITE EVALUATION (section 1.2)
VEGETATION ESTABLISHMENT (section 3.3)

Background

The wildfowl collection at Slimbridge is the largest in the country and also supports large numbers of feral and wild birds. Approximately 2.2 million litres of water passes through the enclosures daily, and is discharged to a nearby watercourse. Artificial feeding, fertiliser run-off and bird faeces enrich the water giving peak BOD values of 25 mg/l. In order to improve effluent quality a constructed wetland was proposed. This comprises an overland flow system, which aims to settle out suspended solids, remove phosphates and break down organic material. The system uses a range of experimental treatment methods, including pools, cascades and different vegetation types, designed to maximise wildlife benefit (Plate 2). Grants from the Department of the Environment's Environmental Action Fund and the BOC Foundation for the Environment funded the project.

Site Evaluation (Planning and design)

- Initial consultation with Penny Anderson Associates produced a design which was experimental and would best suit the needs of WWT regarding water treatment, wildlife and educational aspects.

- An assessment revealed that:
  - The site was virtually flat and a fall of 1 m was needed to achieve a cascading flow. This would necessitate the use of electric pumps.
  - No lining would be necessary as leakage was prevented by an effective sub-soil clay layer.

- It was determined that:
  - A total retention time of 83.5 h would be needed to treat the water (between 3 and 8 h on individual beds).
  - The system would need a capacity of 967 population equivalent.
  - The system would operate optimally with an average water depth of 15 cm.

All excavation work and land forming was done by digger in 1992. The National Rivers Authority carried out the work (an estimated equivalent of £9,000) in exchange for soil for sea wall repair works nearby. Some spoil was used to construct banks and access routes for future management work.

The twin pumps and sluices cost approximately £10,000.

Vegetation Establishment

- The beds were prepared for planting at the construction phase by over-excavating into the clay sub-soil and overlaying with top-soil.

- The beds were planted in early spring of 1993 and in the following proportions:
  - reed 40%
  - reedmace 10%
  - bulrush 10%
  - yellow flag iris and others 10%

Approximately 30% of the wetland is open water.

- Reed was established by:
  - planting pot-grown seedlings (Plate 1)
  - spreading soil with rhizomes
  - planting rhizome cuttings and clumps
  - planting stem cuttings

- All other plants were planted by hand

- The beds were flooded to a depth of 5–10 cm after planting.

Benefits

- Reed and other plants established well.

- By 1994, dragonflies were already using the wetland, with several species breeding.

- Snipe and water rail feed in winter.

- Grass snakes use the site regularly.

- As it develops, this wetland will be able to support an increasing range of wildlife including reed warblers, reed buntings, amphibians and aquatic invertebrates. Many of the latter will have been introduced with the soil, roots and stems of the plants.

P Worrall

Plate 1 Home-produced pot-grown reed plugs being planted.

C Hawke (RSPB)

Plate 2 View of one of the pools containing a floating mat with water plants.

Table 1: Initial results of water analysis

Component	Average % reduction	range (%)
BOD	67	59–75
TSS	90	87–93
Ammonia	15	-22–45
Nitrate	42	20–63
Total Phosphate	70	67–73
Zinc	80	79–82
Lead	79	69–87

(BOD = biochemical oxygen demand; TSS = total suspended solids)

These results are from the first post-commissioning samples and do not represent the full potential of the system. As it matures, soil microbe communities will develop further and sediments stabilise, increasing the efficiency of break-down of substances.

Figure 1 The Slimbridge wetland water treatment system.

A Water supply

1. Drop-board sluice (DS) maintains deep water in ditch

2. Pipe-sluice controls input to pumping chamber (PC)

3. An electric pump transfers water into the stilling pond (a second pump cuts in should the first fail)

B Stilling pond

1. A sensor cuts out pump when maximum level is reached

2. 35-hour retention time facilitates sedimentation of suspended solids and some bacterial breakdown

3. Sluice-pipes permit water to run into one or more treatment beds

4. Minimum of 25 years before desilting required

C Treatment beds

1. Experimental range of vegetation types to break down organic and inorganic pollutants

2. Beds will be drawn-down in rotation to facilitate management and permit oxidation of organic litter

3. Sluice-pipes permit water to run into Lagoon 1

D Lagoon 1

1. Rafts of plants with suspended roots to further break down pollutants

2. Limestone cascade precipitates phosphates and oxygenates water as it enters Lagoon 2

E Lagoon 2

1. Deep pond to store precipitated phosphate

2. Shallow end planted with water plants of wildlife value

F 'Polishing' beds

1. Final polishing of water to remove traces of pollutants

2. Final effluent runs through outlet pipes half filled with limestone to precipitate any remaining phosphate

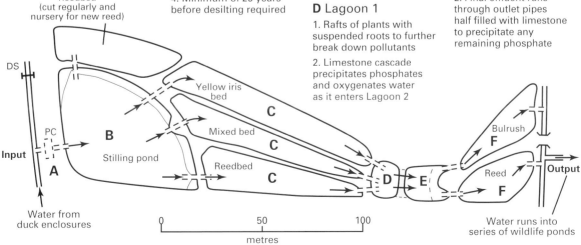

183

Billingham Reedbed

(ICI)

Location:	Billingham, Teesside
	OS 1:50,000 sheet No 93
	GR NZ 464 214
Area:	5 ha reedbed

Objectives:
To construct a water treatment reedbed to treat industrial effluent.

Techniques:
WATER TREATMENT SYSTEM (section 3.5.5)
(Construction and Functioning)

Background

In 1987, ICI's Chemical Products Area at Billingham assessed several options for dealing with effluents from a range of chemical processes. Retrospective modification of the processes had reached practical limits although further advance was considered practicable on new plant. Off-plant effluent treatment was therefore studied. Various biological treatment systems were examined, including an activated sludge system, a packed tower system and a reedbed system. A reedbed system based on the Kikuth horizontal flow design was trialled in view of low running costs (no aeration or sludge disposal), potential longevity and its ability to break down toxic, biodegradable substances. This was set against the initial, moderately high capital costs of constructing and developing such a system.

Samples of effluent were trialled in a greenhouse study to determine suitability for treatment by a constructed reedbed. After successful trials the scale was increased to three 10 m x 5 m trial plots at Billingham. After 18 months, results were sufficiently impressive for work to begin on a full-scale scheme.

Reedbed Construction

- An area of 5 ha of unused industrial land adjacent to the Billingham site was selected (additional land next to this was available for a second reedbed if required in the future).

- A 1- m high bund was constructed to enclose the area and create seven, 0.7-ha bunded units within it (Plate 3). Clay was imported from a construction project proceeding in the locality.

- Access roads were incorporated in the design to facilitate maintenance and operational procedures.

- Each unit was lined with 3-mm thick, high density polythene to prevent leakage of effluent (Plate 1).

- A system of supply pipes was installed to feed the effluent onto the surface of the reedbed. The full-scale reedbed utilises a vertical effluent flow-path.

- The beds incorporated drainage pipes below 0.6 m of top-soil into which the reeds were planted.

- Approximately 106,000 pot-grown reed seedlings were planted in rows at about 2 plants/m^2. Planting was done during the late summer/early autumn of 1990 (Plate 2).

- The newly planted reeds were provided with surface water irrigation as required during the summer months while planting continued.

- The following spring, the beds were shallow-flooded with water to a depth of 5 cm to inhibit the growth of unwanted plants.

- The growth characteristics of reeds varied between units and within units (a consequence of different genotypes/sources) but full cover was achieved by 1994.

Reedbed Functioning

- Effluent containing methanol, acetone, phenol and other substances was fed into the reedbed at a rate of 500 m^3/day. This will increase to the design capacity of 3,000 m^3/day as reed root structure develops.

- Each unit can be operated separately, permitting fine control over inputs, outputs and required retention times. The units are used on rotation to prevent overloading.

- The system operates with no surface water to ensure all effluent reaches the active reed root layer.

- The characteristics of effluent into and final effluent out of the system are carefully monitored.

- Treated effluent collects in a series of outlet sluices and passes into the River Tees via the Billingham site's drains thus achieving a reduction in the effluent load discharged by the site.

- By the end of 1994, the reedbed was four years old and had well developed root structures. Hydraulic capacity had developed in line with root growth.

Benefits

- Despite high construction costs the day-to-day running costs have been very low. This is due to the absence of sludge disposal (not required with reedbeds) and no significant chemical requirement (unlike many other effluent treatments).

- The reeds are generally very vigorous (up to 3 m tall, stems 20 mm diameter, large leaves and seed-heads). This will increase energy production which should further enhance rhizome development and, with time, increase the efficiency of treatment.

● While the reedbed occupies a relatively large area of land it is a significant landscape feature with conservation value. It provides an important habitat and wildlife refuge within the industrial area.

● Monitoring commenced in 1993 and has shown the site has significant wildlife value. Breeding bird census and ringing studies are carried out annually and moth and beetle surveys have been conducted. Tables 1 and 2 summarise the results to date.

Plate 1 Each of the seven units was lined with an impermeable plastic.

Table 1: Birds recorded breeding in the Billingham Reedbed and associated habitats

Species	Number of Breeding Pairs 1993	1994
Little grebe	1	1
Mallard	0	1
Tufted duck	0	1*
Grey partridge	4	3
Coot	1	2
Lapwing	1	*
Skylark	14	9
Carrion crow	0	1
Blackbird	1	3+
Robin	0	1*
Whinchat	1	0
Reed warbler	0	3/4
Sedge warbler	14+	14
Grasshopper warbler	0	1*
Whitethroat	7	8
Meadow pipit	6+	12
Reed bunting	15+	21

* Actual numbers unconfirmed
  Emboldened names are those species which usually or often nest in reed

a Reed warbler is a scarce breeding species in Cleveland with fewer than 20 pairs. The four pairs of the Billingham reedbed are of considerable regional significance therefore.

b 14 pairs of sedge warblers makes the reedbed a major site for this species in the county.

During 1993 and 1994 a total of 57 species of bird have been recorded using the site.

Other species which possibly bred were pheasant, moorhen, snipe, wood pigeon, magpie, goldfinch and linnet.

(All bird data courtesy of D I Griff, Tees Ringing Group, ICI and INCA.)

Plate 2 Commercially produced pot-grown seedlings were planted in the topsoil. Note the pipes along the surface which supply effluent to the reedbed.

Plate 3 An aerial view of the seven, bunded units with reed at different stages of development.

Table 2: Rare and uncommon beetles recorded from the Billingham Reedbed

Species	Number of individuals recorded 1993	1994
Dyschirius luedersi	1	1
Stomis pumicatus	0	1
Agonum thoreyi	0	1
Cercyon lateralis	1	13
Cercyon marinus	19	0
Cercyon tristis	0	1
Platystethus cornutus	1	0
Sternus carbonarius	0	8
Atheta celata	4	6
Atheta deformis	0	2
Atheta liliputana	0	1
Carpelimus zealandicus	0	10
Atomaria barani	2	0
Atomaria mesomela	0	10
Scymnus haemorrhoidalis	0	1

(Data courtesy Les Jessop/Sunderland Museum, ICI and INCA.)

Appendix 1
Assessment of Hydrological Conditions

The initial hydrological assessment for the viability of a site for reedbed creation involves consideration of the climatic conditions ie the average expected precipitation and transpiration (Emerson1995).

Precipitation and transpiration figures can be derived from the *MAFF Technical Bulletin Number 34, Climate and Drainage*. This will give a monthly water balance value for a reedbed using the transpiration from the reedbed minus the rainfall. A monthly water balance for a 10-ha potential reedbed in East Anglia is shown in the table below.

The rainfall and transpiration figures (columns B and C) used in the table are taken directly from 'Climate and Drainage' which provides figures for all England and Wales. The transpiration figures stated in the technical bulletin are for farm crops which do not have a free supply of water. As a reedbed is usually provided with an ample supply of water its transpiration rate is greater than that of farm crops. To allow for this reedbed transpiration rates (column D) are obtained by multiplying transpiration rates (column C) by a factor of 1.4.

By subtracting the reedbed transpiration figure from the monthly rainfall figure a basic water balance for the site is obtained

in mm/month (column E). Reedbed water deficit figures (column F) are periods during which the water balance figure is negative. To calculate the additional water demand in litres per day per hectare (l/day/ha), water deficit figures are multiplied by a factor of 333 (column G). This figure can then be used to estimate the average monthly water demand for the site in litres/second (l/sec) (column H). The figure is reached by multiplying the water demand per day by the area of the reedbed and dividing by 86,400.

By measuring the flows of potential water sources in the area such as streams and rivers and comparing them to the water demands, an initial assessment of the site's viability can be made. In the example given in the table, rivers and streams in the area must provide a combined flow of at least 3.36 l/sec in June to provide enough water to meet the peak average deficits of the reedbed.

This is the first element of any hydrological assessment of a potential reedbed site and is the basis of a water balance. Depending on the complexity of local hydrology, investigations into seepage into and out of the site, the needs of other water users and water courses running onto and off the site will have to be considered in the water balance.

A Month	B rainfall mm/month	C Transpiration mm/month	D = C x 1.4 Reedbed Transpiration mm/month	E = D - B Water balance mm/month	F Reedbed water deficit mm/month	G = F x 333 Water demand per ha l/day/ha	H = G x area /86400 Water demand demand site l/sec
January	48	1	1	47	0	0	0
February	38	10	14	24	0	0	0
March	38	33	47	-9	9	3,000	0.35
April	37	57	81	-44	44	14,667	1.7
May	44	83	119	-75	75	25,000	2.9
June	47	94	134	-87	87	29,000	3.36
July	56	94	134	-78	78	26,000	3.01
August	60	76	109	-49	49	16,333	1.89
September	49	48	69	-20	20	6,667	0.77
October	49	22	31	18	0	0	0
November	58	5	7	51	0	0	0
December	50	0	0	50	0	0	0
Total	**574**	**523**	**746**	**-172**	**362**	**120,667**	**13.98**

Appendix 2
Current Schemes Offering Financial Incentives for Reedbed Management, Rehabilitation and Creation

Scheme	Mechanism	Eligibility	Payments	Administration
Countryside Stewardship (Scheme to be amended in 1996)	10-year agreements for management and creation of waterside landscapes including reedbeds	All farmers and land-owners (including voluntary bodies and local authorities). England only.	£40/ha for 5 years for reedbed creation. £100/ha for reedbed management.	CC (MAFF 1996)
Tir Cymen	10-year agreements to encourage management for wildlife and landscape benefit.	All registered farm holdings within pilot areas of Wales only.	£20–£280/ha	CCW
Environmentally Sensitive Areas (ESAs)	10-year agreements to adopt environmentally beneficial practices to protect important landscape and wildlife areas. Grants for establishing reedbeds as part of Farm Conservation Plan.	All farmers and land-owners within an ESA boundary. All of UK.	£ 8–£400/ha	DANI, MAFF, SOAFD, WOAD.
Habitat Scheme (proposed as part of Agri-environment regulations)	Mostly 10-and 20-year agreements for creation and management of selected habitats such as water margins eg reedbeds. Each country has slightly different arrangements.	All farmers and land-owners in the UK, although may be limited to pilot areas.	£125–£360	DANI, MAFF, SOAFD, WOAD.
Landscape and Nature Conservation Grants	Covers a wide range of projects to encourage the conservation and creation of landscapes, wildlife and habitats. Includes agreements for management of SSSIs and ASSIs.	Open to all farmers and land managers in the UK.	Grants cover part of management costs and capital cost. (Usually up to 50%).	CC, CCW, EN, DoENI, SNH, BA, LA, NPA.

NB: Grants for reedbed creation for treatment of farm effluents currently under the Farm Conservation Grant Scheme are likely to fall under the revised Nitrate Sensitive Areas Scheme in 1996.

The information given here is reviewed from time to time by the relevant organisations. For more detailed and up to date information contact the relevant organisation directly (addresses in Appendix 3).

A summary leaflet entitled *Farming and Wildlife Financial Incentives 1994* is available free from the RSPB, and MAFF has produced a leaflet *Conservation Grants for Farmers* (addresses in Appendix 3).

Appendix 3
Addresses of Government Organisations and Voluntary Organisations

Government organisations

1. Agriculture Departments

Ministry of Agriculture, Fisheries and Food (MAFF), 3 Whitehall Place, London SW1A 2HH. Tel 0645 335577 (Helpline - all calls charged at local rate)

Ministry of Agriculture, Fisheries and Food, Nobel House, 17 Smith Square, London SW1P 3JR. Tel 0645 335577 for information on burning crop residues and pesticides use.

Welsh Office Agriculture Department (WOAD), Cathays Park, Crown Buildings, Cardiff CF1 3NQ. Tel 01222 825111.

Scottish Office Agricultural and Fisheries Department (SOAFD), Pentland House, 47 Robb's Loan, Edinburgh EH14 1TW. Tel 0131 556 8400.

Department of Agriculture for Northern Ireland (DANI), Dundonald House, Upper Newtownards Road, Belfast BT4 3SB. Tel 01232 520000.

2. Countryside and Conservation Departments/Agencies

English Nature (EN), Northminster House, Peterborough PE1 1UA. Tel 01733 340345.

Countryside Council for Wales (CCW), Plas Penrhos, Fford Penrhos, Bangor LL57 2LQ. Tel 01248 370444.

Scottish Natural Heritage (SNH), 12 Hope Terrace, Edinburgh EH9 2AS. Tel 0131 4474784.

Department of the Environment for Northern Ireland (DoENI), Countryside and Wildlife Branch, Calvert House, 23 Castle Place, Belfast BT1 1FY. Tel 01232 254754.

Countryside Commission (CC), John Dower House, Crescent Place, Cheltenham GL50 3RA. Tel 01242 521381.

National Parks Authorities (NPAs). Details in relevant local telephone directory.

Broads Authority (BA), Thomas Harvey House, 18 Colegate, Norwich NR3 1BQ. Tel 01603 610734.

3. Water Management Agencies

National Rivers Authority (NRA), Rivers House, Waterside Drive, Aztec West, Almondsbury, Bristol BS12 4UD. Tel 01454 624400. (NRA will become the Environmental Agency from April 1996.)

Scottish River Purification Boards. There are seven RPB's: Clyde, Forth, Highland, Northeast, Solway, Tweed and Tay. Details from relevant area telephone directory. (The RPBs will become part of the Scottish Environmental Protection Agency from April 1996.)

DANI, Watercourse Management Division, Hydebank, 4 Hospital Road, Belfast BT8 8JP. Tel 01232 253380.

Association of Drainage Authorities (ADA), The Mews, 3 Royal Oak Passage, High Street, Huntingdon PE18 6EA. Tel 01480 411123. (For details of local IDBs).

4. Other Departments

Local Authorities (LAs) including Planning Authorities. Details in relevant local telephone directory.

Voluntary Organisations

The Royal Society for the Protection of Birds (RSPB), The Lodge, Sandy SG19 2DL. Tel 01767 680551.

The Wildlife Trusts, The Green, Witham Park, Waterside South, Lincoln LN5 7JR. Tel 01522 544400.

Wildfowl & Wetlands Trust (WWT), Slimbridge GL2 7BT. Tel 01453 890333.

National Trust (NT), 33 Sheep Street,
Cirencester GL7 1QW. Tel 01285 651818.

British Reed Growers' Association, c/o
Francis Horner and Son, Old Bank of
England Court, Queen Street, Norwich
NR2 4TA. Tel 01603 629871.

Other Organisations

Water Research Centre (WRc), Frankland
Road, Blagrove, Swindon SN5 8YF. Tel
01793 511711.

Penny Anderson Associates, 52 Lower
Lane, Chinley, Stockport SK12 6BD. Tel
01663 750205. (Ecological consultants in
reedbed creation)

Yarningdale Nurseries, 16 Chapel Street,
Warwick CV34 4H. Tel 01926 496656.
(Suppliers of pot-grown reeds)

H S Blundell, The Hollies, Greaves Lane,
Threepwood, Malpas SY14 7AS. Tel 01948
770289. (Supplier of pot-grown reeds)

Appendix 4
Map Showing some other Sites in Britain where Reedbed Management and Creation Techniques have been Practised

Techniques Key:

Pl	Planning Management
WL	Water Level Control
Q	Water Quality Management/Monitoring
D	Ditch Management
Rp	Ditch Reprofiling
OW	Open Water (Management/Creation)
C	Cutting (unspecified)
Rt	Rotational Cutting
CC	Commercial Cutting
SC	Summer Cutting
B	Burning
S	Scrub Management
Rc	Rotational Coppicing
R	Bed Regeneration
L	Land Forming
E	Expansion of Reed
P	Planting Reed
WTS	Water Treatment System
NI	Non-intervention
G	Grazing

Key to Organisations

RSPB	Royal Society for the Protection of Birds
SNH	Scottish Natural Heritage
NWTa	Norfolk Wildlife Trust
NWTb	Northumberland Wildlife Trust
TDC	Teesside Development Corporation
YW	Yorkshire Water
YWT	Yorkshire Wildlife Trust
LTWC	Lincolnshire Trust for Nature Conservation
EN	English Nature
NT	National Trust
SWT	Suffolk Wildlife Trust
EWT	Essex Wildlife Trust
SuWT	Sussex Wildlife Trust
TW	Thames Water
NRA	National Rivers Authority
PA	Pond Action
WBC	Waverley Borough Council
WSCC	West Sussex County Council
DoWT	Dorset Wildlife Trust
CWT	Cornwall Wildlife Trust
HWT	Hampshire Wildlife Trust
STNC	Somerset Trust for Nature Conservation
BBAWT	Bristol, Bath and Avon Wildlife Trust
WWT	Wildfowl & Wetlands Trust
BS	British Steel
DWT	Dyfed Wildlife Trust
WaWt	Warwickshire Wildlife Trust
ShWT	Shropshire Wildlife Trust
MWT	Montgomeryshire Wildlife Trust
BA	Broads Authority
CCW	Countryside Council for Wales
NWWT	North Wales Wildlife Trust

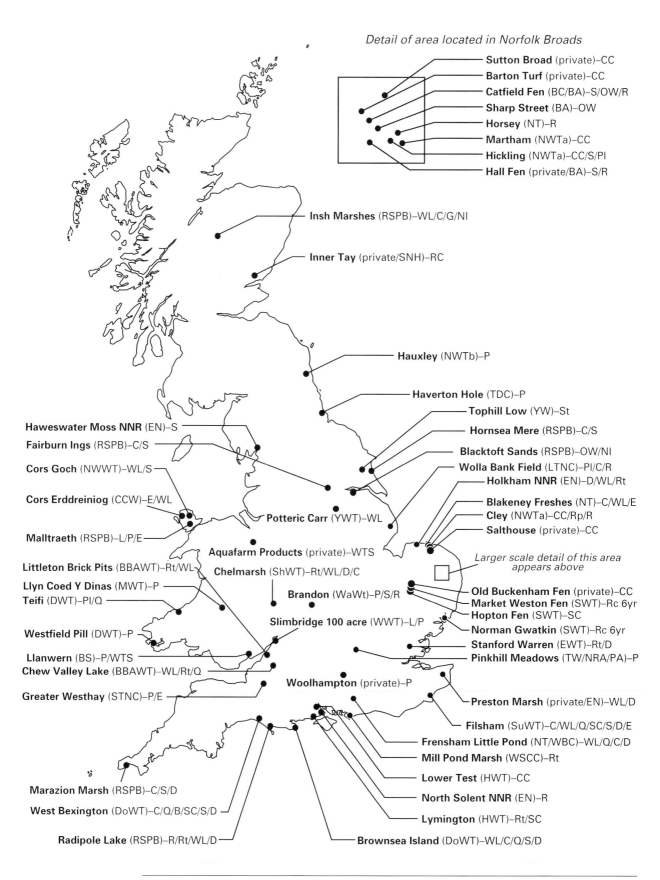

Detail of area located in Norfolk Broads

Sutton Broad (private)–CC
Barton Turf (private)–CC
Catfield Fen (BC/BA)–S/OW/R
Sharp Street (BA)–OW
Horsey (NT)–R
Martham (NWTa)–CC
Hickling (NWTa)–CC/S/PI
Hall Fen (private/BA)–S/R

Insh Marshes (RSPB)–WL/C/G/NI

Inner Tay (private/SNH)–RC

Hauxley (NWTb)–P

Haverton Hole (TDC)–P
Tophill Low (YW)–St
Hornsea Mere (RSPB)–C/S
Blacktoft Sands (RSPB)–OW/NI
Wolla Bank Field (LTNC)–PI/C/R
Holkham NNR (EN)–D/WL/Rt
Blakeney Freshes (NT)–C/WL/E
Cley (NWTa)–CC/Rp/R
Salthouse (private)–CC

Haweswater Moss NNR (EN)–S
Fairburn Ings (RSPB)–C/S
Cors Goch (NWWT)–WL/S
Cors Erddreiniog (CCW)–E/WL
Potteric Carr (YWT)–WL
Malltraeth (RSPB)–L/P/E

Larger scale detail of this area appears above

Littleton Brick Pits (BBAWT)–Rt/WL
Chelmarsh (ShWT)–Rt/WL/D/C
Llyn Coed Y Dinas (MWT)–P
Brandon (WaWt)–P/S/R
Teifi (DWT)–PI/Q
Slimbridge 100 acre (WWT)–L/P
Westfield Pill (DWT)–P
Llanwern (BS)–P/WTS
Chew Valley Lake (BBAWT)–WL/Rt/Q
Woolhampton (private)–P
Greater Westhay (STNC)–P/E

Old Buckenham Fen (private)–CC
Market Weston Fen (SWT)–Rc 6yr
Hopton Fen (SWT)–SC
Norman Gwatkin (SWT)–Rc 6yr
Stanford Warren (EWT)–Rt/D
Pinkhill Meadows (TW/NRA/PA)–P

Preston Marsh (private/EN)–WL/D
Filsham (SuWT)–C/WL/Q/SC/S/D/E
Frensham Little Pond (NT/WBC)–WL/Q/C/D
Mill Pond Marsh (WSCC)–Rt
Lower Test (HWT)–CC
North Solent NNR (EN)–R
Lymington (HWT)–Rt/SC

Marazion Marsh (RSPB)–C/S/D
West Bexington (DoWT)–C/Q/B/SC/S/D
Radipole Lake (RSPB)–R/Rt/WL/D
Brownsea Island (DoWT)–WL/C/Q/S/D

Appendix 5
Health and Safety

Information and Training

Training in pesticides use, the operation of knapsack sprayers, chainsaws, Tirfor winches and brushcutters may be obtained through:

Agricultural Training Board (ATB-Landbase), National Agricultural Centre, Kenilworth CV8 2UG. Tel 01203 696996 for information on local ATB training centres.

National Proficiency Tests Council, Tenth Street, National Agricultural Training Centre, Stoneleigh CV8 2LG. Write for information about the requirements for national testing and other organisations which may offer training courses.

British Trust for Conservation Volunteers (BTCV), 36 St Mary's Street, Wallingford, OX10 0EU. Tel 01491 839766. Run training courses on a range of conservation techniques and equipment use, throughout the UK.

Information on the regulations governing pesticide use and other safety matters may be obtained from:

Health and Safety Executive (HSE), Agricultural Inspectorate, Magdalen House, Stanley Precinct, Bootle L20 3QZ.

Relevant Legislation and Regulations

Health and Safety at Work Act 1974

Health and Safety Regulations 1992

Food and Environment Protection Act 1985

Control of Substances Hazardous to Health Regulations 1988

Control of Pesticides Regulations 1986

Additional safety information on pesticide use includes:

Working with Pesticides, MAFF, 1989

Code of Practice for the Safe Use of Pesticides on Farms and Small Holdings

Guidelines for the Use of Herbicides on Weeds in or near Watercourses

The above are available through MAFF at the address in Appendix 3.

General Safety Precautions in Reedbeds

Reedbeds are potentially dangerous places in which to work, with soft, boggy, uneven ground, deep water and sharp vegetation. Simply walking through such terrain is difficult. Operating equipment such as reed cutters, chainsaws and ATVs can be dangerous. Prior to undertaking any work on a reedbed the following should be considered:

- All persons intending to operate equipment or use tools must be trained.

- A risk assessment should have been carried out for each task by a person responsible for safety and all staff/volunteers be familiar with the assessment. (This is a requirement of the Management of Health and Safety at Work Regulations 1992).

- Under the same regulations, all staff/volunteers should be familiar with the hazards and risks and how to prevent/reduce them.

- All staff/volunteers should be provided with the required personal protective equipment including protection from foul weather.

- An agreed procedure for action in case of an emergency should be established prior to entering the work area.

- A first aid kit should be available on-site containing the minimum required items for the number of staff/volunteers present.

Working alone

Whenever possible, working alone should be avoided. If it is unavoidable, the following precautions should be considered:

- If possible, carry a mobile phone/CB radio/short-wave radio and maintain regular contact with base or home.

- Inform someone of your plans; where you are going, how long you expect to be. Try to give an indication of the time at which you expect to return.

- Avoid undertaking hazardous tasks such as operating machinery.

- Do not take risks.

Leptospirosis (Weil's disease)

Weil's disease is the most serious form of an illness called leptospirosis. In the UK it is most commonly associated with rats, which excrete the bacteria in their urine. The bacteria can survive in fresh water for about four weeks and people can become infected through contact with water or muddy soil contaminated by infected rat urine. The leptospira bacteria can enter the human body through cuts, grazes and sores and mucous membranes of the eyes, nose and mouth. Simple precautions to reduce the chances of contracting the disease are:

- Ensure cuts, scratches and skin abrasions are thoroughly cleansed and covered with a waterproof plaster.

- Avoid submerging hands or other parts of the body with cuts or abrasions in water.

- Avoid rubbing eyes, nose or mouth during work.

- Wear protective clothing where appropriate, eg waders and rubber gloves, and ensure these and other protective equipment are cleaned after use.

- After work and particularly before taking food or drink, wash hands thoroughly.

Working on or near deep water

In addition to the standard safety precautions already outlined special consideration needs to be given to deep water:

- Avoid working on or near deep water if you are unable to swim.

- Ensure life jackets are available for all persons required to work on deep water.

- Persons operating boats should be trained.

- Be aware of the likelihood of flooding, eg tidal river, periods of prolonged heavy rainfall, and avoid working in areas with a high risk.

- Avoid steep or unstable banks adjacent to deep water.

- Do not enter the water if the river/ditch bottom is not visible.

Appendix 6
Contents for a Full Management Plan

(from Alexander 1994)

Part 1 Description

1.1   General Information

1.1.1   Location
1.1.2   Land tenure
1.1.3   Management infrastructure
1.1.4   Map coverage
1.1.5   Photographic coverage
1.1.6   Compartments

1.2   Environmental Information

1.2.1   Physical

1.2.1.1   Climate
1.2.1.2   Hydrology
1.2.1.3   Geology
1.2.1.4   Geomorphology
1.2.1.5   Soils

1.2.2   Biological

1.2.2.1   Flora
1.2.2.2   Fauna
1.2.2.3   Communities

1.2.3   Cultural

1.2.3.1   Archaeology/past land use
1.2.3.2   Present land use
1.2.3.3   Past management - nature conservation
1.2.3.4   Past status/interest
1.2.3.5   Present conservation status
1.2.3.6   Landscape
1.2.3.7   Public interest/community relations
1.2.3.8   Educational use/facilities
1.2.3.9   Research use/facilities
1.2.3.10   Interpretation use/facilities
1.2.3.11   Recreational use/facilities

1.2.4   Environmental relationships which may have implications for management

1.3   Bibliography

Part 2 Evaluation and Objectives

2.1   Evaluation of features

2.1.1   Evaluation

2.1.1.1   Size

Appendix 7 Glossary

AOD Above Ordnance Datum
A measure of the height of land surface relative to sea level.

Aquifer
Water-bearing strata, eg sandstone.

ATV All Terrain Vehicle
Machines designed for operation on difficult terrain, excluding tractors and diggers.

(BOD) Biochemical Oxygen Demand
A measure of organic pollution. (The amount of oxygen used by micro-organisms per unit volume of water at a given temperature and for a given time).

Berm
Shelf at the base of a bank or bund that is at the level of normal water flow and gives extra channel width during high flows.

Biomass
A quantitative estimate of animal and/or plant matter.

Borrow ditch/dyke
Ditch created as a result of excavating soil to create a bund/sea wall.

Brackish
Water that is intermediate in salinity between fresh water and sea water.

Bryophytes
Mosses and liverworts.

Bund
A raised earth bank, eg for retaining water.

Carr
Woodland, usually dominated by willows and alder, growing on water-logged soils (usually peat).

Community
A grouping of populations of different organisms found living together in a particular environment.

Crome
A long-handled fork with tines bent through 90 degrees.

Detritus
Material formed through the break-down and decay of plant and animal remains.

Dibber
Device for creating a hole in the soil of suitable size to receive a plant plug.

Diversity
The number of species present in a community or habitat.

Eutrophic
Nutrient enriched.

Effluent
Liquid waste from industrial, agricultural or sewage outlets.

Evapotranspiration
Combined term for water lost from a soil or water surface (evaporation) and water lost from the surface of a plant (transpiration).

Fen
Area of wet peat, typically fed by alkaline groundwater but sometimes neutral or slightly acidic.

Flash
A small depression with shallow water which may be natural or excavated.

Floodplain
The low relief area of valley floor adjacent to a river that is periodically inundated by flood waters.

Foot-drain
Small ditch/grip in reedbeds designed to assist water distribution and flow.

Genotype
The genetic constitution of an organism.

Grip
Alternative term for a foot-drain designed to enable a flow of water to be maintained in a reedbed.

Groundwater
Water held in water-bearing rocks and underground pores and fissures.

Habitat
The local environment occupied by individuals of a particular species, population or community.

Hover
Floating mattress of reed growth over liquid mud.

Invertebrates
Animals without a backbone, eg insects, spiders, earthworms.

Jetting
Process where a floating reed/vegetation mat is disintegrated using powerful jets of water generated by a floating pump.

Kevlar
Trade mark for an anti-ballistic material used to line certain items of safety clothing.

Ligger

Local term for a plank(s) usually used as a temporary bridge across a ditch.

Litter

An accumulated layer of dead organic matter, mainly derived from plants.

Marsh

More or less permanently wet area of mineral soil.

Mats

Usually wooden structures from which diggers operate if soils are very soft and there is a danger of the machine sinking.

Microhabitat

One of many very small habitats that constitute a larger habitat, eg reed litter is a microhabitat in a reedbed.

Mud pumping

Process where loose or suspended sediments or jetted material is pumped from a watercourse/body.

National Vegetation Classification

A classification system for British plant communities.

Perennial

Plant that normally lives for more than two seasons and, after an initial period, produces flowers annually.

Phenotype

The observable manifestation of a specific genotype, ie an organism's appearance.

Planktonic

Describes organisms that form part of the microscopic animal and plant community that drifts with water movements.

Population equivalent (pe)

A measure of BOD and suspended solid concentration of an effluent; measured in terms of the average wastewater production per individual within the population (200 L/day with a load of 40g BOD/day).

Rhizomatous

Arising from a rhizome.

Rhizome

Persistent, underground stem providing a means of vegetative propagation.

Rond

The area between the river bank and river wall which is occasionally flooded at high tide. Ronds may be areas of reed, sedge or grass.

Saline

Water or soil rich in dissolved salts.

Soke dyke

A ditch on the marsh side of a river bank, which traps saline water, preventing its spread across the reedbed/fen.

Spoil

Soil and/or vegetation removed during dredging/slubbing or excavation

Succession

The natural process by which plants gradually colonise an area.

Swamp

Area of vegetation normally covered by water all year. Often dominated by one or two species of tall plants.

Systemic

Used to describe a herbicide which is taken up and distributed internally, killing the entire plant.

Turf

Section of vegetation lifted complete with root system and soil.

Vegetative propagation

Asexual reproduction involving unspecialised plant parts such as roots, stems or leaves.

Water table

Level below which the soil or rock is permanently saturated.

Wind-rowing

When cut vegetation is laid in continuous rows to facilitate drying, baling or bundling.

Appendix 8
Abbreviations used in text

ADA	Association of Drainage Authorities
AONB	Area of Outstanding Natural Beauty
ASSI	Area of Special Scientific Interest
BA	Broads Authority
CC	Countryside Commission
CCW	Countryside Council for Wales
DANI	Department of Agriculture for Northern Ireland
DoENI	Department of the Environment for Northern Ireland
EN	English Nature
ESA	Environmentally Sensitive Area
IDB	Internal Drainage Board
IoH	Institute of Hydrology
LA	Local Authorities
MAFF	Ministry of Agriculture, Fisheries and Food
N	Nitrogen
NPA	National Parks Authorities
NRA	National Rivers Authority
P	Phosphorus
SNH	Scottish Natural Heritage
SOAFD	Scottish Office Agricultural and Fisheries Department
SSSI	Site of Special Scientific Interest
WOAD	Welsh Office Agricultural Department

Appendix 9
Scientific names of species referred to in text.

Plants

Alder	*Alnus glutinosa*
Arrowhead	*Sagittaria sagittifolia*
Bedstraw, marsh	*Galium palustre*
Birch, silver	*Betula pendula*
Bittersweet	*Solanum dulcamara*
Bog St John's Wort	*Hypericum elodes*
Bogbean	*Menyanthes trifoliata*
Bog Pimpernel	*Anagallis tenella*
Bramble	*Rubus fruticosus*
Bur-marigold, trifid	*Bidens tripartita*
Bur-reed	*Sparganium* spp.
Canary-grass, reed	*Phalaris arundinacea*
Cotton-grass	*Eriophorum angustifolium*
Cowbane	*Cicuta virosa*
Cudweed, marsh	*Gnaphalium uliginosum*
Dock, water	*Rumex hydrolapathum*
Duckweeds	*Lemna* spp.
Fern, crested buckler	*Dryopteris cristata*
Foxtail, marsh	*Alopecurus geniculatus*
Frogbit	*Hydrocharis morsus-ranae*
Hemp-agrimony	*Eupatorium cannibinum*
Iris, yellow	*Iris pseudacorus*
Louse-wort, marsh	*Pedicularis palustris*
Mare's-tail	*Hippuris vulgaris*
Marsh cinquefoil	*Potentilla palustris*
Meadowsweet	*Filipendula ulmaria*
Milk-parsley	*Peucedanum palustre*
Myrtle, bog	*Myrica gale*
Nettle	*Urtica dioica*
Orchid, marsh	*Dactylorhiza* spp.
Pea, marsh	*Lathyrus palustris*
Pondweeds	*Potamogeton* spp.
Purple-loosestrife	*Lythrum salicaria*
Ragged-robin	*Lychnis flos-cuculi*
Reed, common	*Phragmites australis*
Reedmace	*Typha latifolia*
Saw-sedge	*Cladium mariscus*
Sedge, bottle	*Carex rostrata*
cyperus	*C. pseudocyperus*
pond (greater)	*C. riparia*
Sneezewort	*Achillea ptarmica*
Sow-thistle, marsh	*Sonchus palustris*
Spike-rush, common	*Eleocharis palustris*
Sweetgrass, reed	*Glyceria maxima*
Water dropworts	*Oenanthe* spp.
Water lily	*Nymphaea alba*
Water mint	*Mentha aquatica*
Water parsnip, lesser	*Berula erecta*
Water-pepper	*Polygonum hydropiper*
Water plantain, common	*Alisma plantago-aquatica*
Water soldier	*Stratiotes aloides*
Water starworts	*Callitriche* spp.
Willowherb, greater	*Epilobium hirsutum*

Birds

Great crested grebe	*Podiceps cristatus*
Little grebe	*Tachybaptus ruficollis*
Cormorant	*Phalacrocorax carbo*
Grey heron	*Ardea cinerea*
Bittern	*Botaurus stellaris*
Mute swan	*Cygnus olor*
Bewick's swan	*Cygnus colombianus bewickii*
Canada goose	*Branta canadensis*
Greylag	*Anser anser*
Mallard	*Anas platyrhynchus*
Wigeon	*Anas penelope*
Gadwall	*Anas strepera*
Teal	*Anas crecca*
Shoveler	*Anas clypeata*
Garganey	*Anas querquedula*
Pintail	*Anas acuta*
Pochard	*Aythya ferina*
Tufted duck	*Aythya fuligula*
Goldeneye	*Bucephala clangula*

Goosander	*Mergus merganser*
Red-breasted merganser	*Mergus serrator*
Marsh harrier	*Circus aeruginosus*
Peregrine	*Falco peregrinus*
Grey partridge	*Perdix perdix*
Water rail	*Rallus aquaticus*
Moorhen	*Gallinula chloropus*
Coot	*Fulica atra*
Avocet	*Recurvirostra avosetta*
Little ringed plover	*Charadrius dubius*
Lapwing	*Vanellus vanellus*
Redshank	*Tringa totanus*
Snipe	*Gallinago gallinago*
Jack snipe	*Lymnocryptes minimus*
Black-headed gull	*Larus ridibundus*
Common gull	*Larus canus*
Common tern	*Sterna hirundo*
Kingfisher	*Alcedo atthis*
Wren	*Troglodytes troglodytes*
Skylark	*Alauda arvensis*
Sand martin	*Riparia riparia*
Swallow	*Hirundo rustica*
House martin	*Hirundo domestica*
Meadow pipit	*Anthus pratensis*
Yellow wagtail	*Motacilla citreola*
Savi's warbler	*Locustella luscinioides*
Grasshopper warbler	*Locustella naevia*
Reed warbler	*Acrocephalus scirpaceus*
Sedge warbler	*A. schoenobaenus*
Cetti's warbler	*Cettia cetti*
Whitethroat	*Sylvia communis*
Willow warbler	*Phylloscopus collybita*
Wood warbler	*Phylloscopus sibilatrix*
Bearded tit	*Panurus biarmicus*
Whinchat	*Saxicola rubetra*
Robin	*Erithacus rubecula*
Carrion crow	*Corvus corone*
Starling	*Sturnus vulgaris*
Reed bunting	*Emberiza schoeniclus*
Mammals Water shrew	*Neomys fodiens*
Otter	*Lutra lutra*
Rabbit	*Oryctolagus cuniculus*
Harvest mouse	*Micromys minutus*
Roe deer	*Capreolus capreolus*
Fishes Pike	*Esox lucius*
Eel	*Anguilla anguilla*
Rudd	*Scardinius erythrophthalmus*
Roach	*Rutilus rutilus*
Tench	*Tinca tinca*
Stickleback	*Gasterostidae*
Amphibians Common frog	*Rana temporaria*
Common toad	*Bufo bufo*
Common newt	*Triturus vulgaris*
Palmate newt	*Triturus helveticus*
Invertebrates White-faced darter	*Leucorrhinia dubia*
Black-tailed skimmer	*Orthetrum cancellatum*
Norfolk hawker	*Aeshna isosceles*
Silky wainscot	*Chilodes maritimus*
Fen wainscot	*Arenostola phragmitidis*
Fenn's wainscot	*Photedes brevilinea*
Brown-veined wainscot	*Archanara dissoluta*
White-mantled wainscot	*Archanara neurica*
Large wainscot	*Rhizedra lutosa*
Rush wainscot	*Archanara algae*
Flame wainscot	*Senta flammea*
Twin-spotted wainscot	*Archanara geminipunctata*
Reed leopard moth	*Phragmataecia castaneae*
Scarce burnished brass	*Diachrysia chrysitis*
May high flyer	*Hydriomena impluviata*
Dingy footman	*Eilema griseola*
Double kidney	*Ipimorpha retusa*
Ringed China-mark	*Parapoynx stratiotata*
Small China-mark	*Cataclysta lemnata*
Water veneer	*Acentria ephemerella*
Gigantic water veneer	*Schoenobius gigantella*
Great silver beetle	*Hydrophilus piceus*
Waterlouse	*Asellus* spp
Great raft spider	*Dolomedes plantarius*

References

Alexander, M (1994) *Management Planning Handbook*. Countryside Council for Wales.

Andrews, J and Ward, D (1991) The Management and Creation of Reedbeds – especially for rare birds. *British Wildlife* **3 (No.2)**: 81–91.

Andrews, R (1992) Establishment and Management to Produce Reeds for Thatching. In D Ward (ed), *Reedbeds for Wildlife* pp 31–35. RSPB/University of Bristol.

Axell, H E (1966) Eruptions of bearded tits during 1959–65. *British Birds*, **59**: 513–543.

Bateman, S, Turner, R K and Bateman, I J (1990) *Socio-economic Impact of Changes in the Quality of Thatching Reed on the Future of the Reed-growing and Thatching Industries and on the Wider Rural Economy*. Rural Development Commission.

Becker, D and Sills, N (1988) The conversion of saltmarsh into fresh and brackish water habitats at Titchwell Marsh, Norfolk. RSPB.

Bibby, C (1993) Bearded Tit. In D W Gibbons, J B Reid and R A Chapman (eds), *The New Atlas of Breeding Birds in Britain and Ireland 1988–91*, pp 360–361. T & A D Poyser, London.

Bibby, C, Housden, S, Porter, R and Thomas, G (1989) A Conservation Strategy for Birds. RSPB unpublished report.

Bibby, C J and Lunn, J (1982) Conservation of Reed Beds and Their Avifauna in England and Wales. *Biological Conservation* **23**: 167–186.

Bittman, E (1960) Uferschutz durch Schilfanbau; hier Schilfrohrpflanzer. Bundesanstalt fur Gewasserkunde, Koblenz G6/3401/2116 S (mimeographed).

Boar, R R, Leeming, D J and Moss, B (1991) *The Quality of Thatching Reed and its Impact on the Thatching Industry: The Links Between Water and Sediment Chemistry and Reed Quality*. English Nature.

Brett, D (1989) Getting it Clean with Aquatic Plants. *Ecos* **60**: 17–22.

Brooks, A Revised by Agate, E (1981) *Waterways and Wetlands - a practical conservation handbook*. Second edition. BTCV.

Burgess, N, Ward, D, Hobbs, R and Bellamy, D (1995) Reedbeds, Fens and Acid Bogs. In W J Sutherland and D A Hill (eds), *Managing Habitats for Conservation* pp 149–196. Cambridge University Press, UK.

Burgess, N D and Evans, C E (1989) *The Management of Reedbeds for Birds*. RSPB.

Burgess, N D and Hirons, G J M (1990) *Techniques of Hydrological Management at Coastal Lagoons and Lowland Wet Grasslands on RSPB Reserves*. RSPB.

Campbell, S F (1994) A strategy for wetland creation. MSc thesis, Cranfield University (Silsoe College).

Coombes, C (1990). Reed Bed Treatment Systems in Anglian Water. In P F Cooper and B C Findlater (eds), *Constructed Wetlands in Water Pollution Control* pp 223–234. Pergamon Press, Oxford, UK.

Cooper. F W (1972) The Thatcher and the Thatched Roof. In *The Reed* ('Norfolk Reed') pp 58–69. Norfolk Reed Growers' Association. Second Edition.

Cooper, P F (1990) *European Design and Operation Guidelines for Reed Bed Treatment Systems*. Report No. U117, Water Research Centre, Swindon, UK.

Cooper, P F, Hobson, J A and Findlater, C (1990) The Use of Reedbed Treatment Systems in the UK. *Water Science Technology* **22**: 57–64.

Cowie, N R, Sutherland, W J, Ditlhogo, M K M and James, R (1992) The Effects of Conservation Management of Reed Beds II. The Flora and Litter Disappearance. *Journal of Applied Ecology* **29**: 277–284.

Crook, C E, Boar, R R and Moss, B D (1983) The Decline of Reedswamp in the Norfolk Broadland: Causes, Consequences and Solutions. Broads Authority (BARS 6).

Day, J C U and Wilson, J (1978) Breeding Bitterns in Britain. *British Birds* **71**: 285–300.

Ditlhogo, M K M, James, R, Laurence, B R and Sutherland, W J (1992) The effects of Conservation Management of Reed Beds I. The Invertebrates. *Journal of Applied Ecology* **29**: 265–276.

Ekstam, B, Graneli, W and Weisner, S (1992) Establishment of Reedbeds. In D Ward (ed), *Reedbeds for Wildlife* pp 3–19. RSPB/University of Bristol.

Ellis, E A (1965) *The Broads*. Collins, London.

Emerson, V (1995) An Engineering Strategy for the Design of Wetlands. B. Eng. thesis, Silsoe College, Cranfield University.

English Nature (1994a) *Action for Reedbed Birds in England*. EN Action Plan, Peterborough.

English Nature (1994b) *Species Action Plan for Birds. Bittern*. EN Action Plan, Peterborough.

Everett, M J (1989) Reedbeds: a scarce habitat. *RSPB Conservation Review* **3**: 14–19.

Fojt, W (1994) The Conservation of British Fens. *British Wildlife* **5 (No.6)**: 355–366.

Fojt, W and Foster, A (1992) Reedbeds, their wildlife and requirements A. Botanical and invertebrate aspects of reedbeds, their ecological requirements and conservation significance. In D Ward (ed), *Reedbeds for Wildlife* pp 49–56. RSPB/University of Bristol.

George, M (1992) *The Land Use, Ecology and Conservation of Broadland*. Packard Publishing Ltd, Chichester.

Graham, R (1994) Decomposition of *Phragmites australis* (cav) Trin. in Relation to Degree of Submersion. BSc dissertaion, Lancaster University.

Green, M B (1993) Growing Confidence in the Use of Constructed Reed Beds for Polishing Wastewater Effluents. *Proceedings of the Water Environment Federation 66th Annual Conference and Exposition* **9**: 86–96.

Green, M B (1994) Constructed Reedbeds Clean Up Storm Overflows on Small Works. *Proceedings of the Water Environment Federation 67th Annual Conference and Exposition* **8**: 113–124.

Green, M B and Upton, J (1994) Constructed Reed Beds: A Cost-effective Way to Polish Wastewater Effluents for Small Communities. *Water Environment Research* **66**: 188–192.

Grooby, L (1994) Operation Bittern: Reedbed Management at the Barton Clay Pits. In J Redshaw (ed), *Conservation Management No. 16*. Lincolnshire Trust for Nature Conservation.

Gryseels, M (1989a) Nature Management Experiments in a Derelict Reedmarsh. I: Effects of Winter Cutting. *Biological Conservation* **47**: 171–193.

Gryseels. M (1989b) Nature Management Experiments in a Derelict Reedmarsh. II: Effects of Summer Mowing. *Biological Conservation* **48**: 85–99.

Hall, M J, Hockin, D L and Ellis, J B (1992) *The design of Flood Storage Reservoirs*. CIRIA/Butterworth-Heinemann.

Hammer, D A (1992a) *Creating Freshwater Wetlands*. Lewis Publishers.

Hammer, D A (1992b) Designing Constructed Wetlands Systems to Treat Agricultural Nonpoint Source Pollution. *Ecological Engineering* **1**: 49–82.

Haslam, S M (1969) The Development of Shoots in *Phragmites communis* Trin. *Annals of Botany* **33**: 695–709.

Haslam, S M (1970) The performance of *Phragmites communis* Trin. in relation to water supply. *Annals of Botany* **34**: 867–877.

Haslam, S M (1971) Community Regulation in *Phragmites communis* Trin. *Journal of Ecology* **60**: 585–610.

Haslam, S M (1972a) The Reed, *Phragmites communis* Trin. In *The Reed* ('Norfolk Reed') pp 3–48. Norfolk Reed Growers' Association. Second edition.

Haslam, S M (1972b) Biological flora of the British Isles *Phragmites communis* Trin. *Journal of Ecology* **60**: 585–610.

Haslam, S M (1994) *Wetland Habitat Differentiation and Sensitivity to Chemical Pollutants (Non Open Water Wetlands) Vol II*. Annexes pp 103–110. Department of the Environment report no. DoE/HMIP/RR/040.

Hoffman, B (1980) Vergleichend ökologische Untersuchungen über Einflüsse des kontrollierten Brennens auf die Arthropodenfauna einer Riedwiese im Federseegebiet (Südwürttemberg). *Verhoff. Naturschutz Lanschaftspflege. Bad-Württ* **51/52** (2): 691—714.

Hudson, D (1992) The Ecological and Commercial Potential of reedbed Treatment Systems. In D Ward (ed), *Reedbeds for Wildlife* pp 37–41. RSPB/University of Bristol.

James, B B and Bogaert, R (1989) Wastewater Treatment/Disposal in a Combined Marsh and Forest System Provides for Wildlife Habitat and Recreational Use. In D A Hammer (ed), *Constructed Wetlands for Wastewater Treatment*. Lewis Publishers Inc, Chelsea, Michigan, USA.

Jowitt, A J D and Perrow, M R (1993) *The status and habitat preferences of water shrew* (Neomys fodiens) *and harvest mouse* (Micromys minutus) *in Broadland*. A report for the Vincent Wildlife Trust by ECON.

Kelsey, M (1993) Reed Warbler. In D W Gibbons, J B Reid and R A Chapman (eds) *The New Atlas of Breeding Birds in Britain and Ireland 1988–91*: 334–335. T & A D Poyser, London.

Kikuth, R (1970) Okochemische leistungen hoherer Pflanzen. *Die Naturwissenschaften* **57**.

Kirby, P (1992) *Habitat Management for Invertebrates: A Practical Handbook*. RSPB.

Kirby, P (1994) Reedbeds of the South Bank of the Humber. A report commissioned by the Anglia Division of the NRA and prepared by Lapwings Consultants.

Langton, T (1989) *Snakes and Lizards*. Whittet Books, London.

Madgwick, F J, Andrews, R and Kennison, G C B (1994) Conservation Management of Fens in the Broads National Park. In *Proceedings of International Symposium of Conservation and Management of Fens* pp 187–200. Biebrza, Warsaw.

MAFF (1985) *Guidelines for the Use of Herbicides on weed in or near watercourses and lakes*. Booklet 2078.

MAFF (1995) *Pesticides 1995*. HMSO, London.

McDougall, D S A (1972) Marsh Management for Reed and Sedge Production. In *The Reed* ('Norfolk Reed') pp 49–57. Norfolk Reed Growers' Association.

McKee, J and Richards, A J (in prep) A survey of seed production and germinability in *Phragmites australis* (CAV) Trin Ex Steud in Britain. University of Newcastle.

Merritt, A (1994) *Wetlands, Industry and Wildlife: A Manual of Principles and Practices*. Wildfowl and Wetlands Trust.

Moyes, S B (1990) The Effects of Reedbed Management on the Breeding Birds of the Tay Reedbeds, 1989. Report to NCC (Scotland).

Moyes, S B and Robertson, D (1991) Studies of sedge warblers (1989–91) and water rail (1991) in the Tay reedbeds. Report to NCC (Scotland).

Newbold, C, Honnor, J and Buckley, K (1992) *Nature Conservation and the Management of Drainage Channels*. English Nature.

O'Sullivan, J M (1976) Bearded tits in Britain and Ireland 1966–74. *British Birds* **69**: 473–489.

Painter, M (in prep) The UK Reedbed Inventory report. RSPB.

Parr, T W (1987) *Experimental Studies on the Propagation and Establishment of Reeds* (Phragmites australis) *for Root Zone Treatment of Sewage*. Institute of Terrestrial Ecology.

Ranwell, D S, Bird, E F C, Hubbard, J C E and Stebbings, R E (1964) Tidal submergence and chlorinity in Poole Harbour. *Journal of Ecology* **52**: 627–642.

Rodwell, J (1995) *British Plant Communities Volume 4 Aquatic Communities, Swamp and Tall Herb Fen*. Cambridge University Press.

Staniforth, P A (1984) Discussion paper on alternative techniques for the establishment of new reedbeds. (unpubl.)

RSPB (1994) Reedbed Habitat Action Plan. RSPB, unpublished.

RSPB/NRA/RSNC (1994) *The New Rivers and Wildlife Handbook*. RSPB, Sandy.

Sills, N (1988) Transformation at Titchwell: a Wetland Reserve Management Case History. *RSPB Conservation Review 2*: 64–68.

Street, M (1989) *Ponds and Lakes for Wildfowl*. Game Conservancy.

Tickner, M B, Blackburn, M and Evans, C E (1991) The Rehabilitation of a Norfolk Broad at Strumpshaw RSPB Reserve. RSPB unpubl.

Tickner, M, Evans, C and Blackburn, M (1991) Restoration of a Norfolk Broad: A Case Study at Strumpshaw Fen. *RSPB Conservation Review 5*: 72–77.

Toorn, van der J and Mook, J H (1982) The Influence of Environmental Factors and Management on Stands of *Phragmites australis*: II Effects of Burning, Frost and Insect Damage on Shoot Density and Shoot Size. *Journal of Applied Ecology* **19**: 477–499.

Toorn, van der J and Hemminga, M A (1994) Use and Management of Common Reed (*Phragmites australis*) for Land Reclamation (The Netherlands). In B C Patten et al (eds), *Wetlands and Shallow Continental Water Bodies*, vol. 2; pp 363–371. SPB Academic Publishing, The Hague, Netherlands.

Tyler, G (1992) Reedbeds, Their Wildlife and Requirements B: Requirements of Birds in Reedbeds. In D Ward (ed), *Reedbeds for Wildlife* pp 57–64. RSPB/University of Bristol.

Tyler, G (1994a) Management of Reedbeds for Bitterns and Opportunities for Reedbed Creation. *RSPB Conservation Review 8*: 57–62.

Tyler, G (1994b) Bittern. In G M Tucker and M F Heath (eds). *Birds in Europe Their Conservation Status*, pp 88–89. BirdLife International, Cambridge.

Underhill-Day, J (1993) Marsh Harrier. In D W Gibbons, J B Reid and R A Chapman (eds). *The New Atlas of Breeding Birds in Britain and Ireland 1988–91*, pp 102–103. T & A D Poyser, London.

Veber, K (1978) Propagation, Cultivation and Exploitation of Common Reed in Czechoslovakia. In D Dykyjova and J Kvet (eds), *Pond Littoral Ecosystems* pp 416–423. Springer Verlag, Berlin.

Venner, J (1994) Rejuvenating Reedbeds. *Enact* **2** (No.2): 10–11.

Ward, D (1992) Management of Reedbeds for Wildlife. In D Ward (ed), *Reedbeds for Wildlife* pp 65–78. RSPB/University of Bristol.

Ward, D (1993) The establishment of reed for conservation reedbeds and review of the management of water treatment reedbeds. RSPB unpublished.

Wheeler, B D (1980) The plant communities of rich-fen systems in England and Wales. I. Tall reed and sedge communities. *Journal of Ecology*, 68 pp 365–395.

Wheeler, B D (1992) Integrating Wildlife with Commercial Uses. In D Ward (ed), *Reedbeds for Wildlife* pp 79–89. RSPB/University of Bristol.

Wheeler, B D and Giller, K E (1982a) Species Richness of Herbaceous Fen Vegetation in Broadland, Norfolk, in Relation to the Quantity of Above ground Material. *Journal of Ecology* **70**: 179–200.

Wheeler, B D and Giller, K E (1982b) Status of aquatic macrophytes in an undrained area of fen in the Norfolk Broads, England. *Aquatic Botany* **12**: 277–296.

Wilson, J (1990) Annual Report for Leighton Moss RSPB Nature Reserve. RSPB unpublished.

Woodcock, P (1994) Creating a Wetland for Wildlife. *Enact* **2 (2)**: 19–20.

Worrall, P and Peberdy, K (1994) Wastewater to Warblers. *Enact* **2 (No.2)**: 4–6.

Index

RSPB habitat management handbooks

The New Rivers and Wildlife Handbook RSPB,
NRA, RSNC. RSPB 1994. ISBN 0 903138 70 0
£19.95

Gravel Pit Restoration for Wildlife by John
Andrews. RSPB. 1990. ISBN 0 903138 60 3
£12

*Gravel Pit Restoration for Wildlife – Managers
Summary*. RSPB, 1990. ISBN 0 903138 61 1
£5

*Habitat Management for Invertebrates – A
Practical Handbook* by Peter Kirby, RSPB and
JNCC, 1992. ISBN 0 903138 55 7 £9